주한미군지위협정(SOFA)

서명 및 발효 15

주한미군지위협정(SOFA)

서명 및 발효 15

_____

한국외교협회

| 머리말

미국은 오래전부터 우리나라 외교에 있어서 가장 긴밀하고 실질적인 우호·협력관계를 맺어 온 나라다. 6·25전쟁 정전 협정이 체결된 후 북한의 재침을 막기 위한 대책으로서 1953년 11월 한미 상호방위조약이 체결되었다. 이는 미군이 한국에 주둔하는 법적 근거였고, 그렇게 주둔하게 된 미군의 시설, 구역, 사업, 용역, 출입국, 통관과 관세, 재판권 등 포괄적인 법적 지위를 규정하는 것이 바로 주한미군지위협정(SOFA)이다. 그러나 이와 관련한 협상은 계속된 난항을 겪으며 한미 상호방위조약이 체결로부터 10년이 훌쩍 넘은 1967년이 돼서야 정식 발효에 이를 수 있었다. 그럼에도 당시 미군 범죄에 대한 한국의 재판권은 심한 제약을 받았으며, 1980년대 후반 민주화 운동과 함께 미군 범죄 문제가 사회적 이슈로 떠오르자 협정을 개정해야 한다는 목소리가 커지게 되었다. 이에 1991년 2월 주한미군지위협정 1차 개정이 진행되었고, 이후에도 여러 사건이 발생하며 2001년 4월 2차 개정이 진행되어 현재에 이르고 있다.

본 총서는 외교부에서 작성하여 최근 공개한 주한미군지위협정(SOFA) 관련 자료를 담고 있다. 1953년 한미 상호방위조약 체결 이후부터 1967년 발효가 이뤄지기까지의 자료와 더불어, 이후 한미 합동위원회을 비롯해 민·형사재판권, 시설, 노무, 교통 등 각 분과위원회의 회의록과 운영 자료, 한국인 고용인 문제와 관련한 자료, 기타 관련 분쟁 자료 등을 포함해 총 42권으로 구성되었다. 전체 분량은 약 2만 2천여 쪽에 이른다.

2024년 3월
한국학술정보(주)

❘ 일러두기

· 본 총서에 실린 자료는 2022년 4월과 2023년 4월에 각각 공개한 외교문서 4,827권, 76만 여 쪽 가운데 일부를 발췌한 것이다.

· 각 권의 제목과 순서는 공개된 원본을 최대한 반영하였으나, 주제에 따라 일부는 적절히 변경하였다.

· 원본 자료는 A4 판형에 맞게 축소하거나 원본 비율을 유지한 채 A4 페이지 안에 삽입 하였다. 또한 현재 시점에선 공개되지 않아 '공란'이란 표기만 있는 페이지 역시 그대로 실었다.

· 외교부가 공개한 문서 각 권의 첫 페이지에는 '정리 보존 문서 목록'이란 이름으로 기록물 종류, 일자, 명칭, 간단한 내용 등의 정보가 수록되어 있으며, 이를 기준으로 0001번부터 번호가 매겨져 있다. 이는 삭제하지 않고 총서에 그대로 수록하였다.

· 보고서 내용에 관한 더 자세한 정보가 필요하다면, 외교부가 온라인상에 제공하는『대한 민국 외교사료요약집』1991년과 1992년 자료를 참조할 수 있다.

| 차례

정/리/보/존/문/서/목/록

기록물종류	문서-일반공문서철	등록번호	936 9609	등록일자	2006-07-27
분류번호	741.12	국가코드	US	주제	
문서철명	한.미국 간의 상호방위조약 제4조에 의한 시설과 구역 및 한국에서의 미국군대의 지위에 관한 협정 (SOFA) 전59권. 1966.7.9 서울에서 서명 : 1967.2.9 발효 (조약 232호) ＊원본				
생산과	미주과/조약과	생산년도	1952 - 1967	보존기간	영구
담당과(그룹)	조약	조약		서가번호	--
참조분류					
권차명	V.38 실무교섭회의, 제82차. 1966.7.8 (II)				

내용목차

```
* 일지 :
1953.8.7        이승만 대통령-Dulles 미국 국무장관 공동성명
                - 상호방위조약 발효 후 군대지위협정 교섭 약속
1954.12.2       정부, 주한 UN군의 관세업무협정 체결 제의
1955.1월, 5월    미국, 제의 거절
1955.4.28       정부, 군대지위협정 제의 (한국측 초안 제시)
1957.9.10       Hurter 미국 국무차관 방한 시 각서 수교 (한국측 제의 수락 요구)
1957.11.13, 26  정부, 개별 협정의 단계적 체결 제의
1958.9.18       Dawling 주한미국대사, 형사재판관할권 협정 제외 조건으로 행정협정 체결 의사 전달
1960.3.10       정부, 토지, 시설협정의 우선적 체결 강력 요구
1961.4.10       장면 국무총리-McConaughy 주한미국대사 공동성명으로 교섭 개시 합의
1961.4.15, 4.25 제1, 2차 한.미국 교섭회의 (서울)
1962.3.12       정부, 교섭 재개 촉구 공한 송부
1962.5.14       Burger 주한미국대사, 최규하 장관 면담 시 형사재판관할권 문제 제기 않는 조건으로
                교섭 재개 통고
1962.9.6        한.미국 간 공동성명 발표 (9월 중 교섭 재개 합의)
1962.9.20~      제1-81차 실무 교섭회의 (서울)
   1965.6.7
1966.7.8        제82차 실무 교섭회의 (서울)
1966.7.9        서명
1967.2.9        발효 (조약 232호)
```

마/이/크/로/필/름/사/항

촬영연도	＊롤 번호	화일 번호	후레임 번호	보관함 번호
2006-11-23	I-06-0070	06	1-241	

0001

한·미국 간의 상호방위조약 제4조에 의한 시설과 구역 및 한국에서의 미국군대의 지위에 관한 협정(SOFA)
전59권. 1966.7.9 서울에서 서명 : 1967.2.9 발효(조약 232호) (V.38 실무교섭회의, 제82차, 1966.7.8(II))

7

STATUS OF FORCES NEGOTIATIONS: 82nd Meeting

SUBJECTS:

1. Facilities and Areas
2. Non-appropriated Fund Organi-
        zations
3. Invited Contractors
4. Labor
5. Criminal Jurisdiction
6. Claims
7. Entry into Force of Agreement

PLACE: Ministry of Foreign Affairs

DATE: January_____, 1966

PARTICIPANTS:

Republic of Korea   United States

CHANG Sang-mun   Richard A. Ericson, Jr.,
YUN Wun-yong   Brig Gen Carroll H. Dunn
HO Sung-chun   Col Allan G. Pixton, USA
YI Nam-ki   Capt George M. Hagerman, USN
KIM Tong-hui   Col Wilson Freeman, USA
HO Hyong-ku   Frank R. LaMacchia
Col KIM Won-kil, ROKA   Richard M Herndon
Maj YI Ke-hun, ROKA   Robert A. Kinney
KIM Ki-cho   Goodwin Shapiro
PAK Won-chol   Maj Alton Harvey, USA
YI Kun-pal (Interpreter)   David i. C. Lee (Interpreter)

                                              Ogden Reed, Observer
                                              G. W. Flowers, Observer

0002

Proposed Minutes of 82nd Session

Article IV - Facilities and Areas - Return of Facilities

1. Mr. Ericson noted that, at the 81st session the Korean negotiators proposed a new Agreed Minute, to be added as Agreed Minute No. 2 to the US draft. The US negotiators agree that this new Agreed Minute is the corollary to Agreed Minute No. 1. It is logical that all removable properties located in any area or facilities which are provided by the ROK Government should be returned whenever such properties are no longer needed for the US armed forces.

2. Therefore, Mr. Ericson continued, the US negotiators are happy to accept the new proposed Agreed Minute No. 2, and thereby achieve full agreement on this Article.

Article XIII - Non-appropriated Fund Organizations Article

3. Mr. Ericson noted that, at the 81st meeting, the ROK negotiators accepted the Agreed Minute of Article XIII as proposed by the US negotiators. The US side agrees to the understanding for the Agreed Joint Summary proposed by the ROK negotiators at the 81st meeting relating to this Agreed Minute, and full US-ROK agreement on this Article has now been achieved.

Article XV - Invited Contractors

4. Mr. Ericson stated that, at the 81st negotiating session, the Korean negotiators reiterated their objection to Paragraph 8 of the US draft and requested the acceptance of their Paragraph 8. This matter was subsequently extensively discussed at informal meetings between members of the ROK and US negotiating team. As a result of these discussions, the United States negotiators now accept Paragraph 8 as proposed by the Korean negotiators, with minor modifications as follows:

2

0003

한·미국 간의 상호방위조약 제4조에 의한 시설과 구역 및 한국에서의 미국군대의 지위에 관한 협정(SOFA)
전59권. 1966.7.9 서울에서 서명 : 1967.2.9 발효(조약 232호) (V.38 실무교섭회의, 제82차, 1966.7.8(II))

9

"8. The authorities of the Republic of Korea shall have the right to exercise jurisdiction over such persons for offenses committed in the Republic of Korea and punishable by the law of the Republic of Korea. In recognition of the role of such persons in the defense of the Republic of Korea, they shall be subject to the provisions of paragraphs 5, 7(b), and 9 and the related Agreed Minutes, of Article XXII. In those cases in which the authorities of the Republic of Korea decide not to exercise jurisdiction they shall notify the military authorities of the United States as soon as possible. Upon such notification the military authorities of the United States shall have the right to exercise such jurisdiction over the persons referred to as is conferred on them by the law of the United States."

5. Mr. Ericson noted that in the first sentence, the word "primary" was deleted. This was necessary to prevent misunderstanding since the term "primary jurisdiction" relates to the exercise of concurrent jurisdiction. Under the present state of U. S. laws, the Korean jurisdiction over contractor employees is exclusive, although it is understood that the effective administration and disciplinary sanctions available to the United States may be appropriate in certain cases.

6. Mr. Ericson stated that the second sentence is a proposed addition to Paragraph 8. It provides that personnel under this article will be subject to the provisions of the Criminal Jurisdiction Article and its Agreed Minutes relating to custody, confinement and trial safeguards. This takes nothing away from the right of jurisdiction retained by the Republic of Korea. It merely confers upon these persons the same protections relating to custody, confinement and trial safeguards as are accorded members of the civilian component.

3

0004

Mr. Ericson emphasized that invited contractors have an important role in the defense of the Republic of Korea and are indispensable to the United States military forces. It is deemed essential that they receive the minimal protections offered by the custody, confinement and trial safeguard provisions. The last two sentences of Paragraph 8 are accepted as proposed by the ROK without change. The US negotiators trust that these modifications will be acceptable to the Korean negotiators and that full agreement can now be reached on this Article.

7. Mr. Chang replied that, with regard to the modified proposals tabled by the U. S. negotiators regarding Paragraph 8 of the Invited Contractors Article, the Korean negotiators wish to present the following response. The Korean negotiators are prepared to accept deletion of the word "primary" from the first sentence on the basis of the statement by the US negotiators to the effect that:

> "Under the present state of U. S. law, the Korean jurisdiction over contractor employees is exclusive although it is understood that the effective administration and/disciplinary sanctions available to the United States may be appropriate in certain cases."

8. With respect to the proposed new second sentence which is to be incorporated into the provisions of Paragraph 8, which provides that in recognition of the role of such personnel in the defense of the Republic of Korea, the persons referred to in Paragraph 1 shall be subject to the provisions of Paragraph 5, 7(b), 9 and its related Agreed Minutes of Article XXII. Mr. Chang recalled that the U. S. negotiators had in the past placed their special emphasis on guarantees of fair trial for U. S. personnel on the grounds that as U. S. citizens they are entitled to such rights as are guaranteed under the

4

한·미국 간의 상호방위조약 제4조에 의한 시설과 구역 및 한국에서의 미국군대의 지위에 관한 협정(SOFA) 전59권. 1966.7.9 서울에서 서명 : 1967.2.9 발효(조약 232호) (V.38 실무교섭회의, 제82차, 1966.7.8(II)) 11

Constitution of the United States. In the course of negotiations regarding the Invited Contractors Article, they had further stated that although those third-country employees who are present on the effective date of this Agreement will be entitled to enjoy the privileges contained in this Article, there is no intention to bring in any third-country nationals/after the Agreement goes into force, but if any were brought in, they would have no privileges under the terms of this Article, thereby indicating their flexibility toward the extent of privileges to be granted to third-country employees under this Article.

9. Mr. Chang stated that, in the light of the above position of the U.S. negotiators, the Korean negotiators believe that application of such privileges as proposed by the U. S. negotiators in their second sentence of Paragraph 8 pertaining to the provisions of Paragraphs 5, 7(b), 9 and its related Agreed Minutes of the Criminal Jurisdiction Article should naturally be limited to U. S. nationals only. Consequently, it is also the view of the Korean negotiators, Mr. Chang continued, that the privileges to be granted under Agreed Minute No. 2 of this Article to the contractor employees of third-country nationality who are present in the Republic of Korea on the effective date of this Agreement shall, to be consonant with the above observation of Paragraph 8, not include any privilege provided for in the proposed second/sentence of Paragraph 8.

10. Mr. Chang pointed out that in this connection, the Korean negotiators, before accepting the U. S. modifications, wish to seek clarification from the U. S. negotiators on their intention as to the following two points:

a. Whether or not third-country employees and those

5

employees who are ordinarily resident in, but are
not nationals of the United States, and their
dependents will be subject to the provisions of
Paragraph 5, 7(b), 9 and its related Agreed
Minutes of the Criminal Jurisdiction Article?

b. Whether or not the privileges to be granted to
third-country employees under Agreed Minute
No. 2 include the privileges in the proposed
second sentence of Paragraph 8 relating to the
Criminal Jurisdiction Article?

11. Mr. Ericson replied that the United States negotiators, in response
to the ROK queries in Paragraph 10, agree to the following understanding for
the Agreed Joint Summary.

> "Unless otherwise agreed in the Joint Committee,
> the privileges provided for in the second sentence of
> Paragraph 8 of this Article shall be extended only to
> United States nationals."

The US negotiators also can assure the Koreans, as indicated in the informal
discussions, that such requests for Joint Committee consideration on this
point are expected to be rare.

12. Mr. Chang stated that, with these explanations and understandings
in the Joint Summary Record, the Korean negotiators now accept the proposed
U. S. modifications regarding Paragraph 8, thereby reaching full agreement
on this Article.

Article XVII - Labor

13. Mr. Ericson tabled a revised Labor Article, which he stated was

6

responsive to the proposals made by the ROK negotiators at the 81st session, and at subsequent informal meetings. He expressed the belief that this revised Labor Article fully meets the ROK requirements, and he anticipates full agreement can now be reached on the revised text of the Labor Article.

14. Mr. Ericson stated that the following comments refer to specific changes in the previously tabled United States draft, made in response to the Korean proposals at the 81st session:

a. <u>Paragraph 1(b)</u>. The US negotiators accept the ROK proposal for the inclusion of a new sentence in Paragraph 1(b), as follows: "Such employees shall be nationals of the Republic of Korea." This sentence is accepted on the condition of ROK acceptance of two understandings for the Agreed Summary Record, as follows:

> (1) "Local residents, who are third-country nationals and are also local-hire USFK employees and local-hire contractor employees paid in won, on the effective date of the agreement, shall be excluded from the application of this provision."

There are only a few USFK employees in this category, who have been working with USFK in good faith for some years, and the US negotiators feel their exclusion from this provision would not present problems and would only be fair to all concerned.

> (2) The second understanding is as follows:
> "The provisions of Paragraph 1(b) do not preclude the United States armed forces from bringing into Korea, without <u>privileges</u>, third-country contractor employees

7

0008

possessing special skills not available from the
Korean labor force."

The US negotiators believe general US-ROK agreement on this point is
reflected in previous informal discussions. In adding the new sentence to
Paragraph 1(b), it is also necessary to add, in the parenthetical phrase
"(other than a member of the civilian component)" the phrase " or a contractor
employee under Article XV," to enable invited contractors to hire American
personnel. Mr. Ericson pointed out that invited contractor employees are
not included as part of the civilian component in the Definitions Article (I).
Therefore, this added phrase is made necessary by the ROK-proposed added
sentence, and it makes it clear that the word "employee" as used in this
Article does not refer to non-Korean employees of invited contractors.

b. <u>Paragraph 2 and Agreed Minutes No. 1, 2, 3</u>. The U.S. negotiators believe the two sides are now in full agreement regarding Paragraph
2 and Agreed Minutes 1, 2, and 3 as previously tabled by the US. Mr. Ericson
noted that, during the informal discussions which took place since the 81st
meeting, it was mutually agreed that the ROK-proposed understanding relating
to Agreed Minute No. 2, reported in Paragraph 27 of the Agreed Summary Record
of the 81st meeting, would be withdrawn.

c. <u>Paragraph 3 and Agreed Minute No. 4</u>. The US negotiators accept
the revisions in Paragraph 3, as tabled by the ROK negotiators at the 81st
meeting. With regard to the related Agreed Minute No. 4, the US negotiators
believe both sides are now in agreement on revised language of this Agreed
Minute, as follows:

"4. When employers cannot conform with provisions of
labor legislation of the Republic of Korea applicable under

8

0009

this Article on account of the military requirements of the United States armed forces, the matter shall be referred, in advance whenever possible, to the Joint Committee for consideration and appropriate action. In the event mutual agreement cannot be reached in the Joint Committee regarding appropriate action, the issue may be made the subject of review through discussions between appropriate officials of the Government of the Republic of Korea and the diplomatic mission of the United States of America."

Mr. Ericson stated that in informal discussions, agreement was reached that an agreed understanding will be included in the Agreed Joint Summary as follows:

"It is understood that the deviation from Korean labor legislation need not be referred to the Joint Committee in cases when such referral would seriously hamper military operations." in an emergency

There had been some discussion as to whether the word "need" or "may" should be used in this understanding, but the word "need," as better English, had been agreed upon.

  d. Paragraph 4: The US side concurs in the proposed ROK changes at the end of Para 4 (a) (5), changing the number in parentheses from "3" to "2" in the following phrase: "as stipulated in subparagraph (2), above,"

  e. Paragraph 5: The US side accepts the ROK-proposed added phrase, "through mutual consultation," after the word "deferred."

  f. Agreed Minute No. 5: The US negotiators also accept the

9

0010

modifications of Agreed Minute No. 5, as proposed by the ROK negotiators at the 81st meeting, with the addition of the phrase "by the employers" as agreed upon in informal discussions. The full text of Agreed Minute No. 5 is as follows:

> "5. A union or other employee group shall be recognized by the employers unless its objectives are inimical to the common interests of the United States and the Republic of Korea. Membership or non-membership in such groups shall not be a factor in employment or other actions affecting employees."

15. Mr. Ericson stated that he felt the revised text of the Labor Article, as tabled at this meeting, will be fully acceptable to the ROK negotiators. These proposals are presented as a package and the US revisions of its draft in response to ROK proposals are contingent upon ROK acceptance of the rest of the text and understandings.

16. Mr. Chang stated that the Korean negotiators appreciate the general acceptance of the revised draft of the Labor Article, as tabled at 81st session. The Korean side accepts, with certain remarks, the US modifications effected in Paragraph 1(b) and Agreed Minutes No. 4 and No. 5, as well as the understandings, as proposed by the US negotiators.

17. In agreeing to this Article, Mr. Chang stated that the Korean negotiators would like to reiterate following four points for the record in the Agreed Joint Summary:

a. First, the Korean side has come to accept the phrase "military requirements" provided for in Paragraph 3 and Agreed Minutes No. 2 and 4,

10

0011

which provides that employers, if required, may deviate from Korean labor legislation without referring the matter in advance to the Joint Committee. We still believe the phrase "military requirements" is broad and ambiguous, and could sometimes lead to undesirable controversy over interpretation during implementation of the Agreement. Whenever such controversy arises in the future, the Korean side would like to have it settled in the light of the text of the Article and Agreed Minutes as well as statements made by the US negotiators for the Agreed Joint Summary. Specifically, the Korean side expects that, as the US Chief Negotiator stated at the 73rd session, "the US armed forces only rarely, if ever, will not be able to conform to ROK labor legislation applicable under this Article, except in emergency situations."

  b. Secondly, the provisions of Agreed Minute No. 4 is understood to apply to the proviso of Paragraph 3 and, therefore, any deviation from the provisions of labor legislation of the Republic of Korea because of military requirements, as stated in Paragraph 3 and Agreed Minutes No. 2 and No. 4, shall be subject of referral to the Joint Committee for consideration and appropriate action in advance or afterward.

  c. Thirdly, the Korean side has accepted the phrase "for consideration and appropriate action" in place of the phrase "for mutual agreement" in Agreed Minute No. 4. In accepting this phrase, the Korean side takes the view that the "appropriate action" will be taken as a result of consideration by the Joint Committee, or of diplomatic consultation in the event mutual agreement cannot be reached in the Joint Committee regarding appropriate action.

11

0012

d. Fourthly, the Agreed Minute No. 4 provides that deviation from Korean labor legislation shall be referred, in advance ~~whenever possible~~, to the Joint Committee for consideration and appropriate action. While this provision states that deviation from ROK labor legislation shall be referred ~~whenever possible~~ in advance, it implies that such deviation shall be referred to the Joint Committee as soon as such referral becomes possible. Whenever the matter is referred to the Joint Committee after the deviation had already been made on account of military requirements, it is presumed that the Korean side could raise objection in the Joint Committee to the action taken by the employer and request that appropriate action, i.e., corrective action or measures for remedy be taken. It is understood that such corrective action will be taken as and when the Joint Committee so directs. In the event that mutual agreement cannot be reached in the Joint Committee regarding appropriate action, the matter may be discussed between officials of the Government of the Republic of Korea and the US diplomatic mission.

18. Mr. Chang indicated that these remarks are not intended to introduce any new understanding, but rather are intended to provide guidance to the members of the Joint Committee in their interpretation and implementation of the new agreed Labor Article.

Article XXII - Criminal Jurisdiction

19. Mr. Ericson noted that, at the 81st negotiating session, the Korean negotiators accepted the US draft of the Criminal Jurisdiction Article with certain modifications. The United States negotiators are now pleased to accept the proposals made by the ROK negotiators at that session, subject to

12

0013

Korean acceptance of several minor changes. Specifically, the US side accepts:

    a. The Korean proposals relating to Paragraph 7(b), verbatim.

    b. The understanding on the Agreed Minute Re Para 2, as follows:

> "It is understood that the United States authorities
> shall exercise utmost restraint in requesting waivers
> of exclusive jurisdiction as provided for in the
> Agreed Minute Re Paragraph 2 of this Article."

    c. The understanding on Agreed Minute Re Para 3(a), with deletion of the previously proposed phrase "or his designee," as follows:

> "A duty certificate shall be issued only upon the advice
> of a Staff Judge Advocate, and the competent auth-
> ority issuing the duty certificates shall be a General
> Grade officer."

    d. Addition of the ROK-proposed sentence in Agreed Minute No. 4 Re Para 3(b).

    e. Mr. Ericson stated the US side accepts the Korean proposal to delete the word "civil" from Para 1(b) and to reinsert the second sentence of Agreed Minute Re Para 9(a), on the condition ROK negotiators accept the following understanding on Para 1(b) for inclusion in the Agreed Joint Summary:

> "The civil authorities of the Republic of Korea will
> retain full control over the arrest, investigation and
> trial of a member of the United States armed forces
> or civilian component or a dependent."

13

0014

The US negotiators believe that this statement represents the positions of both sides and that this is a mutually agreeable understanding.

f. Regarding the definition of official duty, the US side is prepared to compromise by including the first sentence of the official duty definition as the second sentence of Agreed Minute No. 1 Re Para 3(a). The second sentence will be included as an understanding in the Agreed Joint Summary, as follows:

> "With regard to the Agreed Minute Re Paragraph 3(a), a substantial departure from the acts a person is required to perform in a particular duty usually will indicate an act outside of his "official duty,"

g. With reference to Agreed Minute Re Para 9(g), the additional language proposed by the Korean negotiators at the 81st session is unacceptable. It is recognized that similar language contained in subpara (b) of Agreed Minute No. 6 Re Para 3(b) of the US draft is likewise objectionable to the Korean negotiators. Therefore, the US side proposes deletion of the following portion of the second sentence of subpara (b):

> "... except where his presence is incompatible with the rules of the court of the United States or with the security requirements of the United States, which are not at the same time the security requirements of the Republic of Korea."

This proposal is conditioned on acceptance by the Korean negotiators of the US draft Agreed Minute Re Para 9(g) as tabled.

14

0015

h. Regarding Agreed Minute Re Para 10(a) and 10(b), the US negotiators have given careful consideration to the Korean proposal tabled at the 81st session and also the informal discussions held thereafter. The US negotiators are now tabling a modification of this US draft which it is believed will more than fulfill the desires of the Korean negotiators. It should be noted that the language is virtually identical to the similar provisions of the Japanese SOFA.

20. Mr. Ericson emphasized that the US negotiators agree to all of the foregoing ROK proposals made at the 81st meeting, on the condition that the ROK accept the few proposed changes the US side has made. Mr. Ericson stated that he is confident that these changes will be agreeable to the Korean negotiators and that full agreement can be reached on this Article as now tabled.

21. Mr. Chang expressed the appreciation of the Korean negotiators to the United States negotiators for the most careful consideration and acceptance of those proposals tabled by the Korean negotiators at the 81st session, i.e.:

    a. The additional proposals relating to Paragraph 7(b).

    b. The understanding on the Agreed Minute Re Paragraph 2.

    c. The understanding on Agreed Minute Re Paragraph 3(a).

    d. The additional sentence for Agreed Minute No. 4 Re Paragraph 3(b).

22. Mr. Chang stated that the Korean negotiators are now prepared to accept the following proposals tabled by the US negotiators:

15

0016

a. The Agreed Minute No. 1 Pe Paragraph 1(b), verbatim.

b. The US proposal regarding the definition of official duty which includes the first sentence of the definition as the second sentence of the Agreed Minute No. 1 Re Paragraph 3(a) and the second sentence of the definition as an understanding in the Agreed Joint Summary.

c. The US proposals relating to Agreed Minute Re Paragraph 9(g) and subparagraph (b) of Agreed Minute No. 6 of Re Paragraph 3(b) with deletion of the following identical languages therefrom:

"...except where his presence is incompatible with the rules of the court of the United States or with the security requirements of the United States, which are not at the same time the security requirements of the Republic of Korea."

d. The modification of the US draft regarding Agreed Minute Re Paragraph 10(a) and 10(b).

23. Mr. Chang stated that, with respect to Paragraph 1(b) of the US draft, the Korean negotiators express their thanks to the U.S. side for deletion of the word "civil" from their draft coupled with reinsertion of the second sentence of Agreed Minute Re Paragraph 9(a). However, the Korean negotiators have noted that the deletion of the word "civil" from their draft is conditioned upon ROK acceptance of the following understanding in the Agreed Joint Summary:

"The civil authorities of the Republic of Korea will retain full control over the arrest, investigation and

16

0017

trial of a member of the United States armed forces or civilian component or a dependent."

To accommodate the U.S. concern over this problem, the Korean negotiators had in the past reiterated their assurances that the U. S. personnel shall under no circumstances be tried by the military tribunal of the Republic of Korea, and thus have accepted the second sentence of Agreed Minute Re Paragraph 9(a) and Agreed Minute No. 1 of Re Paragraph 1(b) of the U.S. draft regarding martial law. In the light of the trend of the past negotiations on this problem, the Korean negotiators, to expedite and complete the negotiations as soon as practicable, and at the same time to fulfill the requirements of the US negotiators, accept the proposed U.S. understanding with the Korean interpretation of the understanding that the US negotiators are merely reaffirming their basic position that the U.S. personnel referred to in Paragraph 1(b) of this Article shall under no circumstances be arrested, investigated, or tried by the military authorities or military tribunals of the Republic of Korea.

24. Mr. Chang stated that, with these acceptances by the Korean negotiators of the U.S. proposals, both sides have now reached full agreement on the Article dealing with Criminal Jurisdiction, the heart of the Status of Forces Agreement between the United States and the Republic of Korea.

Article XXIII - Claims.

25. Mr. Ericson noted that, at the 81st negotiating session, the Korean negotiators tabled a revised draft of the Claims Article, including modifications of Paragraph 5(e) (iii) and Agreed Minute No. 1 and Paragraph 12 relating to the Korean Service Corps. The United States negotiators are

17

0018

pleased to accept this revised Claims Article, subject to ROK acceptance of an agreed understanding for the Agreed Joint Summary.

26. With regard to Agreed Minute No. 1, Mr. Ericson indicated that the US negotiators agree with the Korean negotiators that claims settlement authority for all areas of the Republic of Korea should be transferred to the Korea Claims Service at the earliest date practicable, as determined by the Joint Committee. The US side believes the record makes clear that the extension of these claims responsibilities to areas beyond Seoul Special City will depend upon the development of the ROK Claims Service. The primary US concern in this matter is to insure prompt and equitable settlements for Korea claimants against the USFK. Therefore, Mr. Ericson stated, the US negotiators accept the ROK draft of this Article as tabled, contingent upon US-ROK agreement on the following understanding in the Agreed Joint Summary:

> "With regard to Agreed Minute No. 1(b), the extension
> of the provisions of Paragraphs 5, 6, 7, and 8 to
> other areas of Korea will be based upon the capa-
> bility of the Korean Claims Service to implement
> these provisions."

27. Mr. Chang stated that the Korean negotiators accept the US proposal regarding the Claims Article in order to reach full agreement at the present session. Mr. Chang continued that the Korean negotiators also believe, as just stated by the US negotiators, that the primary concern of the Korean negotiators in this matter is to insure prompt and equitable

18

0019

settlements of the claims for damages caused by USFK. Therefore, extension of these claims responsibility to the areas beyond Seoul Special City should be made at the earliest date practicable, as determined by the Joint Committee. The Korean negotiators firmly believe that decision of the Joint Committee to effectuate this Article throughout the Republic of Korea should be made as soon as the Korean Claims Service is well prepared to bear its responsibilities under this Article. Mr. Chang noted that with this fact in mind, the Korean negotiators accept the understanding in the Agreed Joint Summary as proposed by the US negotiators, thereby reaching full agreement on this Article.

28. The ROK and US Chief Negotiators agreed the two sides are now in full agreement on the Claims Article, on the basis of the ROK draft tabled at the 81st meeting and the agreed understanding set forth in Paragraph 26.

Article XXIX - Entry into Force of Agreement.

29. Mr. Ericson stated that the United States Government will accept the Ratification Article proposed by the ROK negotiators at the 81st session, subject to minor modifications in which it is understood the ROK side concurs.

30. Mr. Ericson stated that the US side accepts the full text of the ROK proposal made at the 81st session, verbatim, with only the following two modifications:

a. In Paragraph 1, the phrase "three months" is substitute for the phrase "sixty days." There is mutual agreement regarding the need for the longer time interval between ratification and the entry into force of the Agreement. It is proposed that the precise date of entry into force should be mutually acknowledged at the time of the receipt of the ROK Government's written notification that it has approved the Agreement in

19

0020

accordance with its legal procedures (probably the same date three months later).

       b. In Paragraph 2, a change is proposed which it is believed will make the sentence read more smoothly without changing its meaning. Substitution of the word "the" for "its" in the last clause of the sentence is proposed. This change makes the last clause read "to give effect to the provisions of this Agreement."

31. In accepting the ROK draft of this Article, with these minor modifications, Mr. Ericson indicated he would like to reiterate the US views concerning implementation of the Agreement, as previously presented at the 80th session. The US negotiators believe both sides are in full agreement on the importance of careful planning and action by their respective governments to insure the maximum possible efficiency and effectiveness in the implementation of the SOFA. In the language of Paragraph 2, the ROK Government will endeavor to take "all legislative and budgetary action necessary to give effect to the provisions of this Agreement." The US negotiators believe such necessary action also includes any other necessary implementing action, such as issuing appropriate administrative regulations. United States authorities in Korea will inform the Government of the Republic of Korea, on a continuing basis, of their progress in implementation of the Agreement. The US side expects that the ROK Government, similarly, will inform appropriate United States officials of its progress in implementation of the SOFA and that copies of pertinent documents and regulations issued by ROK and United States authorities will be exchanged. We believe both sides

20

0021

are in mutual agreement on the necessity for consistent and coordinated action, to insure smooth implementation of the SOFA.

32. Mr. Chang stated that the Korean negotiators appreciate the concurrence of the U. S. negotiators to the revised Korean draft of the Ratification Article and accept the two modifications proposed by the U.S. side in Paragraphs 1 and 2. Both sides, thereby, have also reached full agreement on this Article. Mr. Chang further stated that, similarly, the Korean side has no objection to exchange, on a continuous basis, of copies of pertinent documents and regulations issued by authorities of both Governments to give effect to the provisions of the Agreement, as well as any other information on the progress of the Korean Government in carrying out the Agreement, in order to insure the maximum possible efficiency and effectiveness in the implementation of the present Status of Forces Agreement between the Republic of Korea and the United States.

33. Mr. Chang replied that the ROK negotiators are in full agreement with the US negotiators on this Article, and with this agreement the US and ROK negotiators have now achieved agreement on all 31 Articles of the US-ROK Status of Forces Agreement. Therefore, formal negotiation of this Status of Forces Agreement is finally concluded, after 40-months of negotiation.

34. In concluding the final session of the negotiations, both the Republic of Korea and the United States negotiators exchanged their heartfelt praise for the patience and friendly cooperation rendered by those who have tirelessly participated in one of the most lengthy yet epoch-making negotiations, which resulted in the achievement of a US-ROK Status of Forces Agreement.

21

0022

<u>US-ROK SOFA 82nd MEETING MINUTES ARE AS PREVIOUSLY DISTRIBUTED, EXCEPT</u>

<u>AS PRESENTED BELOW</u>:

I. Regarding the Labor Article, the following is substituted for the minutes beginning on Page 8, Paragraph 14. c. and continuing through Paragraph 18, page 12:

c. <u>Paragraph 3 and Agreed Minute No. 4.</u> Mr. Ericson stated that the US negotiators accept the revisions in Paragraph 3, as tabled by the ROK negotiators at the 81st meeting. With regard to the related Agreed Minute No. 4, subsequent to the 81st meeting the ROK negotiators proposed revision of the text of this Agreed Minute which they had previously tabled, Their new proposal is, as follows:

"4. When employers cannot conform with provisions of labor legislation of the Republic of Korea applicable under this Article on account of the military requirements of the United States armed forces, the matter shall be referred, in advance, to the Joint Committee for consideration and appropriate action. In the event mutual agreement cannot be reached in the Joint Committee regarding appropriate action, the issue may be made the subject of review through discussions between appropriate officials of the Government of the Republic of Korea and the diplomatic mission of the United States of America."

8

0023

Mr. Chang noted that the ROK negotiators had revised their previously tabled Agreement Minute No. 4, deleting the words "whenever possible". In proposing this revised language, Mr. Chang stated that the ROK Government is appreciative of the need for the United States armed forces to have the flexibility in an emergency to deviate from ROK labor legislation without referral to the Joint Committee, as presented by the US negotiators at the 71st meeting (Paragraph 15 of the Agreed Joint Summary) and at the 73rd meeting (Paragraph 5 of the Agreed Joint Summary). Therefore, the ROK negotiators proposed the following agreed understanding which will be included in the Agreed Joint Summary, as follows:

> "It is understood that the deviation from Korean labor legislation need not be referred to the Joint Committee in cases when such referral would seriously hamper military operations in an emergency."

Mr. Ericson stated that the US negotiators were authorized to accept the ROK proposal to delete the phrase "whenever possible" in Agreed Minute 4 on the basis that the ROK-proposed agreed understanding, which the US accepts, clearly indicates that the United States military authorities can deviate from Korean labor legislation without referral to the Joint Committee when such would seriously hamper military operations in an emergency.

d. Paragraph 4: The US side concurs in the proposed ROK changes at the end of Para 4 (a) (5), changing the number in parentheses from "3" to "2" in the following phrase: "as stipulated in subparagraph

9

0024

(2), above."

The US side also accepts the revised Paragraph 4 (b), as proposed by the ROK side, as follows:

> "Employees or any employee organization shall have the right of further collective action in the event a labor dispute is not resolved by the foregoing procedures except in cases where the Joint Committee determines such action seriously hampers military operations of the United States armed forces for the joint defense of the Republic of Korea. In the event an agreement cannot be reached on this question in the Joint Committee, it may be made the subject of review through discussions between appropriate officials of the Government of the Republic of Korea and the diplomatic mission of the United States of America."

In accepting this ROK proposal on this important point, the US side should like it understood and agreed that the Joint Committee will take up as one of its earliest items of business the delineation of those activities the interruption of which would seriously hamper military operations of the United States armed forces for the joint defense of the ROK. In the Joint Committee's consideration of this matter, the Korean Labor Disputes Act of 1953 should be used as a general guide.

e. Paragraph 5: The US side accepts the ROK-proposed added phrase, "through mutual consultation," after the word "deferred."

f. Agreed Minute No. 5: The US negotiators also accept the

한·미국 간의 상호방위조약 제4조에 의한 시설과 구역 및 한국에서의 미국군대의 지위에 관한 협정(SOFA)
전59권. 1966.7.9 서울에서 서명 : 1967.2.9 발효(조약 232호) (V.38 실무교섭회의, 제82차, 1966.7.8(II))   31

modifications of Agreed Minute No. 5, as proposed by the ROK negotiators at the 81st meeting, with the addition of the phrase "by the employers" as agreed upon in informal discussions. The full text of Agreed Minute No. 5 is as follows:

> "5. A union or other employee group shall be recognized by the employers unless its objectives are inimical to the common interests of the United States and the Republic of Korea. Membership or non-membership in such groups shall not be a factor in employment or other actions affecting employees."

15. Mr. Ericson states that he felt that the revisions of text of the Labor Article, as tabled by the US side at this meeting, will be fully acceptable to the ROK negotiators. These proposals are presented as a package and the US revisions of its draft in response to ROK proposals are contingent upon ROK acceptance of the rest of the text and understandings.

16. Mr. Chang stated that the Korean negotiators appreciate the general acceptance of the revised draft of the Labor Article, as tabled at 81st session and as revised as a result of informal discussions. The Korean side accepts the modifications effected in Paragraph 1 (b) and Agreed Minutes No. 4 and No. 5, as well as in the agreed understandings, and therefore full agreement has been reached on the Labor Article.

11

0026

UNITED STATES FORCES KOREA

US – ROK STATUS OF FORCES AGREEMENT

7 JUL 1966

한·미국 간의 상호방위조약 제4조에 의한 시설과 구역 및 한국에서의 미국군대의 지위에 관한 협정(SOFA)
전59권. 1966.7.9 서울에서 서명 : 1967.2.9 발효(조약 232호) (V.38 실무교섭회의, 제82차, 1966.7.8(II))

AGREEMENT UNDER ARTICLE IV OF THE MUTUAL DEFENSE TREATY
BETWEEN THE UNITED STATES OF AMERICA AND THE REPUBLIC
OF KOREA, REGARDING FACILITIES AND AREAS AND THE STATUS
OF UNITED STATES ARMED FORCES IN THE REPUBLIC OF KOREA

0028

Agreed Minutes

- 2 -

0029

3

AGREEMENT UNDER ARTICLE IV OF THE MUTUAL DEFENSE TREATY BETWEEN THE UNITED STATES OF AMERICA AND THE REPUBLIC OF KOREA, REGARDING FACILITIES AND AREAS AND THE STATUS OF UNITED STATES ARMED FORCES IN THE REPUBLIC OF KOREA

Whereas the United States of America has disposed its armed forces in and about the territory of the Republic of Korea pursuant to the resolutions of the United Nations Security Council of June 25, 1950, June 27, 1950, and July 7, 1950, and pursuant to Article IV of the Mutual Defense Treaty between the United States of America and the Republic of Korea, signed on October 1, 1953;

Therefore, the United States of America and the Republic of Korea, in order to strengthen the close bonds of mutual interest between their two countries, have entered into this Agreement regarding facilities and areas and the status of United States armed forces in the Republic of Korea in terms as set forth below:

0031

ARTICLE I

Definitions

In this Agreement the expression:

(a) "members of the United States armed forces" means the personnel on active duty belonging to the land, sea, or air armed services of the United States of America when in the territory of the Republic of Korea except for personnel of the United States armed forces attached to the United States Embassy and personnel for whom status has been provided in the Military Advisory Group Agreement of January 26, 1950, as amended;

(b) "civilian component" means the civilian persons of United States nationality who are in the employ of, serving with, or accompanying the United States armed forces in the Republic of Korea, but excludes persons who are ordinarily resident in the Republic of Korea or who are mentioned in paragraph 1 of Article XV; for the purposes of this Agreement only, dual nationals, i.e., persons having the nationality of both the United States and the Republic of Korea, who are brought into the Republic of Korea by the United States shall be considered United States nationals;

(c) "dependents" means

    (i) spouse and children under 21;

    (ii) parents, children over 21, or other relatives dependent for over half their support upon a member of the United States armed forces or civilian component.

2

0032

ARTICLE II

Facilities and Areas - Grant and Return

1.   (a) The United States is granted, under Article IV of the Mutual Defense Treaty, the use of facilities and areas in the Republic of Korea. Agreements as to specific facilities and areas shall be concluded by the two Governments through the Joint Committee provided for in Article XXVIII of this Agreement. "Facilities and areas" include existing furnishings, equipment, and fixtures, wherever located, used in the operation of such facilities and areas.

(b) The facilities and areas of which the United States armed forces have the use at the effective date of this Agreement together with those facilities and areas which the United States armed forces have returned to the Republic of Korea with the reserved right of re-entry, when these facilities and areas have been re-entered by the United States armed forces, shall be considered as the facilities and areas agreed upon between the two Governments in accordance with subparagraph (a) above. Records of facilities and areas of which the United States armed forces have the use or the right of re-entry shall be maintained through the Joint Committee after this Agreement comes into force.

2. At the request of either Government, the Governments of the United States and the Republic of Korea shall review such agreements and may agree that such facilities and areas or portions thereof shall be returned to the Republic of Korea or that additional facilities and areas may be provided.

3

0033

3. The facilities and areas used by the United States shall be returned to the Republic of Korea under such conditions as may be agreed through the Joint Committee whenever they are no longer needed for the purposes of this Agreement and the United States agrees to keep the needs for facilities and areas under continual observation with a view toward such return.

4. (a) When facilities and areas are temporarily not being used and the Government of the Republic of Korea is so advised, the Government of the Republic of Korea may make, or permit nationals of the Republic of Korea to make, interim use of such facilities and areas provided that it is agreed between the two Governments through the Joint Committee that such use would not be harmful to the purposes for which the facilities and areas are normally used by the United States armed forces.

(b) With respect to facilities and areas which are to be used by the United States armed forces for limited periods of time, the Joint Committee shall specify in the agreements covering such facilities and areas the extent to which the provisions of this Agreement shall not apply.

ARTICLE III

Facilities and Areas - Security Measures

1. Within the facilities and areas, the United States may take all the measures necessary for their establishment, operation, safeguarding and control. In order to provide access for the United States armed forces to the facilities and areas for their support, safeguarding and control, the Government of the Republic of Korea shall, at the request of the United States armed forces and upon consultation between the two Governments through the Joint Committee, take necessary measures, within the scope of applicable laws and regulations, with respect to land, territorial waters and airspace adjacent to, or in the vicinities of the facilities and areas. The United States may also take necessary measures for such purposes upon consultation between the two Governments through the Joint Committee.

2.   (a) The United States agrees not to take the measures referred to in paragraph 1 in such a manner as to interfere unnecessarily with navigation, aviation, communication, or land travel, to, from, or within the territories of the Republic of Korea.

   (b) All questions relating to telecommunications including radio frequencies for electromagnetic radiating devices, or like matters, shall continue to be resolved expeditiously in the utmost spirit of coordination and cooperation by arrangement between the designated communications authorities of the two Governments.

5

0035

(c) The Government of the Republic of Korea shall, within the scope of applicable laws, regulations and agreements, take all reasonable measures to avoid or eliminate interference with electro-magnetic radiation sensitive devices, telecommunications devices, or other apparatus required by the United States armed forces.

3. Operations in the facilities and areas in use by the Government of the United States shall be carried on with due regard to the public safety.

6

0036

ARTICLE IV

Facilities and Areas - Return of Facilities

1. The Government of the United States is not obliged, when it returns facilities and areas to the Government of the Republic of Korea on the expiration of this Agreement or at an earlier date, to restore the facilities and areas to the condition in which they were at the time they became available to the United States armed forces, or to compensate the Government of the Republic of Korea in lieu of such restoration.

2. The Government of the Republic of Korea is not obliged to make any compensation to the Government of the United States for any improvements made in facilities and areas or for the buildings and structures left thereon on the expiration of this Agreement or the earlier return of the facilities and areas.

3. The foregoing provisions shall not apply to any construction which the Government of the United States may undertake under special arrangements with the Government of the Republic of Korea.

한·미국 간의 상호방위조약 제4조에 의한 시설과 구역 및 한국에서의 미국군대의 지위에 관한 협정(SOFA)
전59권. 1966.7.9 서울에서 서명 : 1967.2.9 발효(조약 232호) (V.38 실무교섭회의, 제82차, 1966.7.8(II))   43

ARTICLE V

Facilities and Areas - Cost and Maintenance

1. It is agreed that the United States will bear for the duration of this Agreement without cost to the Republic of Korea all expenditures incident to the maintenance of the United States armed forces in the Republic of Korea, except those to be borne by the Republic of Korea as provided in paragraph 2.

2. It is agreed that the Republic of Korea will furnish for the duration of this Agreement without cost to the United States and make compensation where appropriate to the owners and suppliers thereof all facilities and areas and rights of way, including facilities and areas jointly used such as those at airfields and ports as provided in Articles II and III. The Government of the Republic of Korea assures the use of such facilities and areas to the Government of the United States and will hold the Government of the United States as well as its agencies and employees harmless from any third party claims which may be advanced in connection with such use.

8

ARTICLE VI

Utilities and Services

1. The United States armed forces shall have the use of all utilities and services which are owned, controlled or regulated by the Government of the Republic of Korea or local administrative subdivisions thereof. The term "utilities and services" shall include, but not be limited to, transportation and communications facilities and systems, electricity, gas, water, steam, heat, light, power, and sewage disposal. The use of utilities and services as provided herein shall not prejudice the right of the United States to operate military transportation, communication, power and such other utilities and services deemed necessary for the operations of the United States armed forces. This right shall not be exercised in a manner inconsistent with the operation by the Government of the Republic of Korea of its utilities and services.

2. The use of such utilities and services by the United States shall be in accordance with priorities, conditions, and rates or tariffs no less favorable than those accorded any other user.

9

0030

ARTICLE VII

Respect for Local Law

It is the duty of members of the United States armed forces, the civilian component, the persons who are present in the Republic of Korea pursuant to Article XV, and their dependents, to respect the law of the Republic of Korea and to abstain from any activity inconsistent with the spirit of this Agreement, and, in particular, from any political activity in the Republic of Korea.

10

0040

46   주한미군지위협정(SOFA) 서명 및 발효 15

ARTICLE VIII

Entry and Exit

1.   The United States may bring into the Republic of Korea persons who are members of the United States armed forces, the civilian component, and their dependents, subject to the provisions of this Article. The Government of the Republic of Korea will be notified at regular intervals, in accordance with procedures to be agreed between the two Governments, of numbers and categories of persons entering and departing.

2.   Members of the United States armed forces shall be exempt from passport and visa laws and regulations of the Republic of Korea. Members of the United States armed forces, the civilian component, and their dependents shall be exempt from laws and regulations of the Republic of Korea on the registration and control of aliens, but shall not be considered as acquiring any right to permanent residence or domicile in the territory of the Republic of Korea.

3.   Upon entry into or departure from the Republic of Korea members of the United States armed forces shall be in possession of the following documents:

(a)   personal identity card showing name, date of birth, rank and service number, service, and photograph; and

(b)   individual or collective travel order certifying to the status of the individual or group as a member or members of the United States armed forces and to the travel ordered. For purposes

11

0041

of their identification while in the Republic of Korea, members of the United States armed forces shall be in possession of the foregoing personal identity card which must be presented on request to the appropriate authorities of the Republic of Korea.

4. Members of the civilian component, their dependents, and the dependents of members of the United States armed forces shall be in possession of appropriate documentation issued by the United States authorities so that their status may be verified by the authorities of the Republic of Korea upon their entry into or departure from the Republic of Korea, or while in the Republic of Korea.

5. If the status of any person brought into the Republic of Korea under paragraph 1 of this Article is altered so that he would no longer be entitled to such admission, the authorities of the United States shall notify the authorities of the Republic of Korea and shall, if such person be required by the authorities of the Republic of Korea to leave the Republic of Korea, assure that transportation from the Republic of Korea will be provided within a reasonable time at no cost to the Government of the Republic of Korea.

6. If the Government of the Republic of Korea has requested the removal from its territory of a member of the United States armed forces or civilian component or has made an expulsion order against an ex-member of the United States armed forces or the civilian component or against a dependent of a member or an ex-member, the

12

0042

authorities of the United States shall be responsible for receiving
the person concerned into its own territory or otherwise disposing
of him outside the Republic of Korea. This paragraph shall apply
only to persons who are not nationals of the Republic of Korea and
have entered the Republic of Korea as members of the United States
armed forces or civilian component or for the purpose of becoming
such members, and to the dependents of such persons.

13

한·미국 간의 상호방위조약 제4조에 의한 시설과 구역 및 한국에서의 미국군대의 지위에 관한 협정(SOFA)
전59권. 1966.7.9 서울에서 서명 : 1967.2.9 발효(조약 232호) (V.38 실무교섭회의, 제82차, 1966.7.8(II))
49

ARTICLE IX

Customs and Duties

1. Save as provided in this Agreement, members of the United States armed forces, the civilian component, and their dependents shall be subject to the laws and regulations administered by the customs authorities of the Republic of Korea.

2. All materials, supplies and equipment imported by the United States armed forces (including their authorized procurement agencies and their non-appropriated fund organizations provided for in Article XIII), for the official use of the United States armed forces or for the use of the members of the United States armed forces, the civilian component, and their dependents, and materials, supplies and equipment which are to be used exclusively by the United States armed forces or are ultimately to be incorporated into articles or facilities used by such forces, shall be permitted entry into the Republic of Korea; such entry shall be free from customs duties and other such charges. Appropriate certification shall be made that such materials, supplies and equipment are being imported by the United States armed forces (including their authorized procurement agencies and their non-appropriated fund organizations provided for in Article XIII), or, in the case of materials, supplies and equipment to be used exclusively by the United States armed forces or ultimately to be incorporated into articles or facilities used by such forces, that delivery thereof is to be taken by the United States armed forces for the purposes specified above. The exemptions provided in this paragraph shall

14

0044

extend to materials, supplies and equipment imported by the United
States armed forces for the use of other armed forces in Korea under
[the Republic of]
the Unified Command which receive logistical support from the United
States armed forces.

3.   Property consigned to and for the personal use of members of
the United States armed forces, the civilian component, and their
dependents, shall be subject to customs duties and other such charges,
except that no duties or charges shall be paid with respect to:

(a)   furniture, household goods, and personal effects for
their private use imported by the members of the United States armed
forces or civilian component when they first arrive to serve in the
Republic of Korea or by their dependents when they first arrive for
reunion with members of such forces or civilian component;

(b)   vehicles and parts imported by members of the United
States armed forces or civilian component for the private use of
themselves or their dependents;

(c)   reasonable quantities of personal effects and household goods of a type which would ordinarily be purchased in the United
States for the private use of members of the United States armed forces,
civilian component, and their dependents, which are mailed into the
Republic of Korea through United States military post offices.

4.   The exemptions granted in paragraphs 2 and 3 shall apply
only to cases of importation of goods and shall not be interpreted as
refunding customs duties and domestic excises collected by the customs
authorities at the time of entry in cases of purchase of goods on
which such duties and excises have already been collected.

15

0045

5. Customs examination shall not be made in the following cases:

(a) members of the United States armed forces under orders, other than leave orders, entering or leaving the Republic of Korea;

(b) official documents under official seal and First Class letter mail in the United States military postal channels under official postal seal;

(c) military cargo consigned to the United States armed forces.

6. Except as such disposal may be authorized by the authorities of the United States and of the Republic of Korea in accordance with mutually agreed conditions, goods imported into the Republic of Korea free of duty shall not be disposed of in the Republic of Korea to persons not entitled to import such goods free of duty.

7. Goods imported into the Republic of Korea free from customs duties and other such charges pursuant to paragraphs 2 and 3, may be re-exported free from customs duties and other such charges.

8. The United States armed forces, in cooperation with the authorities of the Republic of Korea, shall take such steps as are necessary to prevent abuse of privileges granted to the United States armed forces, members of such forces, the civilian component, and their dependents in accordance with this Article.

9. (a) In order to prevent offenses against laws and regulations administered by the customs authorities of the Government of the Republic of Korea, the authorities of the Republic of Korea and the United States armed forces shall assist each other in the conduct of inquiries and the collection of evidence.

16

0046

(b) The United States armed forces shall render all assistance within their power to ensure that articles liable to seizure by, or on behalf of, the customs authorities of the Government of the Republic of Korea are handed over to those authorities.

(c) The United States armed forces shall render all assistance within their power to ensure the payment of duties, taxes, and penalties payable by members of such forces or of the civilian component, or their dependents.

(d) The authorities of the United States armed forces shall provide all practicable assistance to the customs officials dispatched to military controlled piers and airports for the purpose of customs inspection.

(e) Vehicles and articles belonging to the United States armed forces seized by the customs authorities of the Government of the Republic of Korea in connection with an offense against its customs or fiscal laws or regulations shall be handed over to the appropriate authorities of such forces.

17

0047

ARTICLE X

Access of Vessels and Aircraft

1. United States and foreign vessels and aircraft operated by, for, or under the control of the United States for official purposes shall be accorded access to any port or airport of the Republic of Korea free from toll or landing charges. When cargo or passengers not accorded the exemptions of this Agreement are carried on such vessels and aircraft, notification shall be given to the appropriate authorities of the Republic of Korea, and the entry into and departure from the Republic of Korea of such cargo and passengers shall be according to the laws and regulations of the Republic of Korea.

2. The vessels and aircraft mentioned in paragraph 1, United States Government-owned vehicles including armor, and members of the United States armed forces, the civilian component, and their dependents shall be accorded access to and movement between facilities and areas in use by the United States armed forces and between such facilities and areas and the ports or airports of the Republic of Korea. Such access to and movement between facilities and areas by United States military vehicles shall be free from toll and other charges.

3. When the vessels mentioned in paragraph 1 enter ports of the Republic of Korea, appropriate notification shall, under normal conditions, be made to the proper authorities of the Republic of Korea. Such vessels shall have freedom from compulsory pilotage, but if a pilot is taken pilotage shall be paid for at appropriate rates.

0048

ARTICLE XI

Meteorological Services

The Government of the Republic of Korea undertakes to furnish the United States armed forces with the following meteorological services in accordance with arrangements between the appropriate authorities of the two Governments:

    (a) meteorological observations from land and ocean areas including observations from ships;

    (b) climatological information including periodic summaries and historical data wherever available;

    (c) telecommunications service to disseminate meteorological information;

    (d) seismographic data.

19

0049

ARTICLE XII

Air Traffic Control and Navigational Aids

1. All civil and military air traffic control shall be developed in close coordination and shall be integrated to the extent necessary for the operation of this Agreement. Procedures, and any subsequent changes thereto, necessary to effect this coordination and integration will be established by arrangements between the appropriate authorities of the two Governments.

2. The United States is authorized to establish, construct and maintain aids to navigation for vessels and aircraft, both visual and electronic as required, throughout the Republic of Korea and in the territorial waters thereof. Such navigation aids shall conform generally to the system in use in the Republic of Korea. The authorities of the United States and the Republic of Korea which have established navigation aids shall duly notify each other of their positions and characteristics and shall give advance notification where practicable before making any changes in them or establishing additional navigation aids.

ARTICLE XIII

Non-appropriated Fund Organizations

1.   (a) Military exchanges, messes, social clubs, theaters, newspapers and other non-appropriated fund organizations authorized and regulated by the United States military authorities may be established by the United States armed forces for the use of members of such forces, the civilian component, and their dependents. Except as otherwise provided in this Agreement such organizations shall not be subject to Korean regulations, licenses, fees, taxes, or similar controls.

(b) When a newspaper authorized and regulated by the United States military authorities is sold to the general public, it shall be subject to Korean regulations, licenses, fees, taxes, or similar controls so far as such circulation is concerned.

2.   No Korean tax shall be imposed on sales of merchandise or services by such organizations, except as provided in paragraph 1 (b) of this Article. Purchases within the Republic of Korea of merchandise and supplies by such organizations shall be subject to the Korean taxes to which other purchasers of such merchandise and supplies are subject unless otherwise agreed between the two Governments.

3.   Except as such disposal may be permitted by the authorities of the United States and the Republic of Korea in accordance with mutually agreed conditions, goods which are sold by such organizations shall not be disposed of in the Republic of Korea to persons not authorized to make purchases from such organizations.

21

0051

4. The organizations referred to in this Article shall, through consultation between the representatives of the two Governments in the Joint Committee, provide such information to the tax authorities of the Republic of Korea as is required by tax legislation of the Republic of Korea.

22

0052

ARTICLE XIV

Taxation

1. The United States armed forces shall not be subject to taxes or similar charges on property held, used or transferred by such forces in the Republic of Korea.

2. Members of the United States armed forces, the civilian component, and their dependents shall not be liable to pay any Korean taxes to the Government of the Republic of Korea or to any other taxing agency in the Republic of Korea on income received as a result of their service with or employment by the United States armed forces, including the organizations provided for in Article XIII. Persons in the Republic of Korea solely by reason of being members of the United States armed forces, the civilian component, or their dependents shall not be liable to pay any Korean taxes to the Government of the Republic of Korea or to any taxing agency in the Republic of Korea on income derived from sources outside of the Republic of Korea, nor shall periods during which such persons are in the Republic of Korea be considered as periods of residence or domicile in the Republic of Korea for the purpose of Korean taxation. The provisions of this Article do not exempt such persons from payment of Korean taxes on income derived from Korean sources, other than those sources referred to in the first sentence of this paragraph, nor do they exempt United States citizens who claim residence in the Republic of Korea for United States income tax purposes from payment of Korean taxes on income.

23

0053

3. Members of the United States armed forces, the civilian
component, and their dependents shall be exempt from taxation in the
Republic of Korea on the holding, use, transfer _inter se_, or transfer
by death of movable property, tangible or intangible, the presence of
which in the Republic of Korea is due solely to the temporary presence
of these persons in the Republic of Korea, provided that such exemption shall not apply to property held for the purpose of investment
or the conduct of business in the Republic of Korea or to any
intangible property registered in the Republic of Korea.

24

0054

ARTICLE XV

Invited Contractors

1. Persons, including (a) corporations organized under the laws of the United States, (b) their employees who are ordinarily resident in the United States, and (c) the dependents of the foreoging, present in the Republic of Korea solely for the purpose of executing contracts with the United States for the benefit of the United States armed forces or other armed forces in the Republic of Korea under the Unified Command receiving logistical support from the United States armed forces, who are designated by the Government of the United States in accordance with the provisions of paragraph 2 below, shall, except as provided in this Article, be subject to the laws and regulations of the Republic of Korea.

2. The designation referred to in paragraph 1 above shall be made upon consultation with the Government of the Republic of Korea and shall be restricted to cases where open competitive bidding is not practicable due to security considerations, to the technical qualifications of the contractors involved, to the unavailability of materials or services required by the United States standards, or to limitations of United States law. The designation shall be withdrawn by the Government of the United States:

(a) upon completion of contracts with the United States armed forces or other armed forces in the Republic of Korea under the Unified Command receiving logistical support from the United States armed forces;

25

0055

한·미국 간의 상호방위조약 제4조에 의한 시설과 구역 및 한국에서의 미국군대의 지위에 관한 협정(SOFA) 전59권. 1966.7.9 서울에서 서명 : 1967.2.9 발효(조약 232호) (V.38 실무교섭회의, 제82차, 1966.7.8(II))

(b) upon proof that such persons are engaged in business activities in the Republic of Korea other than those pertaining to the United States armed forces or other armed forces in the Republic of Korea under the Unified Command receiving logistical support from the United States armed forces;

(c) upon proof that such persons are engaged in practices illegal in the Republic of Korea.

3. Upon certification by appropriate United States authorities as to their identity, such persons shall be accorded the following benefits of this Agreement:

(a) accession and movement, as provided for in Article X, paragraph 2;

(b) entry into the Republic of Korea in accordance with the provisions of Article VIII;

(c) the exemption from customs duties, and other such charges provided for in Article IX, paragraph 3, for members of the United States armed forces, the civilian component, and their dependents;

(d) if authorized by the Government of the United States, the use of the services of the organizations provided for in Article XIII;

(e) those provided in Article XVIII, paragraph 2, for members of the United States armed forces, the civilian component, and their dependents;

(f) if authorized by the Government of the United States, the use of military payment certificates, as provided for in Article XIX;

(g) the use of postal facilities provided for in Article XX;

(h) the use of utilities and services in accordance with those priorities, conditions, rates or tariffs accorded the United States armed forces by Article VI relating to utilities and services;

(i) exemption from the laws and regulations of the Republic of Korea with respect to terms and conditions of employment, and licensing and registration of businesses and corporations.

4. The arrival, departure, and place of residence in the Republic of Korea of such persons shall from time to time be notified by the United States armed forces to the authorities of the Republic of Korea.

5. Upon certification by an authorized representative of the United States armed forces, depreciable assets, except houses, held, used or transferred by such persons exclusively for the execution of contracts referred to in paragraph 1 shall not be subject to taxes or similar charges of the Republic of Korea.

6. Upon certification by an authorized representative of the United States armed forces, such persons shall be exempt from taxation in the Republic of Korea on the holding, use, transfer by death, or transfer to persons or agencies entitled to tax exemption under this Agreement, of movable property, tangible or intangible, the presence of which in the Republic of Korea is due solely to the temporary presence of these persons in the Republic of Korea, provided that such

0057

exemption shall not apply to property held for the purpose of investment or the conduct of other business in the Republic of Korea or to any intangible property registered in the Republic of Korea.

7. Such persons shall not be liable to pay income or corporation taxes to the Government of the Republic of Korea or to any other taxing agency in the Republic of Korea on any income derived under a contract with the Government of the United States in connection with the construction, maintenance or operation of any of the facilities or areas covered by this Agreement. Such persons shall not be liable to pay any Korean taxes to the Government of the Republic of Korea or to any taxing agency in the Republic of Korea on income derived from sources outside of the Republic of Korea nor shall periods during which such persons are in the Republic of Korea be considered periods of residence or domicile in the Republic of Korea for the purposes of Korean taxation. The provisions of this paragraph do not exempt such persons from payment of income or corporation taxes on income derived from Korean sources, other than those sources referred to in the first sentence of this paragraph, nor do they exempt such persons who claim residence in the Republic of Korea for United States income tax purposes from payment of Korea taxes on income.

8. The authorities of the Republic of Korea shall have the right to exercise jurisdiction over such persons for offenses committed in the Republic of Korea and punishable by the law of the Republic of Korea. In recognition of the role of such persons in the defense of the

28

Republic of Korea, they shall be subject to the provisions of paragraphs 5, 7(b), and 9 and the related Agreed Minutes, of Article XXII. In those cases in which the authorities of the Republic of Korea decide not to exercise jurisdiction they shall notify the military authorities of the United States as soon as possible. Upon such notification the military authorities of the United States shall have the right to exercise such jurisdiction over the persons referred to as is conferred on them by the law of the United States.

29

한·미국 간의 상호방위조약 제4조에 의한 시설과 구역 및 한국에서의 미국군대의 지위에 관한 협정(SOFA)
전59권. 1966.7.9 서울에서 서명 : 1967.2.9 발효(조약 232호) (V.38 실무교섭회의, 제82차, 1966.7.8(II))

65

ARTICLE XVI

Local Procurement

1. The United States may contract for any materials, supplies, equipment and services (including construction work) to be furnished or undertaken in the Republic of Korea for purposes of, or authorized by, this Agreement, without restriction as to choice of contractor, supplier or person who provides such services. Such materials, supplies, equipment and services may, upon agreement between the appropriate authorities of the two Governments, also be procured through the Government of the Republic of Korea.

2. Materials, supplies, equipment and services which are required from local sources for the maintenance of the United States armed forces and the procurement of which may have an adverse effect on the economy of the Republic of Korea shall be procured in coordination with, and, when desirable, through or with the assistance of, the competent authorities of the Republic of Korea.

3. Materials, supplies, equipment and services procured for official purposes in the Republic of Korea by the United States armed forces, including their authorized procurement agencies, or procured for ultimate use by the United States armed forces shall be exempt from the following Korea taxes upon appropriate certification in advance by the United States armed forces:

    (a) commodity tax;

    (b) traffic tax;

    (c) petroleum tax;

    (d) electricity and gas tax;

    (e) business tax.

30

0060

With respect to any present or future Korean taxes not specifically referred to in this Article which might be found to constitute a significant and readily identifiable part of the gross purchase price of materials, supplies, equipment and services procured by the United States armed forces, or for ultimate use by such forces, the two Governments will agree upon a procedure for granting such exemption or relief therefrom as is consistent with the purpose of this Article.

4. Neither members of the United States armed forces, civilian component, nor their dependents, shall by reason of this Article enjoy any exemption from taxes or similar charges relating to personal purchases of goods and services in the Republic of Korea chargeable under legislation of the Republic of Korea.

5. Except as such disposal may be authorized by the authorities of the United States and the Republic of Korea in accordance with mutually agreed conditions, goods purchased in the Republic of Korea exempt from taxes referred to in paragraph 3, shall not be disposed of in the Republic of Korea to persons not entitled to purchase such goods exempt from such taxes.

한·미국 간의 상호방위조약 제4조에 의한 시설과 구역 및 한국에서의 미국군대의 지위에 관한 협정(SOFA)
전59권. 1966.7.9 서울에서 서명 : 1967.2.9 발효(조약 232호) (V.38 실무교섭회의, 제82차, 1966.7.8(II))

ARTICLE XVII

Labor

1. In this Article the expression:

    (a) "employer" refers to the United States armed forces (including non-appropriated fund organizations) and the persons referred to in the first paragraph of Article XV;

    (b) "employee" refers to any civilian (other than a member of the civilian component or a contractor employee under Article XV) employed by an employer, except (1) a member of the Korean Service Corps and (2) a domestic employed by an individual member of the United States armed forces, civilian component or dependent thereof. Such employees shall be nationals of the Republic of Korea.

2. Employers may recruit, employ and administer their personnel. Recruitment services of the Government of the Republic of Korea will be utilized insofar as is practicable. In case employers accomplish direct recruitment of employees, employers will provide such relevant information as may be required for labor administration to the Office of Labor Affairs of the Republic of Korea.

3. To the extent not inconsistent with the provisions of this Article or the military requirements of the United States armed forces, the conditions of employment, compensation, and labor-management relations established by the United States armed forces for their employees shall conform with provisions of labor legislation of the Republic of Korea.

0062

4. (a) In consideration of provision for collective action in labor legislation of the Republic of Korea, any dispute between employers and employees or any recognized employee organization, which cannot be settled through grievance or labor relations procedures of the United States armed forces, shall be settled as follows:

(i) The dispute shall be referred to the Office of Labor Affairs of the Republic of Korea for conciliation.

(ii) In the event that the dispute is not settled by the procedure described in (i) above, the matter will be referred to the Joint Committee, which may refer the matter to a special committee designated by the Joint Committee for further conciliation efforts.

(iii) In the event that the dispute is not settled by the procedures outlined above, the Joint Committee will resolve the dispute, assuring that expeditious procedures are followed. The decisions of the Joint Committee shall be binding.

(iv) Failure of any recognized employee organization or employee to abide by the decision of the Joint Committee on any dispute, or engaging in practices disruptive of normal work requirements during settlement procedures, shall be considered just cause for the withdrawal of recognition of that organization and the discharge of that employee.

(v) Neither employee organizations nor employees shall engage in any practices disruptive of normal work requirements unless a period of at least 70 days has elapsed after the dispute is referred to the Joint Committee, as stipulated in subparagraph (ii), above.

33

0063

(b) Employees or any employee organization shall have the right of further collective action in the event a labor dispute is not resolved by the foregoing procedures except in cases where the Joint Committee determines such action seriously hampers military operations of the United States armed forces for the joint defense of the Republic of Korea. In the event an agreement cannot be reached on this question in the Joint Committee, it may be made the subject of review through discussions between appropriate officials of the Government of the Republic of Korea and the diplomatic mission of the United States of America.

(c) In the event of a national emergency, such as war, hostilities, or situations where war or hostilities may be imminent, the application of this Article shall be limited in accordance with emergency measures taken by the Government of the Republic of Korea in consultation with the military authorities of the United States.

5. (a) Should the Republic of Korea adopt measures allocating labor, the United States armed forces shall be accorded allocation privileges no less favorable than those enjoyed by the armed forces of the Republic of Korea.

(b) In the event of a national emergency, such as war, hostilities, or situations where war or hostilities may be imminent, employees who have acquired skills essential to the mission of the United States armed forces shall, upon request of the United States

34

armed forces, be deferred through mutual consultation from Republic of Korea military service or other compulsory service. The United States armed forces shall furnish in advance to the Republic of Korea lists of those employees deemed essential.

6. Members of the civilian component shall not be subject to laws or regulations of the Republic of Korea with respect to their terms and condition of employment.

0065

35

ARTICLE XVIII

Foreign Exchange Controls

1. Members of the United States armed forces, the civilian component and their dependents, shall be subject to the foreign exchange controls of the Government of the Republic of Korea.

2. The preceding paragraph shall not be construed to preclude the transmission into or out of the Republic of Korea of United States dollars or dollar instruments representing the official funds of the United States or realized as a result of service or employment in connection with this Agreement by members of the United States armed forces and the civilian component, or realized by such persons and their dependents from sources outside of the Republic of Korea.

3. The United States authorities shall take suitable measures to preclude the abuse of the privileges stipulated in the preceding paragraph or circumvention of the foreign exchange controls of the Republic of Korea.

0066

ARTICLE XIX

Military Payment Certificates

1. (a) United States military payment certificates denominated in dollars may be used by persons authorized by the United States for internal transactions. The Government of the United States will take appropriate action to ensure that authorized personnel are prohibited from engaging in transactions involving military payment certificates except as authorized by United States regulations. The Government of the Republic of Korea will take necessary action to prohibit unauthorized persons from engaging in transactions involving military payment certificates and with the aid of United States authorities will undertake to apprehend and punish any person or persons under its jurisdiction involved in the counterfeiting or uttering of counterfeit military payment certificates.

(b) It is agreed that the United States authorities will, to the extent authorized by United States law, apprehend and punish members of the United States armed forces, the civilian component, or their dependents, who tender military payment certificates to unauthorized persons and that no obligation will be due to such unauthorized persons or to the Government of the Republic of Korea or its agencies from the United States or any of its agencies as a result of any unauthorized use of military payment certificates within the Republic of Korea.

0067

한·미국 간의 상호방위조약 제4조에 의한 시설과 구역 및 한국에서의 미국군대의 지위에 관한 협정(SOFA)
전59권. 1966.7.9 서울에서 서명 : 1967.2.9 발효(조약 232호) (V.38 실무교섭회의, 제82차, 1966.7.8(II)) 73

2.   In order to exercise control of military payment certificates the United States may designate certain American financial institutions to maintain and operate, under United States supervision, facilities for the use of persons authorized by the United States to use military payment certificates. Institutions authorized to maintain military banking facilities will establish and maintain such facilities physically separated from their Korean commercial banking business, with personnel whose sole duty is to maintain and operate such facilities. Such facilities shall be permitted to maintain United States currency bank accounts and to perform all financial transactions in connection therewith including receipt and remission of funds to the extent provided by Article XVIII, paragraph 2, of this Agreement.

ARTICLE XX

Military Post Offices

The United States may establish and operate, within the facilities and areas in use by the United States armed forces, United States military post offices for the use of members of the United States armed forces, the civilian component, and their dependents, for the transmission of mail between United States military post offices in the Republic of Korea and between such military post offices and other United States post offices.

0069

한·미국 간의 상호방위조약 제4조에 의한 시설과 구역 및 한국에서의 미국군대의 지위에 관한 협정(SOFA)
전59권. 1966.7.9 서울에서 서명 : 1967.2.9 발효(조약 232호) (V.38 실무교섭회의, 제82차, 1966.7.8(II))

ARTICLE XXI

Accounting Procedures

It is agreed that arrangements will be effected between the Governments of the United States and the Republic of Korea for accounting applicable to financial transactions arising out of this Agreement.

0070

40

ARTICLE XXII

Criminal Jurisdiction

1.   Subject to the provisions of this article,

(a) the military authorities of the United States shall have the right to exercise within the Republic of Korea all criminal and disciplinary jurisdiction conferred on them by the law of the United States over members of the United States armed forces or civilian component, and their dependents;

(b) the authorities of the Republic of Korea shall have jurisdiction over the members of the United States armed forces or civilian component, and their dependents, with respect to offenses committed within the territory of the Republic of Korea and punishable by the law of the Republic of Korea.

2.   (a) The military authorities of the United States shall have the right to exercise exclusive jurisdiction over members of the United States armed forces or civilian component, and their dependents, with respect to offenses, including offenses relating to its security, punishable by the law of the United States, but not by the law of the Republic of Korea.

(b) The authorities of the Republic of Korea shall have the right to exercise exclusive jurisdiction over members of the United States armed forces or civilian component, and their dependents, with respect to offenses, including offenses relating to the security of the Republic of Korea, punishable by its law

0071

41

but not by the law of the United States.

(c) For the purpose of this paragraph and of paragraph 3 of this Article, a security offense against a State shall include:

(i) treason against the State;

(ii) sabotage, espionage or violation of any law relating to official secrets of that State, or secrets relating to the national defense of that State.

3. In cases where the right to exercise jurisdiction is concurrent the following rules shall apply:

(a) The military authorities of the United States shall have the primary right to exercise jurisdiction over members of the United States armed forces or civilian component, and their dependents, in relation to:

(i) offenses solely against the property or security of the United States, or offenses solely against the person or property of another member of the United States armed forces or civilian component or of a dependent;

(ii) offenses arising out of any act or omission done in the performance of official duty.

(b) In the case of any other offense, the authorities of the Republic of Korea shall have the primary right to exercise jurisdiction.

0072

42

(c) If the State having the primary right decides not to exercise jurisdiction, it shall notify the authorities of the other State as soon as practicable. The authorities of the State having the primary right shall give sympathetic consideration to a request from the authorities of the other State for a waiver of its right in cases where that other State considers such waiver to be of particular importance.

4. The foregoing provisions of this Article shall not imply any right for the military authorities of the United States to exercise jurisdiction over persons who are nationals of or ordinarily resident in the Republic of Korea, unless they are members of the United States armed forces.

5. (a) The military authorities of the United States and the authorities of the Republic of Korea shall assist each other in the arrest of members of the United States armed forces, the civilian component, or their dependents in the territory of the Republic of Korea and in handing them over to the authority which is to have custody in accordance with the following provisions.

(b) The authorities of the Republic of Korea shall notify promptly the military authorities of the United States of the arrest of any member of the United States armed forces, or civilian component, or a dependent. The military authorities of the United States shall promptly notify the authorities of the Republic of Korea of the arrest of a member of the United States

43

armed forces, the civilian component, or a dependent in any case in which the Republic of Korea has the primary right to exercise jurisdiction.

(c) The custody of an accused member of the United States armed forces or civilian component, or of a dependent, over whom the Republic of Korea is to exercise jurisdiction shall, if he is in the hands of the military authorities of the United States, remain with the military authorities of the United States pending the conclusion of all judicial proceedings and until custody is requested by the authorities of the Republic of Korea. If he is in the hands of the Republic of Korea, he shall, on request, be handed over to the military authorities of the United States and remain in their custody pending completion of all judicial proceedings and until custody is requested by the authorities of the Republic of Korea. When an accused has been in the custody of the military authorities of the United States, the military authorities of the United States may transfer custody to the authorities of the Republic of Korea at any time, and shall give sympathetic consideration to any request for the transfer of custody which may be made by the authorities of the Republic of Korea in specific cases. The military authorities of the United States shall promptly make any such accused available to the authorities of the Republic of Korea upon their request for purposes of investigation and trial, and shall take all appropriate

0074

44

measures to that end and to prevent any prejudice to the course
of justice. They shall take full account of any special request
regarding custody made by the authorities of the Republic of
Korea. The authorities of the Republic of Korea shall give sympathetic consideration to a request from the military authorities of
the United States for assistance in maintaining custody of an
accused member of the United States armed forces, the civilian
component, or a dependent.

(d) In respect of offenses solely against the security
of the Republic of Korea provided in paragraph 2(c), an accused
shall be in the custody of the authorities of the Republic of
Korea.

6. (a) The military authorities of the United States and
the authorities of the Republic of Korea shall assist each other
in the carrying out of all necessary investigations into offenses,
and in the collection and production of evidence, including the
seizure and, in proper cases, the handing over of objects
connected with an offense. The handing over of such objects may,
however, be made subject to their return within the time specified
by the authority delivering them.

(b) The military authorities of the United States and
the authorities of the Republic of Korea shall notify each other
of the disposition of all cases in which there are concurrent
rights to exercise jurisdiction.

한·미국 간의 상호방위조약 제4조에 의한 시설과 구역 및 한국에서의 미국군대의 지위에 관한 협정(SOFA)
전59권. 1966.7.9 서울에서 서명 : 1967.2.9 발효(조약 232호) (V.38 실무교섭회의, 제82차, 1966.7.8(II))   81

7. (a) A death sentence shall not be carried out in the Republic of Korea by the military authorities of the United States if the legislation of the Republic of Korea does not provide for such punishment in a similar case.

(b) The authorities of the Republic of Korea shall give sympathetic consideration to a request from the military authorities of the United States for assistance in carrying out a sentence of imprisonment pronounced by the military authorities of the United States under the provisions of this Article within the territory of the Republic of Korea. The authorities of the Republic of Korea shall also give sympathetic consideration to a request from the authorities of the United States for the custody of any member of the United States armed forces or civilian component or a dependent, who is serving a sentence of confinement imposed by a court of the Republic of Korea. If such custody is released to the military authorities of the United States, the United States shall be obligated to continue the confinement of the individual in an appropriate confinement facility of the United States until the sentence to confinement shall have been served in full or until release from such confinement shall be approved by competent authorities of the Republic of Korea. In such cases, the authorities of the United States shall furnish relevant information on a routine basis to the authorities of the

0076

46

Republic of Korea, and a representative of the Government of the Republic of Korea shall have the right to have access to a member of the United States armed forces, the civilian component, or a dependent who is serving a sentence imposed by a court of the Republic of Korea in confinement facilities of the United States.

8. Where an accused has been tried in accordance with the provisions of this Article either by the military authorities of the United States or the authorities of the Republic of Korea and has been acquitted, or has been convicted and is serving, or has served, his sentence, or his sentence has been remitted or suspended, or he has been pardoned, he may not be tried again for the same offense within the territory of the Republic of Korea by the authorities of the other State. However, nothing in this paragraph shall prevent the military authorities of the United States from trying a member of its armed forces for any violation of rules of discipline arising from an act or omission which constituted an offense for which he was tried by the authorities of the Republic of Korea.

9. Whenever a member of the United States armed forces or civilian component or a dependent is prosecuted under the jurisdiction of the Republic of Korea he shall be entitled:

한·미국 간의 상호방위조약 제4조에 의한 시설과 구역 및 한국에서의 미국군대의 지위에 관한 협정(SOFA)
전59권. 1966.7.9 서울에서 서명 : 1967.2.9 발효(조약 232호) (V.38 실무교섭회의, 제82차, 1966.7.8(II)) 83

(a) to a prompt and speedy trial;

(b) to be informed, in advance of trial, of the specific charge or charges made against him;

(c) to be confronted with the witnesses against him;

(d) to have compulsory process for obtaining witnesses in his favor, if they are within the jurisdiction of the Republic of Korea;

(e) to have legal representation of his own choice for his defense or to have free or assisted legal representation under the conditions prevailing for the time being in the Republic of Korea;

(f) if he considers it necessary, to have the services of a competent interpreter; and

(g) to communicate with a representative of the Government of the United States and to have such a representative present at his trial.

10. (a) Regularly constituted military units or formations of the United States armed forces shall have the right to police any facilities or areas which they use under Article II of this Agreement. The military police of such forces may take all appropriate measures to ensure the maintenance of order and security within such facilities and areas.

0078

(b) Outside these facilities and areas, such military police shall be employed only subject to arrangements with the authorities of the Republic of Korea and in liaison with those authorities, and in so far as such employment is necessary to maintain discipline and order among the members of the United States armed forces, or ensure their security.

11. In the event of hostilities to which the provisions of Article II of the Mutual Defense Treaty apply, the provisions of this Agreement pertaining to criminal jurisdiction shall be immediately suspended and the military authorities of the United States shall have the right to exercise exclusive jurisdiction over members of the United States armed forces, the civilian component, and their dependents.

12. The provisions of this Article shall not apply to any offenses committed before the entry into force of this Agreement. Such cases shall be governed by the provisions of the Agreement between the United States of America and the Republic of Korea effected by an exchange of notes at Taejon on July 12, 1950.

0079

49

ARTICLE XXIII

Claims

1.   Each party waives all its claims against the other Party
for damage to any property owned by it and used by its armed forces,
if such damage--

(a) was caused by a member or an employee of the armed
forces of the other Party, in performance of his official duties; or

(b) arose from the use of any vehicle, vessel or aircraft owned by the other Party and used by its armed forces,
provided either that the vehicle, vessel or aircraft causing the
damage was being used for official purposes or that the damage was
caused to property being so used.
Claims for maritime salvage by one Party against the other Party
shall be waived, provided that the vessel or cargo salved was
owned by the other Party and being used by its armed forces for
official purposes.

2.   (a) In the case of damage caused or arising as stated in
paragraph 1 to other property owned by either Party, the issue of
liability of the other Party shall be determined and the amount of
damage shall be assessed, unless the two Governments agree otherwise, by a sole arbitrator selected in accordance with subparagraph
(b) of this paragraph. The arbitrator shall also decide any
counterclaims arising out of the same incident.

0080

(b) The arbitrator referred to in subparagraph (a) above shall be selected by agreement between the two Governments from among the nationals of the Republic of Korea who hold or have held high judicial office.

(c) Any decision taken by the arbitrator shall be binding and conclusive upon the Parties.

(d) The amount of any compensation awarded by the arbitrator shall be distributed in accordance with the provisions of paragraph 5(e)(i), (ii) and (iii) of this Article.

(e) The compensation of the arbitrator shall be fixed by agreement between the two Governments and shall, together with the necessary expenses incidental to the performance of his duties, be defrayed in equal proportions by them.

(f) Each Party waives its claim in any such case up to the amount of 1,400 United States dollars or its equivalent in Korean currency at the rate of exchange provided for in the Agreed Minute to Article XVIII at the time the claim is filed.

3. For the purpose of paragraphs 1 and 2 of this Article the expression "owned by a Party" in the case of a vessel includes a vessel on bare boat charter to that Party or requisitioned by it on bare boat terms or seized by it in prize (except to the extent that the risk of loss or liability is borne by some person other than such Party).

0081

한·미국 간의 상호방위조약 제4조에 의한 시설과 구역 및 한국에서의 미국군대의 지위에 관한 협정(SOFA)
전59권. 1966.7.9 서울에서 서명 : 1967.2.9 발효(조약 232호) (V.38 실무교섭회의, 제82차, 1966.7.8(II)) 87

4. Each Party waives all its claims against the other Party for injury or death suffered by any member of its armed forces while such member was engaged in the performance of his official duties.

5. Claims (other than contractual claims and those to which paragraph 6 or 7 of this Article apply) arising out of acts or omissions of members or employees of the United States armed forces, including those employees who are nationals of or ordinarily resident in the Republic of Korea, done in the performance of official duty, or out of any other act, omission or occurrence for which the United States armed forces are legally responsible, and causing damage in the Republic of Korea to third parties, other than the Government of the Republic of Korea, shall be dealt with by the Republic of Korea in accordance with the following provisions:

(a) Claims shall be filed, considered and settled or adjudicated in accordance with the laws and regulations of the Republic of Korea with respect to the claims arising from the activities of its own armed forces.

(b) The Republic of Korea may settle any such claims, and payment of the amount agreed upon or determined by adjudication shall be made by the Republic of Korea in won.

(c) Such payment, whether made pursuant to a settlement or to adjudication of the case by a competent tribunal of the Republic of Korea, or the final adjudication by such a tribunal denying payment, shall be binding and conclusive upon the Parties.

0082

52

(d) Every claim paid by the Republic of Korea shall be communicated to the appropriate ~~United States~~ authorities ~~of the United States~~ together with full particulars and a proposed distribution in conformity with subparagraph (e)(i) and (ii) below. In default of a reply within two months, the proposed distribution shall be regarded as accepted.

(e) The cost incurred in satisfying claims pursuant to the preceding subparagraph and paragraph 2 of this Article shall be distributed between the Parties as follows:

(i) Where the United States alone is responsible, the amount awarded or adjudged shall be distributed in the proportion of 25 percent chargeable to the Republic of Korea and 75 percent chargeable to the United States.

(ii) Where the Republic of Korea and the United States are responsible for the damage, the amount awarded or adjudged shall be distributed equally between them. Where the damage was caused by the armed forces of the Republic of Korea or of the United States and it is not possible to attribute it specifically to one or both of those armed forces, the amount awarded or adjudged shall be distributed equally between the Republic of Korea and the United States.

(iii) Every half year, a statement of the sums paid by the Republic of Korea in the course of the half-yearly period in respect of every case regarding which the liability, amount, and proposed distribution on a percentage basis has been approved by

0083

53

both Governments shall be sent to the appropriate authorities of the United States, together with a request for reimbursement. Such reimbursement shall be made in won within the shortest possible time. The approval by both Governments as referred to in this subparagraph shall not prejudice any decision taken by the arbitrator or adjudication by a competent tribunal of the Republic of Korea as set forth in paragraphs 2(c) and 5(c) respectively.

(f) Members or employees of the United States armed forces, including those employees who are nationals of or ordinarily resident in the Republic of Korea, shall not be subject to any proceedings for the enforcement of any judgment given against them in the Republic of Korea in a matter arising from the performance of their official duties.

(g) Except insofar as subparagraph (e) of this paragraph applies to claims covered by paragraph 2 of this Article, the provisions of this paragraph shall not apply to any claim arising out of or in connection with the navigation or operation of a ship or the loading, carriage, or discharge of a cargo, other than claims for death or personal injury to which paragraph 4 of this Article does not apply.

6. Claims against members or employees of the United States armed forces (except employees who are nationals of or ordinarily resident in the Republic of Korea) arising out of tortious acts or omissions in the Republic of Korea not done in the performance of official duty shall be dealt with in the following manner:

0084

(a) The authorities of the Republic of Korea shall consider the claim and assess compensation to the claimant in a fair and just manner, taking into account all the circumstances of the case, including the conduct of the injured person, and shall prepare a report on the matter.

(b) The report shall be delivered to the appropriate United States authorities, who shall then decide without delay whether they will offer an _ex gratia_ payment, and if so, of what amount.

(c) If an offer of _ex gratia_ payment is made, and accepted by the claimant in full satisfaction of his claim, the United States authorities shall make the payment themselves and inform the authorities of the Republic of Korea of their decision and of the sum paid.

(d) Nothing in this paragraph shall affect the jurisdiction of the courts of the Republic of Korea to entertain an action against a member or employee of the United States armed forces unless and until there has been payment in full satisfaction of the claim.

7. Claims arising out of the unauthorized use of any vehicle of the United States armed forces shall be dealt with in accordance with paragraph 6 of this Article, except insofar as the United States armed forces are legally responsible.

0085

55

8.   If a dispute arises as to whether a tortious act or omission of a member or an employee of the United States armed forces was done in the performance of official duty or as to whether the use of any vehicle of the United States armed forces was unauthorized, the question shall be submitted to an arbitrator appointed in accordance with paragraph 2(b) of this Article, whose decision on this point shall be final and conclusive.

9.   (a) The United States shall not claim immunity from the jurisdiction of the courts of the Republic of Korea for members or employees of the United States armed forces in respect of the civil jurisdiction of the courts of the Republic of Korea except in respect of proceedings for the enforcement of any judgment given against them in the Republic of Korea in a matter arising from the performance of their official duties or except after payment in full satisfaction of a claim.

(b) In the case of any private movable property, excluding that in use by the United States armed forces, which is subject to compulsory execution under the law of the Republic of Korea, and is within the facilities and areas in use by the United States armed forces, the authorities of the United States shall, upon the request of the courts of the Republic of Korea, render all assistance within their power to see that such property is turned over to the authorities of the Republic of Korea.

0086

(c) The authorities of the United States and the Republic of Korea shall cooperate in the procurement of evidence for a fair disposition of claims under this Article.

10. Disputes arising out of contracts concerning the procurement of materials, supplies, equipment, or services by or for the United States armed forces, which are not resolved by the Parties to the contract concerned, may be submitted to the Joint Committee for conciliation, provided that the provisions of this paragraph shall not prejudice any right, which Parties to the contract may have, to file a civil suit.

11. Paragraphs 2 and 5 of this Article shall apply only to claims arising incident to non-combat activities.

12. For the purposes of this Article, members of the Korean Augmentation to the United States Army (KATUSA) shall be considered as members of the United States armed forces.

13. The provisions of this Article shall not apply to any claims which arose before the entry into force of this Agreement. Such claims shall be processed and settled by the authorities of the United States.

한·미국 간의 상호방위조약 제4조에 의한 시설과 구역 및 한국에서의 미국군대의 지위에 관한 협정(SOFA)
전59권. 1966.7.9 서울에서 서명 : 1967.2.9 발효(조약 232호) (V.38 실무교섭회의, 제82차, 1966.7.8(II))

ARTICLE XXIV

Vehicle and Driver's Licenses

1.   The Republic of Korea shall accept as valid, without a driving test or fee, the driving permit or license or military driving permit issued by the United States, or political subdivision thereof, to a member of the United States armed forces, the civilian component, and their dependents.

2.   Official vehicles of the United States armed forces and the civilian component shall carry distinctive numbered plates or individual markings which will readily identify them.

3.   The Government of the Republic of Korea will license and register those vehicles privately owned by members of the United States armed forces, the civilian component, or dependents. The names of the owners of such vehicles and such other pertinent information as is required by the law of the Republic of Korea to effect the licensing and registration of such vehicles shall be furnished to the Government of the Republic of Korea by officials of the Government of the United States through the Joint Committee. Except for the actual cost of the issuance of license plates, members of the United States armed forces, the civilian component, and their dependents shall be exempt from the

0088

57

payment of all fees and charges relating to the
licensing, registration, or operation of vehicles
in the Republic of Korea and, in accordance with the
provisions of Article XIV, from the payment of all
taxes relating thereto.

0089

한·미국 간의 상호방위조약 제4조에 의한 시설과 구역 및 한국에서의 미국군대의 지위에 관한 협정(SOFA)
전59권. 1966.7.9 서울에서 서명 : 1967.2.9 발효(조약 232호) (V.38 실무교섭회의, 제82차, 1966.7.8(Ⅱ)) 95

ARTICLE XXV

Security Measures

The United States and the Republic of Korea will cooperate in taking such steps as may from time to time be necessary to ensure the security of the United States armed forces, the members thereof, the civilian component, the persons who are present in the Republic of Korea pursuant to Article XV, their dependents and their property. The Government of the Republic of Korea agrees to seek such legislation and to take such other action as may be necessary to ensure the adequate security and protection within its territory of installations, equipment, property, records, and official information of the United States and, consistent with Article XXII, to ensure the punishment of offenders under the applicable laws of the Republic of Korea.

0090

ARTICLE XXVI

Health and Sanitation

Consistent with the right of the United States to furnish medical support for its armed forces, civilian component and their dependents, matters of mutual concern pertaining to the control and prevention of diseases and the coordination of other public health, medical, sanitation, and veterinary services shall be resolved by the authorities of the two Governments in the Joint Committee established under Article XXVIII.

한·미국 간의 상호방위조약 제4조에 의한 시설과 구역 및 한국에서의 미국군대의 지위에 관한 협정(SOFA)
전59권. 1966.7.9 서울에서 서명 : 1967.2.9 발효(조약 232호) (V.38 실무교섭회의, 제82차, 1966.7.8(II))

97

ARTICLE XXVII

Enrollment and Training of Reservists

The United States may enroll in its reserve forces and train, in the Republic of Korea, eligible United States citizens who are in the Republic of Korea.

0092

ARTICLE XXVIII

Joint Committee

1.   A Joint Committee shall be established as the means for consultation between the Government of the United States and the Government of the Republic of Korea on all matters requiring mutual consultation regarding the implementation of this Agreement except where otherwise provided. In particular, the Joint Committee shall serve as the means for consultation in determining the facilities and areas in the Republic of Korea which are required for the use of the United States in carrying out the purposes of this Agreement.

2.   The Joint Committee shall be composed of a representative of the Government of the United States and a representative of the Government of the Republic of Korea, each of whom shall have one or more deputies and a staff. The Joint Committee shall determine its own procedures, and arrange for such auxiliary organs and administrative services as may be required. The Joint Committee shall be so organized that it may meet immediately at any time at the request of the representative of either the Government of the United States or the Government of the Republic of Korea.

3.   If the Joint Committee is unable to resolve any matter, it shall refer that matter to the respective Governments for further consideration through appropriate channels.

0033

ARTICLE XXIX

Entry Into Force of Agreement

1.   This Agreement shall enter into force three months after the date of a written notification from the Government of the Republic of Korea to the Government of the United States that it has approved the Agreement in accordance with its legal procedures.

2.   The Government of the Republic of Korea shall undertake to seek from its legislature all legislative and budgetary action necessary to give effect to the provisions of this Agreement.

3.   Subject to the provisions of Article XXII, paragraph 12, this Agreement shall, upon its entry into force, supersede and replace the Agreement between the Government of the United States and the Government of the Republic of Korea on jurisdictional matters, effected by an exchange of notes at Taejon on July 12, 1950.

4.   Within the scope of this Agreement, paragraph 13 of Article III of the Agreement on Economic Coordination between the Republic of Korea and the Unified Command of May 24, 1952, shall not apply to members of the United States armed forces, civilian component, invited contractors, or dependents thereof.

63

0094

ARTICLE XXX

Revision of Agreement

Either Government may at any time request the revision of any Article of this Agreement, in which case the two Governments shall enter into negotiations through appropriate channels.

64

한·미국 간의 상호방위조약 제4조에 의한 시설과 구역 및 한국에서의 미국군대의 지위에 관한 협정(SOFA)
전59권. 1966.7.9 서울에서 서명 : 1967.2.9 발효(조약 232호) (V.38 실무교섭회의, 제82차, 1966.7.8(II)) 101

ARTICLE XXXI

Duration of Agreement

This Agreement, and agreed revisions thereof, shall remain in force while the Mutual Defense Treaty between the United States and the Republic of Korea remains in force unless terminated earlier by agreement between the two Governments.

In witness whereof the undersigned, being duly authorized by their respective Governments, have signed this Agreement.

Done in duplicate, in the English and Korean languages. Both texts shall have equal authenticity, but in case of divergence the English text shall prevail.

Done at Seoul this   day of January 1966.

65

0036

Agreed Minutes to the Agreement Under Article IV of

the Mutual Defense Treaty Between the United States

of America and the Republic of Korea, Regarding

Facilities and Areas and the Status of United States

Armed Forces in the Republic of Korea

The Plenipotentiaries of the United States of America and the Republic of Korea wish to record the following understanding which they have reached during the negotiations for the Agreement under Article IV of the Mutual Defense Treaty between the United States and the Republic of Korea, Regarding Facilities and Areas and the Status of United States Armed Forces in the Republic of Korea, signed today:

<u>ARTICLE I</u>

With regard to subparagraph (b), it is recognized that persons possessing certain skills, not available from United States or Korean sources, who are nationals of third states, may be brought into the Republic of Korea by the United States armed forces solely for employment by the United States armed forces. Such persons, and third state nationals who are employed by, serving with, or accompanying the United States armed forces in the Republic of Korea when this Agreement becomes effective, shall be considered as members of the civilian component.

66

0097

ARTICLE III

It is agreed that in the event of an emergency, the United States armed forces shall be authorized to take such measures in the vicinity of the facilities and areas as may be necessary to provide for their safeguarding and control.

ARTICLE IV

1. All removable facilities erected or constructed by or on behalf of the United States at its expense and all equipment, material and supplies brought into or procured in the Republic of Korea by or on behalf of the United States in connection with the construction, development, operation, maintenance, safeguarding and control of the facilities and areas will remain the property of the United States Government and may be removed from the Republic of Korea.

2. All removable facilities, equipment and material or portions thereof provided by the Republic of Korea under this Agreement and located within the facilities and areas referred to in this Article shall be returned to the Republic of Korea whenever they are no longer needed for the purpose of this Agreement.

ARTICLE VI

1. It is understood that any changes determined by the authorities of the Republic of Korea in priorities, conditions, and rates or tariffs, applicable to the United States armed forces shall be the subject of

67

0098

consultation in the Joint Committee prior to their effective date.

2. This Article will not be construed as in any way abrogating the Utilities Claims Settlement Agreement of December 18, 1958, which continues in full force and effect unless otherwise agreed by the two Governments.

3. In an emergency the Republic of Korea agrees to take appropriate measures to assure provision of utilities and services necessary to meet the needs of the United States armed forces.

ARTICLE VIII

1. With regard to paragraph 3(a), United States armed forces law enforcement personnel (such as Military Police, Shore Patrol, Air Police, Office of Special Investigations, Criminal Investigation Division, and Counterintelligence Corps), who engage in military police activities in the Republic of Korea, will carry a bilingual identity card containing the bearer's name, position, and the fact that he is a member of a law enforcement agency. This card will be shown upon request to persons concerned when the bearer is in the performance of duty.

2. The United States armed forces will furnish, upon request, to the authorities of the Republic of Korea, the form of the identification cards of the members of the United States armed forces, the civilian component, and their dependents and descriptions of the various uniforms of the United States armed forces in the Republic of Korea.

3. The final sentence of paragraph 3 means that members of the United States armed forces will display their identity cards upon request but will not be required to surrender them to authorities of the Republic of Korea.

4. Following a change of status pursuant to paragraph 5, the responsibilities of the United States authorities under paragraph 6 shall arise only if the expulsion order is issued within a reasonable time after the notice under paragraph 5 has been communicated to the authorities of the Republic of Korea.

ARTICLE IX

1. The quantity of goods imported under paragraph 2 by non-appropriated fund organizations of the United States armed forces for the use of persons authorized by Article XIII and its Agreed Minute shall be limited to the extent reasonably required for such use.

2. Paragraph 3(a) does not require concurrent shipment of goods with travel of owner nor does it require single loading or shipment. In this connection, members of the United States armed forces or civilian component and their dependents may import free of duty reasonable quantities of their furniture, household goods and personal effects during a period of six months from the date of their first arrival.

3. The term "military cargo" as used in paragraph 5(c) is not confined to arms and equipment but refers to all cargo consigned to the United States armed forces (including their authorized procurement agencies and their non-appropriated fund organizations provided for in Article XIII). Pertinent

69

information on cargo consigned to non-appropriated fund organizations will be furnished on a routine basis to the authorities of the Republic of Korea. The extent of the pertinent information will be determined by the Joint Committee.

4. The United States armed forces will take every practicable measure to ensure that goods will not be imported into the Republic of Korea by or for the members of the United States armed forces, the civilian component, or their dependents, the entry of which would be in violation of customs laws and regulations of the Republic of Korea. The United States armed forces will promptly notify customs authorities of the Republic of Korea whenever the entry of such goods is discovered.

5. The customs authorities of the Republic of Korea may, if they consider that there has been an abuse or infringement in connection with the entry of goods under Article IX, take up the matter with the appropriate authorities of the United States armed forces.

6. The words "The United States armed forces shall render all assistance within their power," etc., in paragraph 9(b) and (c) refer to reasonable and practicable measures by the United States armed forces.

7. It is understood that the duty-free treatment provided in paragraph 2 shall apply to materials, supplies and equipment imported for sale through commissaries and non-appropriated fund organizations, under such regulations as the United States armed forces may promulgate, to those individuals and organizations referred to in Article XIII and its Agreed Minute.

0101

ARTICLE X

1. "United States and foreign vessels...operated by, for, or under the control of the United States for official purposes" means public vessels and chartered vessels (bare boat charter, voyage charter and time charter). Space charter is not included. Commercial cargo and private passengers are carried by them only in exceptional cases.

2. The ports of the Republic of Korea mentioned herein will ordinarily mean "open ports".

3. The exemption from making the "appropriate notification" referred to in paragraph 3 will apply only in unusual cases where such is required for security of the United States armed forces or similar reasons.

4. The laws and regulations of the Republic of Korea will be applicable except as specifically provided otherwise in this Article.

ARTICLE XII

Installation by the United States armed forces of permanent navigational aids for vessels and aircraft outside of facilities and areas in use by the United States armed forces will be effected in accordance with the procedures established under paragraph 1 of Article III.

0102

ARTICLE XIII

The United States armed forces may grant the use of the organizations referred to in paragraph I of Article XIII to: (a) other officers or personnel of the Government of the United States ordinarily accorded such privileges; (b) those other non-Korean armed forces in the Republic of Korea under the Unified Command which receive logistical support from the United States armed forces, and their members; (c) those non-Korean persons whose presence in the Republic of Korea is solely for the purpose of providing contract services financed by the Government of the United States; (d) those organizations which are present in the Republic of Korea primarily for the benefit and service of the United States armed forces, such as the American Red Cross and the United Service Organizations, and their non-Korean personnel; (e) dependents of the foregoing; and (f) other persons and organizations with the express consent of the Government of the Republic of Korea.

ARTICLE XV

1. The execution of contracts with the United States in addition to those specified in paragraph 1 of Article XV shall not exclude the persons provided for in Article XV from the application of that Article.

2. Contractor employees who are present in the Republic of Korea on the effective date of this Agreement and who would qualify for the privileges contained in Article XV but for the fact that they are not ordinarily resident in the United States shall be entitled to enjoy such privileges so

72

0103

long as their presence is for the purpose stated in paragraph 1 of Article XV.

ARTICLE XVI

1. The United States armed forces will furnish the authorities of the Republic of Korea with appropriate information as far in advance as practicable on anticipated major changes in their procurement program in the Republic of Korea.

2. The problem of a satisfactory settlement of difficulties with respect to procurement contracts arising out of differences between economic laws and business practices of the Republic of Korea and the United States will be studied by the Joint Committe or other appropriate representatives.

3. The procedures for securing exemptions from taxation on purchases of goods for ultimate use by the United States armed forces will be as follows:

(a) Upon appropriate certification by the United States armed forces that materials, supplies and equipment consigned to or destined for such forces, are to be used, or wholly or partially used up, under the supervision of such forces, exclusively in the execution of contracts for the construction, maintenance or operation of the facilities and areas referred to in Article V or for the support of the forces therein, or are ultimately to be incorporated into articles or facilities used by such

73

0104

forces, an authorized representative of such forces shall take delivery of such materials, supplies and equipment directly from manufacturers thereof. In such circumstances the collection of taxes referred to in Article XIV, paragraph 3, shall be held in abeyance.

(b) The receipt of such materials, supplies and equipment in the facilities and areas shall be confirmed by an authorized representative of the United States armed forces to the authorities of the Republic of Korea.

(c) Collection of the taxes on such materials, supplies and equipment shall be held in abeyance until

(i) the United States armed forces confirm and certify the quantity or degree of consumption of the above referred to materials, supplies and equipment, or

(ii) the United States armed forces confirm and certify the amount of the above referred to materials, supplies, and equipment which have been incorporated into articles or facilities used by the United States armed forces.

(d) Materials, supplies and equipment certified under (c) (i) or (ii) shall be exempt from taxes referred to in Article XIV, paragraph 3, insofar as the price thereof is paid out of appropriations of the Government of the United States or out of funds contributed by the Government of the Republic of Korea for disbursement by the Government of the United

States.

4. Regarding paragraph 3 it is understood that "materials, supplies, equipment and services procured for official purposes" refers to direct procurement by the United States armed forces or their authorized procurement agencies from Korean suppliers. "Materials, supplies, equipment and services procured for ultimate use" refers to procurement by contractors of the United States armed forces from Korean suppliers of items to be incorporated into or necessary for the production of the end product of their contracts with the United States armed forces.

ARTICLE XVII

1. It is understood that the Government of the Republic of Korea shall be reimbursed for direct costs incurred in providing assistance requested pursuant to paragraph 2.

2. The undertaking of the Government of the United States to conform to the provisions of labor legislation of the Republic of Korea does not imply any waiver by the Government of the United States of its immunities under international law. The Government of the United States may terminate employment at any time the continuation of such employment is inconsistent with the military requirements of the United States armed forces.

3. Employers will withhold from the pay of their employees, and pay over to the Government of the Republic of Korea, withholdings required by the income tax legislation of the Republic of Korea.

75

0106

4. When employers cannot conform with provisions of labor legislation of the Republic of Korea applicable under this Article on account of the military requirements of the United States armed forces, the matter shall be referred, in advance ~~whenever possible~~, to the Joint Committee for consideration and appropriate action. In the event mutual agreement cannot be reached in the Joint Committee regarding appropriate action, the issue may be made the subject of review through discussions between appropriate officials of the Government of the Republic of Korea and the diplomatic mission of the United States of America.

5. A union or other employee group shall be recognized by the employers unless its objectives are inimical to the common interests of the United States and the Republic of Korea. Membership or non-membership in such groups shall not be a factor in employment or other actions affecting employees.

ARTICLE XVIII

Payment in the Republic of Korea by the United States armed forces, including those organizations provided for in Article XIII, to persons other than members of the United States armed forces, civilian component, their dependents and those persons referred to in Article XV shall be effected in accordance with the Foreign Exchange Control Law and regulations of the Republic of Korea. The funds to be used for these transactions shall be convertible into currency of the Republic of Korea at the highest rate in terms of the number of Korean won per United States dollar

76

0107

which, at the time the conversion is made, is not unlawful in the Republic of Korea.

ARTICLE XX

United States military post offices may be used by other officers and personnel of the Government of the United States, and their dependents, ordinarily accorded such privileges abroad.

ARTICLE XXII

The provisions of this Article shall not affect existing agreements, arrangements, or practices, relating to the exercise of jurisdiction over personnel of the United Nations forces present in the Republic of Korea other than forces of the United States.

Re Paragraph 1(a)

It is understood that under the present state of United States law, the military authorities of the United States have no effective criminal jurisdiction in peacetime over members of the civilian component or dependents. If the scope of United States military jurisdiction changes as a result of subsequent legislation, constitutional amendment, or decision by appropriate authorities of the United States, the Government of the United States shall inform the Government of the Republic of Korea through diplomatic channels.

Re Paragraph 1(b)

1. In the event that martial law is declared by the Republic of Korea, the provisions of this Article shall be immediately suspended in the part of the Republic of Korea under martial law, and the military authorities of the United States shall have the right to exercise

exclusive jurisdiction over members of the United States armed forces
or civilian component, and their dependents, in such part until
martial law is ended.

2. The jurisdiction of the authorities of the Republic of
Korea over members of the United States armed forces or civilian
component, and their dependents, shall not extend to any offenses
committed outside the Republic of Korea.

Re Paragraph 2

The Republic of Korea, recognizing the effectiveness in
appropriate cases of the administrative and disciplinary sanctions
which may be imposed by the United States authorities over members
of the United States armed forces or civilian component, and their
dependents, may at the request of the military authorities of the
United States waive its right to exercise jurisdiction under Paragraph 2.

Re Paragraph 2(c)

Each Government shall inform the other of the details of all
security offenses mentioned in this subparagraph, and of the provisions regarding such offenses in its legislation.

Re Paragraph 3(a)

1. Where a member of the United States armed forces or civilian
component is charged with an offense, a certificate issued by competent
military authorities of the United States stating that the alleged
offense, if committed by him, arose out of an act or omission done in
the performance of official duty shall be sufficient evidence of
the fact for the purpose of determining primary jurisdiction. The

78

0109

term "official duty" as used in this Article and Agreed Minute is not meant to include all acts by members of the United States armed forces and the civilian component during periods when they are on duty, but is meant to apply only to acts which are required to be done as functions of those duties which the individuals are performing.

2. In those exceptional cases where the Chief Prosecutor for the Republic of Korea considers that there is proof contrary to a certificate of official duty, it shall be made the subject of review through discussions between appropriate officials of the Government of the Republic of Korea and the diplomatic mission of the United States in the Republic of Korea.

Re Paragraph 3(b)

1. The authorities of the Republic of Korea, recognizing that it is the primary responsibility of the United States military authorities to maintain good order and discipline where persons subject to United States military laws are concerned, will, upon the request of the military authorities of the United States pursuant to Paragraph 3(c), waive their primary right to exercise jurisdiction under Paragraph 3(b) except when they determine that it is of particular importance that jurisdiction be exercised by the authorities of the Republic of Korea.

2. With the consent of the competent authorities of the Republic of Korea, the military authorities of the United States may transfer to the courts or authorities of the Republic of Korea for investigation, trial and decision, particular criminal cases in which jurisdiction rests with the United States.

79

0110

With the consent of the military authorities of the United States, the competent authorities of the Republic of Korea may transfer to the military authorities of the United States for investigation, trial and decision, particular criminal cases in which jurisdiction rests with the Republic of Korea.

3. (a) Where a member of the United States armed forces or civilian component, or a dependent, is arraigned before a court of the United States, for an offense committed in the Republic of Korea against Korean interests, the trial shall be held within the Republic of Korea

(i) except where the law of the United States requires otherwise, or

(ii) except where, in cases of military exigency or in the interests of justice, the military authorities of the United States intend to hold the trial outside the Republic of Korea. In this event they shall afford the authorities of the Republic of Korea timely opportunity to comment on such intention and shall give due consideration to any comments the latter may make.

(b) Where the trial is held outside of the Republic of Korea the military authorities of the United States shall inform the authorities of the Republic of Korea of the place and date of the trial. A representative of the Republic of Korea shall be entitled to be present at the trial. The authorities of the United States shall inform the authorities of the Republic of Korea of the judgment and the final outcome of the proceedings.

0111

4. In the implementation of the provisions of this Article, and to facilitate the expeditious disposal of offenses, arrangements may be made between the United States military authorities and the competent authorities of the Republic of Korea.

Re Paragraph 6

1. The military authorities of the United States and the authorities of the Republic of Korea shall assist each other in obtaining the appearance of witnesses necessary for the proceedings conducted by such authorities within the Republic of Korea.

When a member of the United States armed forces in the Republic of Korea is summoned to appear before a court of the Republic of Korea, as a witness or as a defendant, United States military authorities shall, unless military exigency requires otherwise, secure his attendance provided such attendance is compulsory under the law of the Republic of Korea. If military exigency prevents such attendance, the military authorities of the United States shall furnish a certificate stating the estimated duration of such disability.

Service of process upon a member of the United States armed forces or civilian component, or a dependent required as a witness or a defendant must be personal service in the English language. Where the service of process is to be effected by a process server of the Republic of Korea upon any person who is inside a military installation or area, the military authorities of the United States shall take all measures

81

0112

necessary to enable the process server to effect such service.

In addition, the authorities of the Republic of Korea shall promptly give copies of all criminal writs (including warrants, summonses, indictments, and subpoenas) to an agent designated by the United States military authorities to receive them in all cases of criminal proceedings of the Republic of Korea involving a member of the United States armed forces or civilian component, or a dependent.

When citizens or residents of the Republic of Korea are required as witnesses or experts by the military authorities of the United States, the courts and authorities of the Republic of Korea shall, in accordance with the law of the Republic of Korea, secure the attendance of such persons. In these cases the military authorities of the United States shall act through the Attorney General of the Republic of Korea, or such other agency as is designated by the authorities of the Republic of Korea.

Fees and other payments for witnesses shall be determined by the Joint Committee established under Article XXVIII.

2. The privileges and immunities of witnesses shall be those accorded by the law of the court, tribunal or authority before which they appear. In no event shall a witness be required to provide testimony which may tend to incriminate him.

3. If, in the course of criminal proceedings before authorities of the United States or the Republic of Korea, the disclosure of an official secret of either of these States or the disclosure of any

8482

한·미국 간의 상호방위조약 제4조에 의한 시설과 구역 및 한국에서의 미국군대의 지위에 관한 협정(SOFA)
전59권. 1966.7.9 서울에서 서명 : 1967.2.9 발효(조약 232호) (V.38 실무교섭회의, 제82차, 1966.7.8(II))

information which may prejudice the security of either appears necessary for the just disposition of the proceedings, the authorities concerned shall seek written permission to make such disclosure from the appropriate authority of the State concerned.

Re Paragraph 9 (a)

The right to a prompt and speedy trial by the courts of the Republic of Korea shall include public trial by an impartial tribunal composed exclusively of judges who have completed their probationary period. A member of the United States armed forces, or civilian component, or a dependent, shall not be tried by a military tribunal of the Republic of Korea.

Re Paragraph 9 (b)

A member of the United States armed forces or civilian component, or a dependent, shall not be arrested or detained by the authorities of the Republic of Korea without adequate cause, and he shall be entitled to an immediate hearing at which such cause must be shown in open court in his presence and the presence of his counsel. His immediate release shall be ordered if adequate cause is not shown. Immediately upon arrest or detention he shall be informed of the charges against him in a language which he understands.

He shall also be informed a reasonable time prior to trial of the nature of the evidence that is to be used against him. Counsel for the accused shall, upon request, be afforded the opportunity before

8583

0114

trial to examine and copy the statements of witnesses obtained by
authorities of the Republic of Korea which are included in the file forwarded to the court of the Republic of Korea scheduled to try the
case.

Re Paragraph 9(c) and (d)

A member of the United States armed forces or civilian component,
or a dependent, who is prosecuted by the authorities of the Republic
of Korea shall have the right to be present throughout the testimony
of all witnesses, for and against him, in all judicial examinations,
pretrial hearings, the trial itself, and subsequent proceedings, and
shall be permitted full opportunity to examine the witnesses.

Re Paragraph 9(e)

The right to legal representation shall exist from the moment of
arrest or detention and shall include the right to have counsel
present, and to consult confidentially with such counsel, at all
preliminary investigations, examinations, pretrial hearings, the trial
itself, and subsequent proceedings, at which the accused is present.

Re Paragraph 9(f)

The right to have the services of a competent interpreter shall
exist from the moment of arrest or detention.

8684

0115

Re Paragraph 9(g)

The right to communicate with a representative of the Government
of the United States shall exist from the moment of arrest or detention,
and no statement of the accused taken in the absence of such a representative shall be admissible as evidence in support of the guilt of
the accused. Such representative shall be entitled to be present at
all preliminary investigations, examinations, pretrial hearings, the
trial itself, and subsequent proceedings, at which the accused is present.

Re Paragraph 9

A member of the United States armed forces or civilian component,
or a dependent, tried by the authorities of the Republic of Korea
shall be accorded every procedural and substantive right granted by
law to the citizens of the Republic of Korea. If it should appear
that an accused has been, or is likely to be, denied any procedural or
substantive right granted by law to the citizens of the Republic of
Korea, representatives of the two Governments shall consult in the
Joint Committee on the measures necessary to prevent or cure such
denial of rights.

In addition to the rights enumerated in items (a) through (g) of
paragraph 9 of this Article, a member of the United States armed
forces or civilian component, or a dependent, who is prosecuted by the
authorities of the Republic of Korea:

8785

0116

(a) shall have the right to appeal a conviction or sentence;

(b) shall have credited to any sentence of confinement his period of pretrial confinement in a confinement facility of the United States or Republic of Korea;

(c) shall not be held guilty of a criminal offense on account of any act or omission which did not constitute a criminal offense under the law of the Republic of Korea at the time it was committed;

(d) shall not be subject to a heavier penalty than the one that was applicable at the time the alleged criminal offense was committed or was adjudged by the court of first instance as the original sentence;

(e) shall not be held guilty of an offense on the basis of rules of evidence or requirements of proof which have been altered to his prejudice since the date of the commission of the offense;

(f) shall not be compelled to testify against or otherwise incriminate himself;

(g) shall not be subject to cruel or unusual punishment;

(h) shall not be subject to prosecution or punishment by legislative or executive act;

(i) shall not be prosecuted or punished more than once for the same offense;

(j) shall not be required to stand trial if he is physically or mentally unfit to stand trial and participate in his defense;

한·미국 간의 상호방위조약 제4조에 의한 시설과 구역 및 한국에서의 미국군대의 지위에 관한 협정(SOFA)
전59권. 1966.7.9 서울에서 서명 : 1967.2.9 발효(조약 232호) (V.38 실무교섭회의, 제82차, 1966.7.8(II)) 123

(k) shall not be subject to trial except under conditions
consonant with the dignity of the United States armed forces, including
appearing in appropriate military or civilian attire and unmanacled.

No confession, admission or other statement, obtained by torture,
violence, threat, deceit, or after prolonged arrest, or detention, or
which has been made involuntarily, and no real evidence which has been
obtained by torture, violence, threat, deceit, or as a result of an
unreasonable search and seizure without a warrant, will be considered
by the courts of the Republic of Korea as evidence in support of the
guilt of the accused under this Article.

In any case prosecuted by the authorities of the Republic of Korea
under this Article no appeal will be taken by the prosecution from a
judgment of not guilty or an acquittal nor will an appeal be taken by
the prosecution from any judgment which the accused does not appeal,
except upon ground of errors of law.

The military authorities of the United States shall have the
right to inspect any confinement facility of the Republic of Korea in
which a member of the United States armed forces, civilian component, or a
dependent is confined, or in which it is proposed to confine such an
individual.

In the event of hostilities, the Republic of Korea will take all
possible measures to safeguard members of the United States armed
forces, members of the civilian component, and their dependents who

8987

0118

are confined in confinement facilities of the Republic of Korea, whether waiting trial or serving a sentence imposed by the courts of the Republic of Korea. The Republic of Korea shall give sympathetic consideration to requests for release of these persons to the custody of responsible United States military authorities. Necessary implementing provisions shall be agreed upon between the two Governments through the Joint Committee.

Facilities utilized for the execution of a sentence to death or a period of confinement, imprisonment, or penal servitude, or for the detention of members of the United States armed forces or civilian component or dependents, will meet minimum standards as agreed by the Joint Committee. The military authorities of the United States shall have the right upon request to have access at any time to members of the United States armed forces, the civilian component, or their dependents who are confined or detained by authorities of the Republic of Korea. During the visit of these persons at confinement facilities of the Republic of Korea, military authorities of the United States shall be authorized to provide supplementary care and provisions for such persons, such as clothing, food, bedding, and medical and dental treatment.

Re Paragraph 10(a) and 10(b)

1. The military authorities of the United States will normally make all arrests within facilities and areas in use by the United States armed forces. This shall not preclude the authorities of the Republic

9088

0119

of Korea from making arrests within facilities and areas in cases where the competent authorities of the United States armed forces have given consent, or in cases of pursuit of a flagrant offender who has committed a serious crime.

Where persons whose arrest is desired by the authorities of the Republic of Korea, and who are not members of the United States armed forces or civilian component or dependents, are within facilities and areas in use by the United States armed forces, the military authorities of the United States will undertake, upon request, to arrest such persons. Any person arrested by the military authorities of the United States who is not a member of the United States armed forces or civilian component or a dependent shall immediately be turned over to the authorities of the Republic of Korea.

The military authorities of the United States may arrest or detain in the vicinity of a facility or area any person in the commission or attempted commission of an offense against the security of that facility or area. Any such person who is not a member of the United States armed forces or civilian component or a dependent shall immediately be turned over to the authorities of the Republic of Korea.

2. The authorities of the Republic of Korea will normally not exercise the right of search, seizure, or inspection with respect to

89

0120

any person or property within facilities and areas in use by the United States armed forces or with respect to property of the United States wherever situated, except in cases where the competent military authorities of the United States consent to such search, seizure, or inspection by the authorities of the Republic of Korea of such persons or property.

Where search, seizure, or inspection with respect to persons or property within facilities and areas in use by the United States armed forces or with respect to property of the United States in the Republic of Korea is desired by the authorities of the Republic of Korea, the military authorities of the United States will undertake, upon request, to make such search, seizure, or inspection. In the event of a judgment concerning such property, except property owned or utilized by the Government of the United States or its instrumentalities, the United States will in accordance with its laws turn over such property to the authorities of the Republic of Korea for disposition in accordance with the judgment.

ARTICLE XXIII

1. Unless otherwise provided, the provisions of paragraphs 5, 6, 7 and 8 of this Article will become effective six months from the date of entry into force of this Agreement with respect to claims arising from incidents in the Seoul Special City area, and one year from that date with respect to claims arising elsewhere in the Republic of Korea.

90
72

2. Until such time as the provisions of paragraphs 5, 6, 7 and 8
become effective in any given area,

(a) The United States shall process and settle claims (other
than contractual claims) arising out of the acts or omissions of members
or employees of the United States armed forces done in the performance of
official duty or out of any other act, omission or occurrence for which
the United States armed forces are legally responsible, which cause
damage in the Republic of Korea to parties other than the two
Governments;

(b) The United States shall entertain other non-contractual
claims against members or employees of the armed forces and may offer
an ex gratia payment in such cases and in such amounts as is determined
by the appropriate United States authorities; and

(c) Each Party shall have the right to determine whether
a member or employee of its armed forces was engaged in the performance
of official duties and whether property owned by it was being used by
its armed forces for official purposes.

3. For the purposes of subparagraph 2(d), subparagraph 5(e)
shall be effective throughout the Republic of Korea from the date
of entry into force of this Agreement.

ARTICLE XXVIII

The exception provided for in the first sentence of paragraph 1 is
relevant only to paragraph 2, subparagraphs (b) and (c) of Article III.

0122

ARTICLE IX, CUSTOMS AND DUTIES

PARAGRAPH 5

Reference: 39th meeting, 17 Jan 64 as modified at 40th meeting, 24 Jan 64 and 41st meeting, 14 Feb 64.

1. Examination of parcels in the APO mails in the ROK by ROK customs inspectors will be conducted so as not to damage the contents of the parcels inspected or delay delivery of the mail;

2. Such examinations will be conducted in U.S. APO installations in the presence of U.S. officials;

3. No parcel in the APO mails will be removed from U.S. postal channels except as mutually agreed;

4. It is understood that the right of inspection will be exercised on a "sample check" basis so as not to unduly delay delivery or increase the administrative burden of the postal authorities.

0123

ARTICLE IX, CUSTOMS AND DUTIES

AGREED MINUTE 3

Reference: 57th meeting, 8 Jul 64.

1. Pertinent information shall include cargo manifests and shipping documents;

2. In addition to information provided on a routine basis, other pertinent information will be provided on request through the Joint Committee.

0124

ARTICLE XIII, NON-APPROPRIATED FUND ORGANIZATIONS

AGREED MINUTE

Reference: 81st meeting, 7 Jun 65.

"It is understood that the present use of Non-Appropriated Fund organizations by organizations and persons other than those referred to in items (a), (b), (c), (d), and (e) shall immediately be suspended at the time of the entry into force of this Agreement. The extent of organizations and persons to be granted the use of such organizations under item (f) of this minute shall be left to further negotiations between the appropriate authorities of the two governments."

0125

ARTICLE XV, INVITED CONTRACTORS

PARAGRAPH 1

Reference: 56th meeting, 26 Jun 64.

"If the U.S. authorities determine that there would be significant advantage for U.S.-ROK mutual defense to utilize one or more third-country corporations as USFK-invited contractors, the authorities of the Government of the Republic of Korea shall give sympathetic consideration to a U.S. request to extend the benefits of this agreement to such non-U.S. corporations."

0126

ARTICLE XV, INVITED CONTRACTORS

PARAGRAPH 8

Reference: 82d meeting

"Unless otherwise agreed in Joint Committee, the privileges provided for in the second sentence of Paragraph 8 of this Article shall be extended only to United States Nationals."

0127

Agreed Mind of Article 17.

"4. When employers cannot conform with provisions of labor

legislation of the Republic of Korea applicable under this

Article on account of the military requirement of the United

States armed forces, the matter shall be referred, in

advance, to the Joint Committee for consideration and

appropriate action. In the event mutual agreement cannot be

reached in the Joint Committee regarding appropriate action,

the issue may be made the subject of review through discussions

between appropriate officials of the Government of the

Republic of Korea and the diplomatic mission of the United

States of America."

AGREED UNDERSTANDING IN AGREED JOINT SUMMARY-82ND MEETING

"It is understood that the deviation from Korean labor legislation

need not be referred to the Joint Committee in cases when such

referral would seriously hamper military operations in an emergency.

ARTICLE XVII   LABOR

AGREED UNDERSTANDING TO AGREED MINUTE NO. 4
CONFIDENTIAL

Reference: 82nd Meeting, July 8, 1966

0128

PARAGRAPH 1

Reference: 82d meeting

(1) "Local residents, who are third-country nationals and are also local-hire USFK employees and local-hire contractor employees paid in won, on the effective date of the agreement, shall be excluded from the application of this provision."

0129

ARTICLE XVII, LABOR

PARAGRAPH 1

Reference: 82d meeting

(2) "The provisions of Paragraph 1(b) do not preclude the United States armed forces from bringing into Korea, <u>without privileges</u>, third-country contractor employees possessing special skills not available from the Korean labor force."

0130

ARTICLE XXIII, CLAIMS

AGREED MINUTE re PARAGRAPH 1(b)

Reference: 82d meeting

"With regard to Agreed Minute No. 1(b), the extension of the provisions of Paragraphs five, six, seven, and eight to other areas of Korea will be based upon the capability of the Korean claims service to implement those provisions."

0131

US-ROK AGREED UNDERSTANDINGS IN AGREED JOINT SUMMARY

ARTICLE XXV - SECURITY MEASURES

PARAGRAPH 5

Rererence: 55th meeting, 19 Jun 64, Paragraph 9, and 81st
meeting, 7 Jun 65, Paragraph 5.

"In cooperating with each other under this Article, the two governments agree that each will take such measures as may be necessary to
ensure the security and protection of the U.S. armed forces, the members
thereof, the civilian component, the persons who are present in the
Republic of Korea pursuant to the Article dealing with Invited Contractors, their dependents and their property."

0132

CONFIDENTIAL

THIS IS A COVER SHEET

BASIC SECURITY REQUIREMENTS ARE CONTAINED
IN AR 380-5

THE UNAUTHORIZED DISCLOSURE OF THE INFORMATION CONTAINED IN
THE ATTACHED DOCUMENT(S) COULD BE PREJUDICIAL TO THE DEFENSE
INTERESTS OF THE UNITED STATES.

RESPONSIBILITY OF PERSONS HANDLING THE ATTACHED DOCUMENT(S)

1. Exercise the necessary safeguards to prevent unauthorized disclosure by never leaving the document(s) unattended except
   when properly secured in a locked safe.

2. Transfer the document(s) only to persons who need to know and
   who possess the required security clearance.

3. Obtain a receipt whenever relinquishing control of the document(s)
   if required by local regulations.

STORAGE

Store as prescribed in AR 380-5.

REPRODUCTION

Copies may be made of these documents except when the originating office or
higher authority has specifically denied this authority.

DISPOSITION

This cover sheet should be removed when document(s) are filed in a
permanent file, declassified, destroyed, or mailed.

(This cover sheet is unclassified when separated from classified documents)

CONFIDENTIAL

DA LABEL 22
1 APR 61   PREVIOUS EDITIONS OF THIS LABEL ARE OBSOLETE.   PPRC, Japan

ARTICLE XV - INVITED CONTRACTORS

PARAGRAPH 1

Reference: 56th meeting, 24 Jun 64, Paragraphs 3 - 5.

"If the U.S. authorities determine that there would be significant advantage for U.S.-ROK mutual defense to utilize one or more third-country corporations as USFK-invited contractors, the authorities of the Government of the Republic of Korea shall give sympathetic consideration to a U.S. request to extend the benefits of this agreement to such non-U.S. corporations."

0134

ARTICLE XV - INVITED CONTRACTORS

PARAGRAPH 8

Reference: 82d meeting, 7 July 66, Paragraph 11.

"Unless otherwise agreed in Joint Committee, the privileges provided for in the second sentence of Paragraph 8 of this Article shall be extended only to United States Nationals."

0135

ARTICLE IX – CUSTOMS AND DUTIES

PARAGRAPH 5

Reference: 39th meeting, 17 Jan 64, Paragraph 3, as modified
at 40th meeting, 24 Jan 64, Paragraphs 3 - 7, and
41st meeting, 14 Feb 64, Paragraphs 5 - 8.

"1. Examination of parcels in the MPO mails in the ROK by ROK customs inspectors will be conducted so as not to damage the contents of the parcels inspected or delay delivery of the mail;

"2. Such examinations will be conducted in U.S. MPO installations in the presence of U.S. officials;

"3. No parcel in the MPO mails will be removed from U.S. postal channels except as mutually agreed;

"4. It is understood that the right of inspection will be exercised on a "sample check" basis so as not to unduly delay delivery or increase the administrative burden of the postal authorities."

0136

US-ROK AGREED UNDERSTANDINGS IN AGREED JOINT SUMMARY

ARTICLE IX - CUSTOMS AND DUTIES

2 AGREED MINUTE 3

Reference: 57th meeting, 8 Jul 64, Paragraphs 1 - 3.

"1. Pertinent information shall include cargo manifests and shipping documents;

"2. In addition to information provided on a routine basis, other pertinent information will be provided on request through the Joint Committee."

0137

ARTICLE XIII - NON-APPROPRIATED FUND ORGANIZATIONS

3

AGREED MINUTE

Reference: 81st meeting, 7 Jun 65, Paragraph 6 and 82d
meeting, 7 July 66, Paragraph 3.

"It is understood that the present use of Non-Appropriated Fund
organizations by organizations and persons other than those referred
to in items (a), (b), (c), (d), and (e) shall immediately be suspended
at the time of the entry into force of this Agreement. The extent of
organizations and persons to be granted the use of such organizations
under item (f) of this minute shall be left to further negotiations
between the appropriate authorities of the two governments."

0138

ARTICLE XVII - LABOR

6   PARAGRAPH 1(b)

Reference: 82d meeting, 7 July 66, Paragraph 14.

"(1) Local residents, who are third-country nationals and are also local-hire USFK employees and local-hire contractor employees paid in won, on the effective date of the agreement, shall be excluded from the application of this provision."

"(2) The provisions of Paragraph 1(b) do not preclude the United States armed forces from bringing into Korea, <u>without privileges</u>, third-country contractor employees possessing special skills not available from the Korean labor force."

0139

US-ROK AGREED UNDERSTANDINGS IN AGREED JOINT SUMMARY

ARTICLE XVII - LABOR

PARAGRAPH 3 AND AGREED MINUTE #4

Reference: 82d meeting, 7 July 66, Paragraph 14. c.

"It is understood that the deviation from Korean labor legislation need not be referred to the Joint Committee in cases when such referral would seriously hamper military operations in an emergency."

0140

ARTICLE XIX - MILITARY PAYMENT CERTIFICATES

Reference: 54th meeting, 9 Jun 64, Paragraphs 3
and 4, and 55th meeting, 19 Jun 64,
Paragraph 15.

"The ROK and U.S. negotiators agree that nothing in the Status of Forces Agreement in any way prevents the appropriate authorities of either the Republic of Korea or the United States from raising any appropriate matter at any time with each other. The U.S. negotiators recognize the desire of the ROK authorities to discuss the disposal of Military Payment Certificates under custody of the ROK Government. However, both the ROK and U.S. negotiators have agreed to remove from the SOFA text any reference to the question of compensation for Military Payment Certificates held by unauthorized persons. This agreement does not prejudice the position of either party in connection with discussion of this question through other channels."

한·미국 간의 상호방위조약 제4조에 의한 시설과 구역 및 한국에서의 미국군대의 지위에 관한 협정(SOFA)
전59권. 1966.7.9 서울에서 서명 : 1967.2.9 발효(조약 232호) (V.38 실무교섭회의, 제82차, 1966.7.8(II)) 147

<u>US-ROK AGREED UNDERSTANDINGS IN AGREED JOINT SUMMARY</u>

 <u>ARTICLE XXII - CRIMINAL JURISDICTION</u>

<u>AGREED MINUTE RE PARAGRAPH 1(a)</u>

Reference: 82d meeting, 7 July 66, Paragraphs 26 & 27.

"The Government of the Republic of Korea agrees, that upon notification under the second sentence of the Agreed Minute Re Paragraph 1 (a), the military authorities of the United States may exercise jurisdiction over such persons in accordance with the terms of the Criminal Jurisdiction Article."

0142

ARTICLE XXII – CRIMINAL JURISDICTION

PARAGRAPH 1(b)

Reference: 82d meeting, 7 July 66, Paragraph 19. d.

"The, civil authorities of the Republic of Korea will retain full control over the arrest, investigation and trial of a member of the United States armed forces or civilian component or a dependent."

0143

한·미국 간의 상호방위조약 제4조에 의한 시설과 구역 및 한국에서의 미국군대의 지위에 관한 협정(SOFA)
전59권. 1966.7.9 서울에서 서명 : 1967.2.9 발효(조약 232호) (V.38 실무교섭회의, 제82차, 1966.7.8(II)) 149

US-ROK AGREED UNDERSTANDINGS IN AGREED JOINT SUMMARY

ARTICLE XXII - CRIMINAL JURISDICTION

AGREED MINUTE re PARAGRAPH 2

Reference: 81st meeting, 7 Jun 65, Paragraph 41, and 82d

meeting, 7 July 66, Paragraph 17. b.

"It is understood that the United States authorities shall
exercise utmost restraint in requesting waivers of exclusive jurisdiction as provided for in the Agreed Minute Re Paragraph 2 of
this Article."

0144

ARTICLE XXII - CRIMINAL JURISDICTION

13

AGREED MINUTE re PARAGRAPH 3 (a)

Reference: 66th meeting, 24 Nov 64, Paragraph 6; 77th
meeting, 6 May 64, Paragraph 17. e., and
80th meeting, 28 May 65, Paragraph 16.

"1.   The certificate will be conclusive unless modification is agreed upon. The United States authorities shall give due consideration to any objection which may be raised by the Chief Prosecutor for the Republic of Korea."

"2.   The accused should not be deprived of his entitlement to a prompt and speedy trial as a result of protracted reconsideration of the duty certificate."

0145

US-ROK AGREED UNDERSTANDINGS IN AGREED JOINT SUMMARY

ARTICLE XXII – CRIMINAL JURISDICTION

AGREED MINUTE re PARAGRAPH 3(a)

Reference: 80th meeting, 28 May 65, Paragraph 16;
81st meeting, 7 Jun 65, Paragraphs 47 - 50;
and 82d meeting, 7 July 66, Paragraph 17 c.

"A duty certificate shall be issued only upon the advice of a Staff Judge Advocate, and the competent authority issuing the duty certificate shall be a General Grade officer."

0146

ARTICLE XXII - CRIMINAL JURISDICTION

AGREED MINUTE NO. 1 RE PARAGRAPH 3(a)

Reference: 82d meeting, 7 July 66, Paragraph 17e.

"With regard to the Agreed Minute Re Paragraph 3(a), a substantial departure from the acts a person is required to perform in a particular duty usually will indicate an act outside of his 'official duty.'"

한·미국 간의 상호방위조약 제4조에 의한 시설과 구역 및 한국에서의 미국군대의 지위에 관한 협정(SOFA)
전59권. 1966.7.9 서울에서 서명 : 1967.2.9 발효(조약 232호) (V.38 실무교섭회의, 제82차, 1966.7.8(II)) 153

US-ROK AGREED UNDERSTANDINGS IN AGREED JOINT SUMMARY

ARTICLE XXII – CRIMINAL JURISDICTION

AGREED MINUTE Re PARAGRAPH 3(b)

Reference: 82d Meeting, 7 July 66, Paragraph 22 c.

"1. It is understood that the term 'of particular importance' has reference to those cases in which, after a careful examination of each specific case, the exercise of jurisdiction by the Republic of Korea is deemed essential, and the term has reference, in general but not exclusively, to the following types of offense:

(a) security offenses against the Republic of Korea;

(b) offenses causing the death of a human being, robbery, and rape, except where the offenses are directed against a member of the United States armed forces, the civilian component, or a dependent; and

(c) attempts to commit such offenses or participation therein.

"2. In respect of the offenses referred to in the above paragraph, the authorities concerned shall proceed in particularly close cooperation from the beginning of the preliminary investigation in order to provide the mutual assistance envisaged in paragraph 6 of Article XXII."

ARTICLE XXII - CRIMINAL JURISDICTION

AGREED MINUTE RE PARAGRAPH 3(b)

Reference: 82d meeting, 7 July 66, Paragraph 23.

"In cases where, in the view of the United States authorities, any question arises concerning the determination that a case is one of particular importance, the United States diplomatic mission reserves the right and expects to be afforded an opportunity to confer with the proper authorities of the Republic of Korea."

0149

ARTICLE XXII - CRIMINAL JURISDICTION

PARAGRAPH 5

Reference: 77th meeting, 6 May 65, Paragraph 21. c.

"With regard to the custody of the accused in the hands of the Korean authorities in connection with security offenses:

1. There must be mutual ROK-US agreement as to the circumstances in which such custody is appropriate;

2. Korean confinement facilities must be adequate by US standards."

0150

ARTICLE XXII - CRIMINAL JURISDICTION

AGREED MINUTE re PARAGRAPH 9, SUB-PARAGRAPH (a) OF SECOND UNNUMBERED PARAGRAPH

      Reference: 80th meeting, 28 May 65, Paragraph 18. c., and 81st meeting, 7 Jun 65, Paragraph 42.

     "Under the appellate procedure of the Courts of the Republic of Korea, the accused may request a re-examination of the evidence, including new evidence and witnesses, as a basis for new findings of fact by the appellate court."

0151

ARTICLE XXIII - CLAIMS

PARAGRAPH 12 (Understanding relating to deletion of KSC from
Paragraph 12)

Reference: 81st meeting, 7 Jun 65, Paragraph 20

"The liability for claims generated by KSC personnel will be
determined by other negotiations between the Republic of Korea and
the United States."

(20) Art. XXV
para 5

0152

CONFIDENTIAL

THIS IS A COVER SHEET

BASIC SECURITY REQUIREMENTS ARE CONTAINED
IN AR 380-5

THE UNAUTHORIZED DISCLOSURE OF THE INFORMATION CONTAINED IN
THE ATTACHED DOCUMENT(S) COULD BE PREJUDICIAL TO THE DEFENSE
INTERESTS OF THE UNITED STATES.

RESPONSIBILITY OF PERSONS HANDLING THE ATTACHED DOCUMENT(S)

1. Exercise the necessary safeguards to prevent unauthorized disclosure by never leaving the document(s) unattended except
when properly secured in a locked safe.

2. Transfer the document(s) only to persons who need to know and
who possess the required security clearance.

3. Obtain a receipt whenever relinquishing control of the document(s)
if required by local regulations.

STORAGE

Store as prescribed in AR 380-5.

REPRODUCTION

Copies may be made of these documents except when the originating office or
higher authority has specifically denied this authority.

DISPOSITION

This cover sheet should be removed when document(s) are filed in a
permanent file, declassified, destroyed, or mailed.

(This cover sheet is unclassified when separated from classified documents)

CONFIDENTIAL

DA LABEL 22
1 APR 61   PREVIOUS EDITIONS OF THIS LABEL ARE OBSOLETE.   PPRC, Japan

STATUS OF FORCES ~~~~~~~~

SUBJECTS:
    1. Facilities and Areas
    2. Non-appropriated Fund Organizations
    3. Invited Contractors
    4. Labor
    5. Criminal Jurisdiction
    6. Claims
    7. Entry into Force of Agreement

PLACE: Ministry of Foreign Affairs

DATE: July 8, 1966

PARTICIPANTS:

<u>Republic of Korea</u>

CHANG Sang-mun
YUN Wun-yong
HO Song-chun
YI Nam-ki
KIM Tong-hwi
HO Hyong-ku
Col KIM Won-kil, ROKA
Lt Col Suh In-suk
KIM Ki-cho
PAK Won-chol
YI Kun-pal (Interpreter)

<u>United States</u>

Richard A. Ericson, Jr.
Col Allan G. Pixton, USA
Col Herbert C. Hicks, Jr., USA
Capt George M. Hagerman, USN
Col Wilson Freeman, USA
Richard M. Herndon
Robert A. Kinney
Goodwin Shapiro
Ronald P. Myers
Ogden Reed, Observer

보통문서로 재분류(1968. 12. 31)

2 Inclosures
    1. Ltr from Minister of Foreign
       Affairs Tong Won Lee
    2. Ltr from Ambassador Brown

직권으로재분류(72.8.0)
직위   성명

0154

양측 교섭대표 싸인本
(See last Page)

66-5-7 (33)

미경·문 113-1 (謄)

0155

Article IV - Facilities and Areas - Return of Facilities

1. Mr. Ericson noted that, at the 81st session the Korean negotiators proposed a new Agreed Minute, to be added as Agreed Minute No. 2 to the US draft. The US negotiators agree that this new Agreed Minute is the corollary to Agreed Minute No. 1. It is logical that all removable properties located in any area or facilities which are provided by the ROK Government should be returned whenever such properties are no longer needed for the US armed forces.

2. Therefore, Mr. Ericson continued, the US negotiators are happy to accept the new proposed Agreed Minute No. 2, and thereby achieve full agreement on this Article.

Article XIII - Non-appropriated Fund Organizations Article'

3. Mr. Ericson noted that, at the 81st meeting, the ROK negotiators accepted the Agreed Minute of Article XIII as proposed by the US negotiators. The US side agrees to the understanding for the Agreed Joint Summary proposed by the ROK negotiators at the 81st meeting relating to this Agreed Minute, and full US-ROK agreement on this Article has now been achieved.

Article XV - Invited Contractors

4. Mr. Ericson stated that, at the 81st negotiating session, the Korean negotiators reiterated their objection to Paragraph 8 of the US draft and requested the acceptance of their Paragraph 8. This matter was subsequently extensively discussed at informal meetings between members of the ROK and US negotiating team. As a result of these

2

0156

66-5-7

미으 113-1

0157

discussions, the United States negotiators now accept Paragraph 8, as proposed by the Korean negotiators, with minor modifications as follows:

"8. The authorities of the Republic of Korea shall have the right to exercise jurisdiction over such persons for offenses committed in the Republic of Korea and punishable by the law of the Republic of Korea. In recognition of the role of such persons in the defense of the Republic of Korea, they shall be subject to the provisions of paragraphs 5, 7(b), and 9 and the related Agreed Minutes, of Article XXII. In those cases in which the authorities of the Republic of Korea decide not to exercise jurisdiction they shall notify the military authorities of the United States as soon as possible. Upon such notification the military authorities of the United States shall have the right to exercise such jurisdiction over the persons referred to as is conferred on them by the law of the United States."

5. Mr. Ericson noted that in the first sentence, the word "primary" was deleted. This was necessary to prevent misunderstanding since the term "primary jurisdiction" relates to the exercise of concurrent jurisdiction. Under the present state of U.S. laws, the Korean jurisdiction over contractor employees is exclusive, although it is understood that the effective administration and disciplinary sanctions available to the United States may be appropriate in certain cases.

6. Mr. Ericson stated that the second sentence is a proposed addition to Paragraph 8. It provides that personnel under this article

3

0158

will be subject to the provisions of the Criminal Juristiction Article and its Agreed Minutes relating to custody, confinement and trial safeguards. This takes nothing away from the right of jurisdiction retained by the Republic of Korea. It merely confers upon these persons the same protections relating to custody, confinement and trial safeguards as are accorded members of the civilian component. Mr. Ericson emphasized that invited contractors have an important role in the defense of the Republic of Korea and are indispensable to the United States military forces. It is deemed essential that they receive the minimal protections offered by the custody, confinement and trial safeguard provisions. The last two sentences of Paragraph 8 are accepted as proposed by the ROK without change. The US negotiators trust that these modifications will be acceptable to the Korean negotiators and that full agreement can now be reached on this Article.

7. Mr. Chang replied that, with regard to the modified proposals tabled by the U.S. negotiators regarding Paragraph 8 of the Invited Contractors Article, the Korean negotiators wish to present the following response. The Korean negotiators are prepared to accept deletion of the word "primary" from the first sentence on the basis of the statement by the US negotiators to the effect that:

> "Under the present state of U.S. law, the Korean jurisdiction over contractor employees is exclusive although it is understood that the effective administration and disciplinary sanctions available

4

0160

to the United States may be appropriate in

certain cases."

8. With respect to the proposed new second sentence which is to be
incorporated into the provisions of Paragraph 8, which provides that in
recognition of the role of such personnel in the defense of the Republic
of Korea, the persons referred to in Paragraph 1 shall be subject to the
provisions of Paragraph 5, 7(b), 9 and its related Agreed Minutes of
Article XXII. Mr. Chang recalled that the U.S. negotiators had in the
past placed their special emphasis on guarantees of fair trial for U.S.
personnel on the grounds that as U.S. citizens they are entitled to such
rights as are guaranteed under the Constitution of the United States.
In the course of negotiations regarding the Invited Contractors Article,
they had further stated that although those third-country employees
who are present on the effective date of this Agreement will be entitled
to enjoy the privileges contained in this Article, there is no
intention to bring in any third-country nationals after the Agreement
goes into force, but if any were brought in, they would have no
privileges under the terms of this Article, thereby indicating their
flexibility toward the extent of privileges to be granted to third-
country employees under this Article.

9. Mr. Chang stated that, in the light of the above position of
the U.S. negotiators, the Korean negotiators believe that application
of such privileges as proposed by the U.S. negotiators in their second
sentence of Paragraph 8 pertaining to the provisions of Paragraphs 5,

5

0162

7(b), 9 and its related Agreed Minutes of the Criminal Jurisdiction Article should naturally be limited to U.S. nationals only. Consequently, it is also the view of the Korean negotiators, Mr. Chang continued, that the privileges to be granted under Agreed Minute No. 2 of this Article to the contractor employees of third-country nationality who are present in the Republic of Korea on the effective date of this Agreement shall, to be consonant with the above observation of Paragraph 8, not include any privilege provided for in the proposed second sentence of Paragraph 8.

10. Mr. Chang pointed out that in this connection, the Korean negotiators, before accepting the U.S. modifications, wish to seek clarification from the U.S. negotiators on their intention as to the following two points:

a. Whether or not third-country employees and those employees who are ordinarily resident in, but are not nationals of the United States, and their dependents will be subject to the provisions of Paragraph 5, 7(b), 9 and its related Agreed Minutes of the Criminal Jurisdiction Article?

b. Whether or not the privileges to be granted to third-country employees under Agreed Minute No. 2 include the privileges in the proposed second sentence of Paragraph 8 relating to the Criminal Jurisdiction Article?

6

0164

66-ㅜ-31

11. Mr. Ericson replied that the United States negotiators, in response to the ROK queries in Paragraph 10, agree to the following understanding for the Agreed Joint Summary.

"Unless otherwise agreed in the Joint Committee, the privileges provided for in the second sentence of Paragraph 8 of this Article shall be extended only to United States nationals."

The US negotiators also can assure the Koreans, as indicated in the informal discussions, that such requests for Joint Committee consideration on this point are expected to be rare.

12. Mr. Chang stated that, with these explanations and understandings in the Joint Summary Record, the Korean negotiators now accept the proposed U.S. modifications regarding Paragraph 8, thereby reaching full agreement on this Article.

Article XVII - Labor

13. Mr. Ericson tabled a revised Labor Article, which he stated was responsive to the proposals made by the ROK negotiators at the 81st session, and at subsequent informal meetings. He expressed the belief that this revised Labor Article fully meets the ROK requirements, and he anticipates full agreement can now be reached on the revised text of the Labor Article.

14. Mr. Ericson stated that the following comments refer to specific changes in the previously tabled United States draft, made in response to the Korean proposals at the 81st session:

7

0166

66-ᆞ-3ᆞ

0167

a. __Paragraph 1(b)__. The US negotiators accept the ROK proposal for the inclusion of a new sentence in Paragraph 1(b), as follows: "Such employees shall be nationals of the Republic of Korea." This sentence is accepted on the condition of ROK acceptance of two understandings for the Agreed Summary Record, as follows:

> (1) "Local residents, who are third-country nationals and are also local-hire USFK employees and local-hire contractor employees paid in won, on the effective date of the agreement, shall be excluded from the application of this provision."

There are only a few USFK employees in this category, who have been working with USFK in good faith for some years, and the US negotiators feel their exclusion from this provision would not present problems and would only be fair to all concerned.

> (2) The second understanding is as follows: "The provisions of Paragraph 1(b) do not preclude the United States armed forces from bringing into Korea, __without privileges,__ third-country contractor employees possessing special skills not available from the Korean labor force."

The US negotiators believe general US-ROK agreement on this point is reflected in previous informal discussions. In adding the new sentence to Paragraph 1(b), it is also necessary to add, in the parenthetical phrase "(other than a member of the civilian component)" the phrase "or a contractor employee under Article XV," to enable invited contractors to hire American personnel. Mr. Ericson pointed

8

0168

66-↓-3↓

66-5-7

이은배

0169

out that invited contractor employees are not included as part of the
civilian component in the Definitions Article (I). Therefore, this added
phrase is made necessary by the ROK-proposed added sentence, and it
makes it clear that the word "employee" as used in this Article does not
refer to non-Korean employees of invited contractors.

     b. <u>Paragraph 2 and Agreed Minutes No. 1, 2, 3</u>. The US negoti-
ators believe the two sides are now in full agreement regarding Paragraph
2 and Agreed Minutes 1, 2, and 3 as previously tabled by the US. Mr.
Ericson noted that, during the informal discussions which took place
since the 81st meeting, it was mutually agreed that the ROK-proposed
understanding relating to Agreed Minute No. 2, reported in Paragraph 27
of the Agreed Summary Record of the 81st meeting, would be withdrawn.

     c. <u>Paragraph 3 and Agreed Minute No. 4</u>. Mr. Ericson stated
that the US negotiators accept the revisions in Paragraph 3, as tabled
by the ROK negotiators at the 81st meeting. With regard to the related
Agreed Minute No. 4, subsequent to the 81st meeting the ROK negotiators
proposed revision of the text of this Agreed Minute which they had
previously tabled. Their new proposal is as follows:

> "4. When employers cannot conform with provisions of labor
> legislation of the Republic of Korea applicable under this
> Article on account of the military requirements of the United
> States armed forces, the matter shall be referred, in advance,
> to the Joint Committee for consideration and appropriate action.
> In the event mutual agreement cannot be reached in the Joint
> Committee regarding appropriate action, the issue may be made the
> subject of review through discussions between appropriate
> officials of the Government of the Republic of Korea and the
> diplomatic mission of the United States of America."

9

0170

Mr. Chang noted that the ROK negotiators had revised their previously tabled Agreed Minute No. 4, deleting the words "whenever possible". In proposing this revised language, Mr. Chang stated that the ROK Government is appreciative of the need for the United States armed forces to have the flexibility in an emergency to deviate from ROK labor legislation without referral to the Joint Committee, as presented by the US negotiators at the 71st meeting (Paragraph 15 of the Agreed Joint Summary) and at the 73rd meeting (Paragraph 5 of the Agreed Joint Summary). Therefore, the ROK negotiators proposed the following agreed understanding which will be included in the Agreed Joint Summary, as follows:

> "It is understood that the deviation from Korean labor legislation need not be referred to the Joint Committee in cases when such referral would seriously hamper military operations in an emergency."

Mr. Ericson stated that the US negotiators were authorized to accept the ROK proposal to delete the phrase "whenever possible" in Agreed Minute 4 on the basis that the ROK-proposed agreed understanding, which the US accepts, clearly indicates that the United States military authorities can deviate from Korean labor legislation without referral to the Joint Committee when such would seriously hamper military operations in an emergency. Mr. Chang stated that whenever the matter is referred to the Joint Committee after the deviation had already been made on account of military requirements in an emergency, it is presumed that the Korean side could raise objection in the Joint Committee to the

10

0172

66-5-9

0173

action taken by the employer and request that appropriate action, i.e., corrective action or measures for remedy be taken. It is understood that such corrective action will be taken as and when the Joint Committee so directs. In the event that mutual agreement cannot be reached in the Joint Committee regarding appropriate action, the matter may be discussed between officials of the Government of the Republic of Korea and the US diplomatic mission. Mr. Chang indicated that these remarks are not intended to introduce any new understanding, but rather are intended to provide guidance to the members of the Joint Committee in their inter-pretation and implementation of the new agreed Labor Article.

     d. _Paragraph 4_: The US side concurs in the proposed ROK changes at the end of Paragraph 4 (a) (5), changing the number in parentheses from "3" to "2" in the following phrase: "as stipulated in subparagraph (2), above."

     The US side also accepts the revised Paragraph 4 (b), as proposed by the ROK side, as follows:

> "Employees or any employee organization shall have the
> right of further collective action in the event a labor
> dispute is not resolved by the foregoing procedures
> except in cases where the Joint Committee determines
> such action seriously hampers military operations of the
> United States armed forces for the Joint defense of the
> Republic of Korea. In the event an agreement cannot be
> reached on this question in the Joint Committee, it may
> be made the subject of review through discussions

11

0174

66-1-36

0175

between appropriate officials of the Government of the
Republic of Korea and the diplomatic mission of the United
States of America."

In accepting this ROK proposal on this important point, the US side should
like it understood and agreed that the Joint Committee will take up as one
of its earliest items of business the delineation of those activities the
interruption of which would seriously hamper military operations of the
United States armed forces for the joint defense of the ROK. In the Joint
Committee's consideration of this matter, the Korean Labor Disputes Act
of 1953 should be used as a general guide.

e. Paragraph 5: The US side accepts the ROK-proposed added phrase,
"through mutual consultation," after the word "deferred."

f. Agreed Minute No. 5: The US negotiators also accept the modifications of Agreed Minute No. 5, as proposed by the ROK negotiators at
the 81st meeting, with the addition of the phrase "by the employers" as
agreed upon in informal discussions. The full text of Agreed Minute No. 5
is as follows:

"5. A union or other employee group shall be recognized
by the employers unless its objectives are inimical to the
common interests of the United States and the Republic of
Korea. Membership or non-membership in such groups shall
not be a factor in employment or other actions affecting
employees."

15. Mr. Ericson states that he felt that the revisions of text of
the Labor Article, as tabled by the US side at this meeting, will be fully

12

0176

66-5-39

66-5-7   가. 요. 113-1

0177

acceptable to the ROK negotiators. These proposals are presented as a package and the US revisions of its draft in response to ROK proposals are contingent upon ROK acceptance of the rest of the text and understandings.

16. Mr. Chang stated that the Korean negotiators appreciate the general acceptance of the revised draft of the Labor Article, as tabled at 81st session and as revised as a result of informal discussions. The Korean side accepts the modifications effected in Paragraph 1 (b) and Agreed Minutes No. 4 and No. 5, as well as in the agreed understandings, and therefore full agreement has been reached on the Labor Article.

Article XXII - Criminal Jurisdiction

17. Mr. Ericson noted that, at the 81st negotiating session, the Korean negotiators accepted the US draft of the Criminal Jurisdiction Article with certain modifications. The United States negotiators are now pleased to accept the proposals made by the ROK negotiators at that session, subject to Korean acceptance of several minor changes. Specifically, the US side accepts:

a. The Korean proposals relating to Paragraph 7(b), verbatim.

b. The understanding on the Agreed Minute Re Para 2, as follows:

"It is understood that the United States authorities shall exercise utmost restraint in requesting waivers of exclusive jurisdiction as provided for in the Agreed Minute Re Paragraph 2 of this Article."

c. The Understanding on Agreed Minute Re Para 3(a), with deletion of the previously proposed phrase "or his designee," as follows:

13

0178

66-ㅅ-30

66-5-7

미·문 113-1

0179

한·미국 간의 상호방위조약 제4조에 의한 시설과 구역 및 한국에서의 미국군대의 지위에 관한 협정(SOFA)
전59권. 1966.7.9 서울에서 서명 : 1967.2.9 발효(조약 232호) (V.38 실무교섭회의, 제82차, 1966.7.8(II)) 185

"A duty certificate shall be issued only upon the advice of a Staff Judge Advocate, and the competent authority issuing the duty certificates shall be a General Grade officer."

d. Mr. Ericson stated the US side accepts the Korean proposal to delete the word "civil" from Paragraph 1(b) and to reinsert the second sentence of Agreed Minute Re Paragraph 9(a), on the condition ROK negotiators accept the following understanding on Paragraph 1(b) for inclusion in the Agreed Joint Summary:

"The civil authorities of the Republic of Korea will retain full control over the arrest, investigation and trial of a member of the United States armed forces or civilian component or a dependent."

The US negotiators believe that this statement represents the positions of both sides and that this is a mutually agreeable understanding.

e. Regarding the definition of official duty, the US side is prepared to compromise by including the first sentence of the official duty definition as the second sentence of Agreed Minute No. 1 Re Para 3(a). The second sentence will be included as an understanding in the Agreed Joint Summary, as follows:

"With regard to the Agreed Minute Re Paragraph 3(a), a substantial departure from the acts a person is required to perform in a particular duty usually will indicate an act outside of his "official duty.""

f. With reference to Agreed Minute Re Para 9(g), the additional language proposed by the Korean negotiators at the 81st session is

14

0180

66-5-7 미·분 113-1

0181

unacceptable. It is recognized that similar language contained in subpara (b) of Agreed Minute No. 6 Re Para 3(b) of the US draft is likewise objectionable to the Korean negotiators. Therefore, the US side proposes deletion of the following portion of the second sentence of subpara (b):

> "... except where his presence is incompatible with the rules of the court of the United States or with the security requirements of the United States, which are not at the same time the security requirements of the Republic of Korea."

This proposal is conditioned on acceptance by the Korean negotiators of the US draft Agreed Minute Re Para 9(g) as tabled.

g. Regarding Agreed Minute Re Para 10(a) and 10(b), the US negotiators have given careful consideration to the Korean proposal tabled at the 81st session and also the informal discussions held thereafter. The US negotiators are now tabling a modification of this US draft which it is believed will more than fulfill the desires of the Korean negotiators. It should be noted that the language is virtually identical to the similar provisions of the Japanese SOFA.

18. Mr. Ericson emphasized that the US negotiators agree to all of the foregoing ROK proposals made at the 81st meeting, on the condition that the ROK accept the few proposed changes the US side has made. Mr. Ericson stated that he is confident that these changes will be agreeable to the Korean negotiators and that full agreement can be reached on this Article as now tabled.

15

0182

66-5-1   미분 113-1

0183

한·미국 간의 상호방위조약 제4조에 의한 시설과 구역 및 한국에서의 미국군대의 지위에 관한 협정(SOFA)
전59권. 1966.7.9 서울에서 서명 : 1967.2.9 발효(조약 232호) (V.38 실무교섭회의, 제82차, 1966.7.8(II)) 189

19. Mr. Chang expressed the appreciation of the Korean negotiators to the United States negotiators for the most careful consideration and acceptance of those proposals tabled by the Korean negotiators at the 81st session, i.e.:

    a. The additional proposals relating to Paragraph 7(b).

    b. The understanding on the Agreed Minute Re Paragraph 2.

    c. The understanding on Agreed Minute Re Paragraph 3(a).

20. Mr. Chang stated that the Korean negotiators are now prepared to accept the following proposals tabled by the US negotiators:

    a. The Agreed Minute No. 1 Re Paragraph 1(b), verbatim.

    b. The US proposal regarding the definition of official duty which includes the first sentence of the definition as the second sentence of the Agreed Minute No. 1 Re Paragraph 3(a) and the second sentence of the definition as an understanding in the Agreed Joint Summary.

    c. The US proposals relating to Agreed Minute Re Paragraph 9(g) and subparagraph (b) of Agreed Minute No. 6 of Re Paragraph 3(b) with deletion of the following identical languages therefrom:

> "... except where his presence is incompatible with the rules of the court of the United States or with the security requirements of the United States, which are not at the same time the security requirements of the Republic of Korea."

    d. The modifications of the US draft regarding Agreed Minute Re Paragraph 10(a) and 10(b).

16

0184

66-5-7   마 븐 113-1

0185

21. Mr. Chang stated that, with respect to Paragraph 1(b) of the US draft, the Korean negotiators express their thanks to the U.S. side for deletion of the word "civil" from their draft coupled with reinsertion of the second sentence of Agreed Minute Re Paragraph 9(a). However, the Korean negotiators have noted that the deletion of the word "civil" from their draft is conditioned upon ROK acceptance of the following understanding in the Agreed Joint Summary:

> "The civil authorities of the Republic of Korea will retain full control over the arrest, investigation and trial of a member of the United States armed forces or civilian component or a dependent."

To accommodate the U.S. concern over this problem, the Korean negotiators had in the past reiterated their assurances that the U.S. personnel shall under no circumstances be tried by the military tribunal of the Republic of Korea, and thus have accepted the second sentence of Agreed Minute Re Paragraph 9(a) and Agreed Minute No. 1 of Re Paragraph 1(b) of the U.S. draft regarding martial law. In the light of the trend of the past negotiations on this problem, the Korean negotiators, to expedite and complete the negotiations as soon as practicable, and at the same time to fulfill the requirements of the US negotiators, accept the proposed U.S. understanding with the Korean interpretation of the understanding that the US negotiators are merely reaffirming their basic position that the U.S. personnel referred to in Paragraph 1(b) of this Article shall under no circumstances be arrested, investigated, or tried by the military authorities or military tribunals of the Republic of Korea.

17

0186

22. The US side indicated, in June 1965, acceptance of the addition of the new sentence in Agreed Minute No. 4, Re Paragraph 3(b), as proposed by the ROK side at the 81st meeting. However, in June 1966, when it became clear as a result of informal US-ROK discussions that a new approach to this Agreed Minute was required, if agreement was to be reached, the US side formally proposed a new package approach to the problem. The new package included three interrelated elements, including Agreed Minute Re Paragraph 3(b), an open exchange of letters between the ROK Foreign Minister and the US Ambassador to Korea and new agreed understandings for the Agreed Joint Summary.

a. The text of the new Agreed Minute Re Paragraph 3(b), as modified as a result of informal negotiations, is as follows:

Re Paragraph 3(b)

1. The authorities of the Republic of Korea, recognizing that it is the primary responsibility of the United States military authorities to maintain good order and discipline where persons subject to United States military laws are concerned, will, upon the request of the military authorities of the United States pursuant to Paragraph 3(c), waive their primary right to exercise jurisdiction under Paragraph 3(b) except when they determine that it is of particular importance that jurisdiction be exercised by the authorities of the Republic of Korea.

2. With the consent of the competent authorities of the Republic of Korea, the military authorities of the United States

18

0188

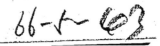

harm transfer to the courts or authorities of the Republic of Korea for investigation, trial and decision, particular criminal cases in which jurisdiction rests with the United States.

With the consent of the military authorities of the United States, the competent authorities of the Republic of Korea may transfer to the military authorities of the United States for investigation, trial and decision, particular criminal cases in which jurisdiction rests with the Republic of Korea.

3. (a) Where a member of the United States armed forces or civilian component, or a dependent, is arraigned before a court of the United States, for an offense committed in the Republic of Korea against Korean interests, the trial shall be held within the Republic of Korea

(i) except where the law of the United States requires otherwise, or

(ii) except where, in cases of military exigency or in the interests of justice, the military authorities of the United States intend to hold the trial outside the Republic of Korea. In this event they shall afford the authorities of the Republic of Korea timely opportunity to comment on such intention and shall give due consideration to any comments the latter may make.

(b) Where the trial is held outside of the Republic of Korea the military authorities of the United States shall inform the authorities of the Republic of Korea of the place and date of

19

0190

66-1-오8

66-5-7   미·문 113-1

0191

미·문113-1

the trial. A representative of the Republic of Korea shall be entitled to be present at the trial. The authorities of the United States shall inform the authorities of the Republic of Korea of the judgment and the final outcome of the proceedings.

4. In the implementation of the provisions of this Article, and to facilitate the expeditious disposal of offenses, arrangements may be made between the United States military authorities and the competent authorities of the Republic of Korea.

b. The full texts of the unclassified letters to be exchanged between the ROK Foreign Minister and the U.S. Ambassador, which were modified as a result of informal negotiations, are attached as Inclosures 1 and 2.

c. The new agreed understandings to be included in the Agreed Joint Summary, as modified as a result of informal negotiations, are as follows:

"1. It is understood that the term "of particular importance" has reference to those cases in which, after a careful examination of each specific case, the exercise of jurisdiction by the Republic of Korea is deemed essential and the term has reference, in general but not exclusively, to the following types of offenses:

(a) security offenses against the Republic of Korea;

(b) offenses causing the death of a human being,

20

0192

66-5-01

66-5-2

기·문·13-1

0193

robbery and rape, except where the offenses are directed against

a member of the United States armed forces, the civilian

component, or a dependent; and

      (c) attempts to commit such offenses or partici-

pation therein.

     "2. In respect of the offenses referred to in the above

paragraph, the authorities concerned shall proceed in particu-

larly close cooperation from the beginning of the preliminary

investigation in order to provide the mutual assistance

envisaged in paragraph 6 of Article XXII."

23. Mr. Chang had indicated the strong desire of the ROK side to

delete the second sentence of the first paragraph of the revised Agreed

Minute Re Paragraph 3(b), as initially proposed by the US side. This

sentence, which had originally been proposed by the ROK side, was as

follows:

    "In cases where any question concerning such determination

    as may be made by the authorities of the Republic of Korea

    in accordance with the foregoing provisions cannot be

    resolved in discussions between the authorities concerned,

    the United States diplomatic mission will be afforded an

    opportunity to confer with the proper authorities of the

    Republic of Korea."

    After informal negotiations, the US agreed to delete this sentence,

if the ROK will accept the following agreed understanding on this point:

21

0194

66-5-7

미톤113-1

0195

"In cases where, in view of the United States authorities, any question arises concerning the determination that a case is one 'of particular importance,' the United States diplomatic mission reserves the right and expects to be afforded an opportunity to confer with the proper authorities of the Republic of Korea."

Mr. Chang stated that the ROK side agrees to this understanding. Notwithstanding the foregoing understanding, however, Mr. Chang stated that authorities of the Republic of Korea shall not be prevented from exercising their primary jurisdiction under Agreed Minute Re Paragraph 3(b) of Article XXII. Mr. Ericson responded that this is also the US interpretation.

24. Mr. Chang stated that the ROK side accepts the US package proposal for Agreed Minute Re Paragraph 3(b), thereby reaching full US-ROK agreement on this key issue of waiver.

25. Mr. Chang indicated, finally, that there were two other minor changes which the ROK side desired to propose, as follows:

a. The first is a new Agreed Minute Re Paragraph 1(a). Mr. Chang stated that notwithstanding the provision of Paragraph 1(a) of the Article, the U.S. military authorities have no criminal jurisdiction in peacetime over members of the civilian component and dependents. Therefore, the Korean negotiators propose the following new Agreed Minute Re Paragraph 1(a) regarding the extent of U.S. military criminal jurisdiction:

"It is understood that under the present state of

22

0196

66-5-7

기문 1137

0197

United States law, the military authorities of the
United States have no effective criminal jurisdiction
in peacetime over members of the civilian component
or dependents. If the scope of United States military
jurisdiction changes as a result of subsequent legislation, constitutional amendment, or decision by
appropriate authorities of the United States, the
Government of the United States shall inform the
Government of the Republic of Korea through diplomatic channels."

b. The second proposed change relates to Agreed Minute Re
Paragraph 2, which the ROK side desires to revise as follows:

"The Republic of Korea, recognizing the effectiveness in
appropriate cases of the administrative and disciplinary
sanctions which may be imposed by the United States
authorities over members of the United States armed
forces or civilian component, and their dependents, may,
at the request of the military authorities of the United
States, waive its right to exercise jurisdiction under
paragraph 2."

26. Mr. Ericson stated that the US side could accept the change
in Agreed Minute Re Paragraph 2 and a new Agreed Minute Re Paragraph
1(a), if the ROK Government would accept the following agreed understanding:

23

0198

66-5-9

마음113거

0199

"The Government of the Republic of Korea agrees
that, upon notification under the second sentence
of the Agreed Minute Re Paragraph 1(a), the
military authorities of the United States may
exercise jurisdiction over such persons in
accordance with the terms of the Criminal Jurisdiction Article."

27. Mr. Chang indicated ROK acceptance of this agreed understanding in paragraph 26, above. He stated that, with the acceptance of
this agreed understanding by the Korean negotiators, both sides have now
reached full agreement on the Article dealing with Criminal Jurisdiction,
the heart of the Status of Forces Agreement between the United States
and the Republic of Korea.

Article XXIII - Claims.

28. Mr. Ericson noted that, at the 81st negotiating session, the
Korean negotiators tabled a revised draft of the Claims Article, including modifications of Paragraph 5(e) (iii) and Agreed Minute No. 1
and paragraph 12 relating to the Korean Service Corps. The United
States negotiators are pleased to accept this revised Claims Article,
subject to ROK acceptance of the following revised Agreed Minute No. 1
of the Claims Article:

"1. Unless otherwise provided, the provisions of paragraphs 5, 6, 7 and 8 of this Article will become effective
six months from the date of entry into force of this

24

0200

66-5-9   가분배3-1

0201

Agreement with respect to claims arising from incidents in the Seoul Special City area, and one year from that date with respect to claims arising elsewhere in the Republic of Korea."

29. Mr. Ericson pointed out that this revised Agreed Minute No. 1 provides for a specific timetable for the progressive turnover of United States Claims Service responsibilities to the ROK Government Claims Service. This progressive US transfer of claims responsibilities to the ROK Government, first in the Seoul Special City area six months after the entry into force of the SOFA, and throughout the Republic of Korea six months later, should provide the basis for an orderly transfer of these complex responsibilities. The primary US concern in this matter is to insure prompt and equitable settlement for Korean claimants against the USFK. This proposal should meet the needs of both Governments and assure justice to deserving Korean claimants in the transition period during which the United States transfers the responsibilities for settlement of claims to the Government of the Republic of Korea.

30. Mr. Chang stated that the Korean negotiators accept the US proposal regarding the Claims Article in order to reach full agreement at the present session. Mr. Chang continued that the Korean negotiators also believe, as just stated by the US negotiators, that the primary concern of the Korean negotiators in this matter is to insure prompt and equitable settlements of the claims for damages caused by USFK.

25

0202

66-5-7   마을 113-1

0203

Mr. Chang noted that with this ect in mind, the Korean negotiators accept the revised Agreed Minute No. 1, which provides for transfer of the claims responsibilities to the ROK in Seoul Special City area six months after entry into force of the SOFA, and throughout the ROK 12 months after the entry into force of the SOFA, thereby reaching full agreement on this Article.

31. The ROK and US Chief Negotiators agreed the two sides are now in full agreement on the Claims Article, on the basis of the ROK draft tabled at the 81st meeting and the revised Agreed Minute No. 1, as set forth in Paragraph 25.

Article XXIX - Entry into Force of Agreement.

32. Mr. Ericson stated that the United States Government will accept the Ratification Article proposed by the ROK negotiators at the 81st session, subject to minor modifications in which it is understood the ROK side concurs.

33. Mr. Ericson stated that the US side accepts the full text of the ROK proposal made at the 81st session, verbatim, with only the following two modifications:

a. In Paragraph 1, the phrase "three months" is substituted for the phrase "sixty days." There is mutual agreement regarding the need for the longer time interval between ratification and the entry into force of the Agreement. It is proposed that the precise date of entry into force should be mutually acknowledged at the time of the receipt of the ROK Government's written notification that it has

26

0204

66-ゲ-17

approved the Agreement in accordance with the legal procedures
(probably the same date three months later).

   b. In Paragraph 2, a change is proposed which it is believed
will make the sentence read more smoothly without changing its meaning.
Substitution of the word "the" for "its" in the last clause of the
sentence is proposed. This change makes the last clause read "to give
effect to the provisions of this Agreement."

   34. In accepting the ROK draft of this Article, with these minor
modifications, Mr. Ericson indicated he would like to reiterate the US
views concerning implementation of the Agreement, as previously
presented at the 80th session. The US negotiators believe both sides are
in full agreement on the importance of careful planning and action by
their respective governments to insure the maximum possible efficiency
and effectiveness in the implementation of the SOFA. In the language
of Paragraph 2, the ROK Government will endeavor to take "all legislative and budgetary action necessary to give effect to the provisions
of this Agreement." The US negotiators believe such necessary action
also includes any other necessary implementing action, such as issuing
appropriate administrative regulations. United States authorities in
Korea will inform the Government of the Republic of Korea, on a continuing basis, of their progress in implementation of the Agreement.
The US side expects that the ROK Government, similarly, will inform
appropriate United States officials of its progress in implementation
of the SOFA and that copies of pertinent documents and regulations

27

0206

66-5-7

미.료 113-1

0207

issued by ROK and United States authorities will be exchanged. We
believe both sides are in mutual agreement on the necessity for
consistent and coordinated action, to insure smooth implementation
of the SOFA.

35. Mr. Chang stated that the Korean negotiators appreciate
the concurrence of the U.S. negotiators to the revised Korean draft
of the Ratification Article and accept the two modifications proposed
by the U.S. side in Paragraphs 1 and 2. Both sides, thereby, have also
reached full agreement on this Article. Mr. Chang further stated that,
similarly, the Korean side has no objection to exchange, on a
continuous basis, of copies of pertinent documents and regulations
issued by authorities of both Governments to give effect to the
provisions of the Agreement, as well as any other information on the
progress of the Korean Government in carrying out the Agreement, in
order to insure the maximum possible efficiency and effectiveness in
the implementation of the present Status of Forces Agreement between
the Republic of Korea and the United States.

36. Mr. Chang replied that the ROK negotiators are in full agreement with the US negotiators on this Article, and with this agreement
the US and ROK negotiators have now achieved agreement on all 31
Articles of the US-ROK Status of Forces Agreement. Therefore, formal
negotiations of this Status of Forces Agreement is finally concluded,
after 45 months of negotiations.

37. In concluding the final session of the negotiations, both

28

0208

0209

the Republic of Korea and the United States negotiators exchanged their heartfelt praise for the patience and friendly cooperation rendered by those who have tirelessly participated in one of the most lengthy yet epoch-making negotiations, which resulted in the achievement of a US-ROK Status of Forces Agreement.

29

0210

66-5-7

마문 ll3거

0211

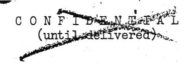

July 9, 1966

His Excellency
Winthrop G. Brown
Ambassador of the United States of America
Seoul, Korea

Excellency:

Today the Governments of the United States and the Republic
of Korea have formally signed the Agreement between the
United States of America and the Republic of Korea regarding
facilities and areas and the status of United States armed
forces in the Republic of Korea. Article XXII of that
Agreement and its agreed minutes provide for the exercise of
jurisdiction over members of the United States armed forces,
the civilian component, and their dependents in the Republic
of Korea. In this regard, the Government of the Republic of
Korea, conscious of the strong ties of mutual respect and
friendship which bind our two countries, and recognizing the
vital role which United States armed forces play in the
defense of the Republic of Korea, proposes the following
understandings for procedural arrangements pursuant to Paragraph 4 of the Agreed Minute Re Paragraph 3(b):

    That, to facilitate the processing of cases
    resulting from the presence of United States armed
    forces deployed in the Republic of Korea for mutual
    defense purposes, in implementation of the provisions
    of the Agreed Minute Re Paragraph 3(b), the Govern-
    ment of the Republic of Korea will not require the
    military authorities of the United States to make a
    request for a waiver in each particular case, and the
    military authorities of the United States shall have
    jurisdiction unless the Government of the Republic of
    Korea determines in a specific case that it is of
    particular importance that jurisdiction be exercised
    therein by the authorities of the Republic of Korea;

    That, in the interest of expediting the
    administration of justice, any such determination by
    the Government of the Republic of Korea shall be

0212

Incl 1

66-1-14

665-7

기로13기

0213

provided in writing by the Minister of Justice to the appropriate military authorities of the United States within fifteen days after the Republic of Korea is notified or is otherwise apprised of the commission of an offense falling within its primary jurisdiction, or such shorter period as may be mutually agreed upon pursuant to Paragraph 4 of the Agreed Minute Re Paragraph 3(b). The military authorities of the United States shall not exercise jurisdiction before the expiration of the fifteen days or other agreed period.

I would be grateful for your confirmation of the above understandings.

Sincerely yours,

2

0214

66-5-16

665-7

마믄ll3-1

0215

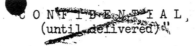

July 9, 1966

His Excellency
Tong Won Lee
Minister of Foreign Affairs
 of the Republic of Korea
Seoul, Korea

Dear Mr. Minister:

I have received your letter of this date on the subject of
the agreement signed today between the Republic of Korea
and the United States of America regarding facilities and
areas and the status of United States armed forces in the
Republic of Korea, and confirm the following understandings
contained therein with respect to the exercise of jurisdiction
over members of the United States armed forces, the civilian
component, and their dependents:

> That, to facilitate the processing of cases
resulting from the presence of United States armed
forces deployed in Korea for mutual defense purposes,
in implementation of the provisions of the Agreed
Minute Re Paragraph 3(b), the Government of the
Republic of Korea will not require the military
authorities of the United States to make a request
for a waiver in each particular case, and the military
authorities of the United States shall have jurisdiction
unless the Government of the Republic of Korea
determines in a specific case that it is of particular
importance that jurisdiction be exercised therein by
the authorities of the Republic of Korea;

> That, in the interest of expediting the adminis-
tration of justice, any such determination by the
Government of the Republic of Korea shall be provided
in writing by the Minister of Justice to the appropriate
military authorities of the United States within fifteen
days after the Republic of Korea is notified or is
otherwise apprised of the commission of an offense
falling within its primary jurisdiction, or such ————

0216

Incl 2

66-5-(7)

66-5-7

미문 113ㅓ

0217

shorter period as may be mutually agreed upon pursuant to
Paragraph 4 of the Agreed Minute Re Paragraph 3(b). The
military authorities of the United States shall not
exercise jurisdiction before the expiration of the fifteen
days or other agreed period.

                    Very sincerely yours,

                    Winthrop G. Brown
                    Ambassador

2

0218

66-5-7 (33)

미주문 13거 (33)

0219

ARTICLES IN US-ROK STATUS OF FORCES AGREEMENT

(Article numbers are tentatively assigned for
mutual convenience and are subject to change)

0220

ARTICLES IN US-ROK STATUS OF FORCES AGREEMENT (cont'd)

2

한·미국 간의 상호방위조약 제4조에 의한 시설과 구역 및 한국에서의 미국군대의 지위에 관한 협정(SOFA)
전59권. 1966.7.9 서울에서 서명 : 1967.2.9 발효(조약 232호) (V.38 실무교섭회의, 제82차, 1966.7.8(II)) 227

PREAMBLE

"Whereas the United States of America has disposed its
armed forces in and about the territory of the Republic of Korea
pursuant to the resolutions of the United Nations Security Council
of June 25, 1950, June 27, 1950, and July 7, 1950, and pursuant to
Article IV of the Mutual Defense Treaty between the United States
of America and the Republic of Korea signed on October 1, 1953,

Therefore, the United States of America and the Republic
of Korea, in order to strengthen the close bonds of mutual interest
between their two countries, have entered into this Agreement
regarding facilities and areas and the status of United States
armed forces in the Republic of Korea in terms as set forth below."

ARTICLE I

DEFINITIONS

In this Agreement the expression

(a)   "members of the United States armed forces" means the personnel on active duty belonging to the land, sea, or air armed services of the United States of America when in the territory of the Republic of Korea except for personnel of the U.S. armed forces attached to the U.S. Embassy and personnel for whose status has been provided in the Military Advisory Group Agreement of January 26, 1950, as amended.

(b)   "civilian component" means the civilian persons of U.S. nationality who are in the employ of, serving with, or accompanying the United States armed forces in the Republic of Korea, but excludes persons who are ordinarily resident in the Republic of Korea or who are mentioned in paragraph ___ of Article ___. For the purposes of this Agreement only, dual nationals, persons having both United States and Korean nationalities who are brought into the Republic of Korea by the United States shall be considered as United States nationals.

(c)   "dependent" means

        (1)   Spouse, and children under 21;

        (2)   Parents, children over 21, or other relatives, dependent for their support upon a member of the United States armed forces or civilian component.

0223

한·미국 간의 상호방위조약 제4조에 의한 시설과 구역 및 한국에서의 미국군대의 지위에 관한 협정(SOFA)
전59권. 1966.7.9 서울에서 서명 : 1967.2.9 발효(조약 232호) (V.38 실무교섭회의, 제82차, 1966.7.8(Ⅱ)) 229

DEFINITIONS ARTICLE

AGREED MINUTE

With regard to subparagraph (c) it is recognized that persons possessing certain skills, not available from United States or Korean sources, who are nationals of third states, may be brought into Korea by the United States armed forces solely for employment by the United States armed forces. Such persons, and third state nationals who are employed by, serving with, or accompanying the United States armed forces in Korea when this Agreement becomes effective, shall be considered as members of the civilian component.

0224

Facilities & Areas
Article "A" -- Grant of and Return

1. (a) The United States is granted, under Article IV of the Mutual Defense Treaty, the use of facilities and areas in the Republic of Korea. Agreements as to specific facilities and areas shall be concluded by the two Governments through the Joint Committee provided for in Article _____ of this Agreement. "Facilities and Areas" include existing furnishings, equipment, and fixtures, wherever located, used in the operation of such facilities and areas.

(b) The facilities and areas of which the United States armed forces have the use at the effective date of this agreement together with those areas and facilities which the United States armed forces have returned to the Republic of Korea with the reserved right of re-entry, when these facilities and areas have been re-entered by U.S. forces, shall be considered as the facilities and areas agreed upon between the two Governments in accordance with subparagraph (a) above. Records of facilities and areas of which the United States armed forces have the use or right of re-entry shall be maintained through the Joint Committee after this Agreement comes into force.

2. At the request of either Government, the Governments of the United States and the Republic of Korea shall review such agreements and may agree that such facilities and areas or portions thereof shall be returned to the Republic of Korea or that additional facilities and areas may be provided.

3. The facilities and areas used by the United States shall be returned to the Republic of Korea under such conditions as may be agreed through the Joint Committee whenever they are no longer needed for the purposes of this Agreement and the United States agrees to keep the needs for facilities and areas under continual observation with a view toward such return.

4. (a) When facilities and areas are temporarily not being used and the Government of the Republic of Korea is so advised, the Government of the Republic of Korea may make, or permit Korean nationals to make, interim use of such facilities and areas provided that it is agreed between the two Governments through the Joint Committee that such use would not be harmful to the purposes for which the facilities and areas are normally used by the United States armed forces.

0225

(b) With respect to facilities and areas which are to be used by the United States armed forces for limited periods of time, the Joint Committee shall specify in the agreements covering such facilities and areas the extent to which the provisions of this Agreement shall not apply.

0226

Facilities & Areas
Article "B" - Security Measures In

1. Within the facilities and areas, the United States may take all
the measures necessary for their establishment, operation, safeguarding
and control. In order to provide access for the United States armed
forces to the facilities and areas for their support, safeguarding, and
control, the Government of the Republic of Korea shall, at the request
of the United States armed forces and upon consultation between the two
Governments through the Joint Committee, take necessary measures
within the scope of applicable laws and regulations over land, territorial
waters and airspace adjacent to, or in the vicinities of the facilities and
areas. The United States may also take necessary measures for such
purposes upon consultation between the two Governments through the
Joint Committee.

2. (a) The United States agrees not to take the measures referred
to in paragraph 1 in such a manner as to interfere unnecessarily with
navigation, aviation, communication, or land travel to or from or
within the territories of the Republic of Korea.

(b) All questions relating to telecommunications including
radio frequencies for electromagnetic radiating devices, or like
matters, shall continue to be resolved expeditiously in the utmost
spirit of coordination and cooperation by arrangement between the
designated communications authorities of the two Governments.

(c) The Government of the Republic of Korea shall, within
the scope of applicable laws, regulations and agreements, take all
reasonable measures to avoid or eliminate interference with
electromagnetic radiation sensitive devices, telecommunications
devices, or other apparatus required by the United States armed
forces.

Agreed Minute

It is agreed that in the event of an emergency, the United
States armed forces shall be authorized to take such measures in
the vicinity of the areas and facilities as may be necessary to
provide for their safeguarding and control.

0227

AREAS AND FACILITIES - RETURN OF FACILITIES

ARTICLE (IV)·

1. The United States is not obliged, when it returns facilities and areas to the Republic of Korea on the expiration of this Agreement or at an earlier date, to restore the facilities and areas to the condition in which they were at the time they became available to the United States armed forces, or to compensate the Republic of Korea in lieu of such restoration.

2. The Government of the Republic of Korea is not obliged to make any compensation to the Government of the United States for any improvements made in facilities and areas or for the buildings and structures left thereon on the expiration of this Agreement or the earlier return of the facilities and areas.

3. The foregoing provisions shall not apply to any construction which the Government of the United States may undertake under special arrangements with the Government of the Republic of Korea.

AGREED MINUTE

All removable facilities erected or constructed by or on behalf of the United States at its expense and all equipment, material and supplies brought into or procured in the Republic of Korea by or on behalf of the United States in connection with the construction, development, operation, maintenance, safeguarding and control of the facilities and areas will remain the property of the United States Government and may be removed from the Republic of Korea.

0228

<u>U.S. DRAFT OF ARTICLE V</u>

<u>AREAS AND FACILITIES - COST AND MAINTENANCE</u>

()

1. It is agreed that the United States will bear for the
duration of the Agreement without cost to the Republic of Korea all
expenditures incident to the maintenance of the United States armed
forces in the Republic of Korea, except those to be borne by the
Republic of Korea as provided in paragraph 2.

2. It is agreed that the Republic of Korea will furnish for the
duration of this Agreement without cost to the United States and make
compensation where appropriate to the owners and suppliers thereof all
facilities and areas and rights of way, including facilities and areas
jointly used such as those at airfields and ports as provided in
Articles II and III. The Government of the Republic of Korea assures
the use of such facilities and areas to the United States Government
and will hold the United States Government as well as its agencies and
employees harmless from any third party claims which may be advanced in
connection with such use.

0229

Utilities and Services

3. (a) The United States armed forces shall have the use of all utilities and services which are owned, controlled or regulated by the Government of the Republic of Korea or local administrative subdivisions thereof. The term "utilities and services" shall include, but not be limited to, transportation and communications facilities and systems, electricity, gas, water, steam, heat, light, power, and sewage disposal. The use of utilities and services as provided herein shall not prejudice the right of the United States to operate military transportation, communication, power and such other utilities and services deemed necessary for the operations of the United States armed forces. This right shall not be exercised in a manner inconsistent with the operation by the Government of the Republic of Korea of its utilities and services.

(b) The use of such utilities and services by the United States shall be in accordance with priorities, conditions, and rates or tariffs no less favorable than those accorded any other user.

Agreed Minutes

1. It is understood that any changes determined by the Korean authorities in priorities, conditions, and rates or tariffs, applicable to the United States armed forces shall be the subject of consultation in the Joint Committee prior to their effective date.

2. Paragraph 3 of Article ____ will not be construed as in any way abrogating the Utilities and Claims Settlement Agreement of December 18, 1958, which continues in full force and effect unless otherwise agreed by the two governments.

3. In an emergency the Republic of Korea agrees to take appropriate measures to assure provision of utilities and services necessary to meet the needs of the United States armed forces.

0230

ARTICLE

1.   All civil and military air traffic control shall be developed in close coordination and shall be integrated to the extent necessary for the operation of this Agreement. Procedures, and any subsequent changes thereto, necessary to effect this coordination and integration will be established by arrangement between the appropriate authorities of the two Governments.

2.   The United States is authorized to establish, construct and maintain aids to navigation for vessels and aircraft, both visual and electronic as required, throughout the Republic of Korea and in the territorial waters thereof.   Such navigation aids shall conform generally to the system in use in Korea. The United States and Korean authorities which have established navigation aids shall duly notify each other of their positions and characteristics and shall give advance notification where practicable before making any changes in them or establishing additional navigation aids.

AGREED MINUTE

Installation by the United States Armed Forces of permanent navigational aids for vessels and aircraft outside of areas and facilities in use by the United States Armed Forces will be effected in accordance with the procedures established under paragraph 1 of Article   .

0231

ARTICLE ___

JOINT COMMITTEE

1. A Joint Committee shall be established as the means for consultation between the Government of the United States and the Government of the Republic of Korea on all matters requiring mutual consultation regarding the implementation of this Agreement except where otherwise provided. In particular, the Joint Committee shall serve as the means for consultation in determining the facilities and areas in the Republic of Korea which are required for the use of the United States in carrying out the purposes of this Agreement.

2. The Joint Committee shall be composed of a representative of the Government of the United States and a representative of the Government of the Republic of Korea, each of whom shall have one or more deputies and a staff. The Joint Committee shall determine its own procedures, and arrange for such auxiliary organs and administrative services as may be required. The Joint Committee shall be so organized that it may meet immediately at any time at the request of the representative of either the Government of the United States or the Government of the Republic of Korea.

3. If the Joint Committee is unable to resolve any matter it shall refer that matter to the respective Governments for further consideration through appropriate channels

Agreed Minute

The exception provided for in the first sentence of paragraph 1 is relevant only to paragraph 2, subparagraphs (b) and (c) of Article ____ .
(Text agreed upon at 15th negotiating meeting, February 25, 1963.)

0232

ARTICLE

ENTRY AND EXIT

1. The United States may bring into the Republic of Korea persons who are members of the United States armed forces, the civilian component, and their dependents, subject to the provisions of this Article. The Government of the Republic of Korea will be notified at regular intervals, in accordance with procedures to be agreed between the two Governments, of numbers and categories of persons entering and departing.

2. Members of the United States Armed Forces shall be exempt from Korean passport and visa laws and regulations. Members of the United States Armed Forces, the civilian component, and their dependents shall be exempt from Korean laws and regulations on the registration and control of aliens, but shall not be considered as acquiring any right to permanent residence or domicile in the territory of the Republic of Korea.

3. Upon entry into or departure from the Republic of Korea members of the United States Armed Forces shall be in possession of the following documents:

(a) Personal identity card showing name, date of birth, rank and service number, service, and photograph; and

(b) Individual or collective travel order certifying to the status of the individual or group as a member or members of the United States Armed Forces and to the travel ordered.

For purposes of their identification while in the Republic of Korea, members of the United States Armed Forces shall be in possession of the foregoing personal identity card which must be presented on request to the appropriate Korean authorities.

0233

4. Members of the civilian component, their dependents, and the dependents of members of the United States Armed Forces shall be in possession of appropriate documentation issued by the United States authorities so that their status may be verified by Korean authorities upon their entry into or departure from the Republic of Korea, or while in the Republic of Korea.

5. If the status of any person brought into the Republic of Korea under paragraph 1 of this Article is altered so that he would no longer be entitled to such admission, the United States authorities shall notify the Korean authorities and shall, if such person be required by the Korean authorities to leave the Republic of Korea, assure that transportation from the Republic of Korea will be provided within a reasonable time at no cost to the Government of the Republic of Korea.

6. If the Government of the Republic of Korea has requested the removal from its Territory of a member of the United States Armed Forces or civilian component or has made an expulsion order against an ex-member of the United States Armed Forces or the civilian component or against a dependent of a member or an ex-member, the authorities of the United States shall be responsible for receiving the person concerned into its own territory or otherwise disposing of him outside the Republic of Korea. This paragraph shall apply only to persons who are not nationals of the Republic of Korea and have entered the Republic of Korea as members of the United States Armed Forces or civilian component or for the purpose of becoming such members, and to the dependents of such persons.

0234

AGREED MINUTES TO ARTICLE

(Entry and Exit)

1. With regard to Paragraph 3(a), United States Armed Forces law enforcement personnel (such as MP, SP, AP, CID and CIC), who engage in military police activities in the Republic of Korea, will carry a bilingual identity card containing the bearer's name, position, and the fact that he is a member of a law enforcement agency. This card will be shown upon request to persons concerned when the bearer is in the performance of duty.

2. The United States Armed Forces will furnish, upon request, to Korean authorities the form of the identification cards of the members of the United States Armed Forces, the civilian component, and their dependents and descriptions of the various uniforms of the United States Armed Forces in the Republic of Korea.

3. The final sentence of Paragraph 3 means that members of the United States Armed Forces will display their identity cards upon request but will not be required to surrender them to Korean authorities.

4. Following a change of status pursuant to Paragraph 5, the responsibilities of the United States authorities under Paragraph 6 shall arise only if the expulsion order is issued within a reasonable time after the notice under Paragraph 5 has been communicated to the Korean authorities.

0235

Customs and Duties

ARTICLE _____

1. Save as provided in this Agreement, members of the United States armed forces, the civilian component, and their dependents shall be subject to the laws and regulations administered by the customs authorities of the Republic of Korea.

2. All materials, supplies and equipment imported by the United States armed forces (including their authorized procurement agencies and their non-appropriated fund organizations provided for in Article _____), for the official use of the United States armed forces or for the use of the members of the United States armed forces, the civilian component, and their dependents, and materials, supplies and equipment which are to be used exclusively by the United States armed forces or are ultimately to be incorporated into articles or facilities used by such forces, shall be permitted entry into the Republic of Korea; such entry shall be free from customs duties and other such charges. Appropriate certification shall be made that such materials, supplies and equipment are being imported by the United States armed forces (including their authorized procurement agencies and their non-appropriated fund organizations provided for in Article _____), or, in the case of materials, supplies and equipment to be used exclusively by the United States armed forces or ultimately to be incorporated into articles or facilities used by such forces, that delivery thereof is to be taken by the United States armed forces for the purposes specified above. The exemptions provided in this

0236

paragraph shall extend to materials, supplies and equipment imported by the United States armed forces for the use of other armed forces in Korea under the Unified Command which receive logistical support from the United States armed forces.

3.　Property consigned to and for the personal use of members of the United States armed forces, the civilian component, and their dependents, shall be subject to customs duties and other such charges, except that no duties or charges shall be paid with respect to:

(a)　Furniture, household goods, and personal effects for their private use imported by the members of the United States armed forces or civilian component when they first arrive to serve in the Republic of Korea or by their dependents when they first arrive for reunion with members of such forces or civilian component;

(b)　Vehicles and parts imported by members of the United States armed forces or civilian component for the private use of themselves or their dependents;

(c)　Reasonable quantities of personal effects and household goods of a type which would ordinarily be purchased in the United States for the private use of members of the United States armed forces, civilian component, and their dependents, which are mailed into the Republic of Korea through United States military post offices.

0237

4. The exemptions granted in paragraphs 2 and 3 shall apply only to cases of importation of goods and shall not be interpreted as refunding customs duties and domestic excises collected by the customs authorities at the time of entry in cases of purchase of goods on which such duties and excises have already been collected.

5. Customs examination shall not be made in the following cases:

(a) Members of the United States armed forces under orders, other than leave orders, entering or leaving the Republic of Korea;

(b) Official documents under official seal and First Class letter mail in the United States military postal channels under official postal seal;

(c) Military cargo consigned to the United States armed forces.

6. Except as such disposal may be authorized by the United States and Korean authorities in accordance with mutually agreed conditions, goods imported into the Republic of Korea free of duty shall not be disposed of in the Republic of Korea to persons not entitled to import such goods free of duty.

7. Goods imported into the Republic of Korea free from customs duties and other such charges pursuant to paragraphs 2 and 3, may be re-exported free from customs duties and other such charges.

8. The United States armed forces, in cooperation with Korean authorities, shall take such steps as are necessary to prevent abuse of privileges granted to the United States armed forces, members of such forces, the civilian component, and their dependents in accordance with this Article.

0238

9.　(a)　In order to prevent offenses against laws and regulations administered by the customs authorities of the Government of the Republic of Korea, the Korean authorities and the United States armed forces shall assist each other in the conduct of inquiries and the collection of evidence.

(b)　The United States armed forces shall render all assistance within their power to ensure that articles liable to seizure by, or on behalf of, the customs authorities of the Government of the Republic of Korea are handed to those authorities.

(c)　The United States armed forces shall render all assistance within their power to ensure the payment of duties, taxes, and penalties payable by members of such forces or of the civilian component, or their dependents.

(d)　The authorities of the United States forces shall provide all practicable assistance to the customs officials dispatched to military controlled piers and airports for the purpose of customs inspection.

(e)　Vehicles and articles belonging to the United States armed forces seized by the customs authorities of the Government of the Republic of Korea in connection with an offense against its customs or fiscal laws or regulations shall be handed over to the appropriate authorities of the forces concerned.

0239

<u>AGREED MINUTES TO ARTICLE ____ (Customs)</u>

1. The quantity of goods imported under paragraph 2 by non-appropriated fund organizations of the United States armed forces for the use of persons authorized by Article _____ and its Agreed Minute shall be limited to the extent reasonably required for such use.

2. Paragraph 3(a) does not require concurrent shipment of goods with travel of owner nor does it require single loading or shipment. In this connection, members of the United States armed forces or civilian component and their dependents may import free of duty reasonable quantities of their personal and household effects during a period of six months from the date of their first arrival.

3. The term "military cargo" as used in paragraph 5(c) is not confined to arms and equipment but refers to all cargo consigned to the United States armed forces (including their authorized procurement agencies and their non-appropriated fund organizations provided for in Article _____). Pertinent information on cargo consigned to non-appropriated fund organizations will be furnished on a routine basis to authorities of the Republic of Korea. The extent of the pertinent information will be determined by the Joint Committee.

4. The United States armed forces will take every practicable measure to ensure that goods will not be imported into the Republic of Korea by or for the members of the United States armed forces, the civilian component,

0240

or their dependents, the entry of which would be in violation of Korean customs laws and regulations. The United States armed forces will promptly notify the Korean customs authorities whenever the entry of such goods is discovered.

5. The Korean customs authorities may, if they consider that there has been an abuse or infringement in connection with the entry of goods under Article   , take up the matter with the appropriate authorities of the United States armed forces.

6. The words "The United States armed forces shall render all assistance within their power," etc., in paragraph 3(b) and (c) refer to reasonable and practicable measures by the United States armed forces.

7. It is understood that the duty free treatment provided in paragraph 2 shall apply to materials, supplies, and equipment imported for sale through commissaries and non-appropriated fund organizations, under such regulations as the United States armed forces may promulgate, to those individuals and organizations referred to in Article _____ and its Agreed Minute.

0241

ARTICLE

1. United States and foreign vessels and aircraft operated by, for, or under the control of the United States for official purposes shall be accorded access to any port or airport of Korea free from toll or landing charges. When cargo or passengers not accorded the exemptions of this Agreement are carried on such vessels and aircraft, notification shall be given to the appropriate Korean authorities, and their entry into and departure from Korea shall be according to the laws and regulations of Korea.

2. The vessels and aircraft mentioned in paragraph 1, United States Government-owned vehicles including armor, and members of the United States Armed Forces, the civilian component, and their dependents shall be accorded access to and movement between facilities and areas in use by the United States Armed Forces and between such facilities and areas and the ports or airports of Korea. Such access to and movement between facilities and areas by United States military vehicles shall be free from toll and other charges.

3. When the vessels mentioned in paragraph 1 enter Korean ports, appropriate notification shall, under normal conditions, be made to the proper Korean authorities. Such vessels shall have freedom from compulsory pilotage, but if a pilot is taken pilotage shall be paid for at appropriate rates.

0242

AGREED MINUTES TO ARTICLE

1. "United States and foreign vessels...operated by, for, or under the control of the United States for official purposes" mean United States public vessels and chartered vessels (bare boat charter, voyage charter and time charter). Space charter is not included. Commercial cargo and private passengers are carried by them only in exceptional cases.

2. The Korean ports mentioned herein will ordinarily mean "open ports".

3. An exception from making the "appropriate notification" referred to in paragraph 3 will apply only in unusual cases where such is required for security of the United States armed forces or similar reasons.

4. The laws and regulations of Korea will be applicable except as specifically provided otherwise in this Article.

0243

METEOROLOGICAL SERVICES

Article .. ..

The Government of the Republic of Korea undertakes to furnish
the United States armed forces with the following meteorological
services in accordance with arrangements between the appropriate
authorities of the two Governments:

 (a) Meteorological observations from land and ocean
areas including observations from ships;

 (b) Climatological information including periodic
summaries and historical data wherever available.

 (c) Telecommunications service to disseminate
meteorological information;

 (d) Seismographic data.

0244

ARTICLE

VEHICLE AND DRIVERS LICENSES

1.   Korea shall accept as valid, without a driving test or fee, the driving permit or license or military driving permit issued by the United States, or political subdivision thereof, to a member of the United States armed forces, the civilian component, and their dependents.

2.   Official vehicles of the United States armed forces and the civilian component shall carry distinctive numbered plates or individual markings which will readily identify them.

3.   The Government of the Republic of Korea will license and register those vehicles privately owned by members of the United States armed forces, the civilian component, or dependents. The names of the owners of such vehicles and such other pertinent information as is required by Korean law to effect the licensing and registration of such vehicles, shall be furnished to the Government of the Republic of Korea by officials of the United States Government through the Joint Committee. Except for the actual cost of the issuance of license plates, members of the United States armed forces, the civilian component, and their dependents shall be exempt from the payment of all fees and charges relating to the licensing, registration, or operation of vehicles in the Republic of Korea and, in accordance with the provisions of Article _____, from the payment of all taxes relating thereto.

0245

ARTICLE (XIII)

NON-APPROPRIATED FUNDS ORGANIZATIONS

(ROK negotiators have agreed to all of this Article except
subpara (f) of the Agreed Minute, as underlined.)

1. (a) Military exchanges, messes, social clubs, theatres,
newspapers and other non-appropriated fund organizations authorized
and regulated by the United States military authorities may be established by the United States armed forces for the use of members of such
forces, the civilian component, and their dependents. Except as
otherwise provided in this Agreement such organizations shall not be
subject to Korean regulations, licenses, fees, taxes, or similar
controls.

(b) When a newspaper authorized and regulated by the United
States military authorities is sold to the general public, it shall be
subject to Korean regulations, licenses, fees, taxes, or similar
controls so far as such circulation is concerned.

2. No Korean tax shall be imposed on sales of merchandise or
services by such organizations, except as provided in paragraph 1 (b)
of this Article. Purchases within the Republic of Korea of merchandise
and supplies by such organizations shall be subject to the Korean
taxes to which other purchasers of such merchandise and supplies are
subject unless otherwise agreed between the two governments.

3. Except as such disposal may be permitted by the United
States and Korean authorities in accordance with mutually agreed

0246

conditions, goods which are sold by such activities shall not be disposed of in Korea to persons not authorized to make purchases from such activities.

4. The organizations referred to in this Article shall, through consultation between the representatives of the two governments in the Joint Committee, provide such information to the Republic of Korea tax authorities as is required by Korean tax legislation.

AGREED MINUTE

The United States Armed Forces may grant the use of the organizations referred to in paragraph 1 of Article (XIII) to: (a) other officers or personnel of the United States Government ordinarily accorded such privileges; (b) those other non-Korean Armed Forces in Korea under the Unified Command which receive logistical support from the United States Armed Forces, and their members; (c) those non-Korean persons whose presence in the Republic of Korea is solely for the purpose of providing contract services financed by the United States Government; (d) those organizations which are present in the Republic of Korea primarily for the benefit and service of the United States Armed forces, such as the American Red Cross and the United Service Organizations, and their non-Korean personnel; (e) dependents of the foregoing; and (f) other persons and organizations with the express consent of the Government of the Republic of Korea.

2

0247

Respect for Local Law

It is the duty of members of the United States Armed Forces, the civilian component, the persons who are present in the Republic of Korea pursuant to Article _____, and their dependents, to respect the law of Korea and to abstain from any activity inconsistent with the spirit of this Agreement, and, in particular, from any political activity in Korea.

0248

ARTICLE

Enrollment and Training of Reservists

The United States may enroll in its reserve forces and train, in Korea, eligible United States citizens who are in the Republic of Korea.

(Text agreed upon at 15th negotiating meeting, February 25, 1963)

0249

ARTICLE (XVI)

SECURITY MEASURES

(US-ROK agreed on following text, but Koreans have
not yet agreed to inclusion of desired US assurance
in Agreed Joint Summary.)

The United States and the Republic of Korea will cooperate in
taking such steps as may from time to time be necessary to ensure the
security of the United States armed forces, the members thereof,
the Civilian component, the persons who are present in the Republic
of Korea pursuant to Article (XVIII), their dependents and their
property. The Government of the Republic of Korea agrees to seek such
legislation and to take such other action as may be necessary to
ensure the adequate security and protection within its territory of
installations, equipment, property, records, and official information
of the United States and, consistent with Article (XXII - Criminal
Jurisdiction), to ensure the punishment of offenders under the applicable
laws of the Republic of Korea.

0250

ARTICLE XVIII

INVITED CONTRACTORS

(US-ROK in agreement, except on para 8, relating to
Criminal Jurisdiction Article. US Text of para 8 underlined; ROK text of para 8 follows in parentheses.)

1. Persons including corporations organized under the laws of
the United States their employees who are ordinarily resident in the
United States, and the dependents of such persons, present in Korea
solely for the purpose of executing contracts with the United States
for the benefit of the United States armed forces or other armed
forces in Korea under the Unified Command receiving logistical support
from the United States armed forces, who are designated by the
Government of the United States in accordance with the provisions of
para 2, below, shall, except as provided in this Article be subject to
the laws and regulations of Korea.

2. The designation referred to in Para 1 above shall be made
upon consultation with the Government of Korea and shall be restricted
to cases where open competitive bidding is not practicable due to
security considerations, to the technical qualifications of the contractors involved, to the unavailability of materials or services
required by the United States standards, or to limitations of United
States law. The designation shall be withdrawn by the Government of
the United States:

(a) Upon completion of contracts with the United States for
the United States armed forces or other armed forces in Korea under the

0251

Unified Command receiving logistical support from the United States armed forces;

(b) Upon proof that such persons are engaged in business activities in Korea other than those pertaining to the United States armed forces or other armed forces in Korea under the Unified Command receiving logistical support from the United States armed forces;

(c) Upon proof that such persons are engaged in practices illegal in Korea.

3. Upon certification by appropriate United States authorities as to their identity, such persons shall be accorded the following benefits of this Agreement:

(a) Accession and movement, as provided for in Article X, para 2;

(b) Entry into Korea in accordance with the provisions of Article VII;

(c) The exemption from customs duties, and other such charges provided for in Article IX, para 3, for members of the United States armed forces, the civilian component, and their dependents;

(d) If authorized by the Government of the United States, the use of the services of the activities provided for in Article (XIII)

(e) Those provided in Article XVII, para 2, for members of the United States armed forces, the civilian component and their dependents;

2

0252

(f) If authorized by the Government of the United States, the use of military payment certificates, as provided for in Article XIX;

(g) The use of postal facilities provided for in Article XX;

(h) The use of utilities and services in accordance with those priorities, conditions, rates or tariffs accorded the United States armed forces by Article V, paragraph 3, relating to utilities and services.

(i) Exemption from the laws and regulations of Korea with respect to terms and conditions of employment, and licensing and registration of businesses and corporations.

4. The arrival, departure, and place of residence in Korea of such persons shall from time to time be notified by the United States Armed Forces to the Korean authorities.

5. Upon certification by an authorized representative of the United States armed forces, depreciable assets, except houses, held, used or transferred by such persons, exclusively for the execution of contracts referred to in paragraph 1 shall not be subject to taxes or similar charges of Korea.

6. Upon certification by an authorized representative of the United States armed forces, such persons shall be exempt from taxation in Korea on the holding, use, transfer by death, or transfer to persons or agencies entitled to tax exemption under this

3

0253

Agreement, of movable property, tangible or intangible the presence of
which in Korea is due solely to the temporary presence of these persons
in Korea, provided that such exemption shall not apply to property held
for the purpose of investment or the conduct of other business in
Korea or to any intangible property registered in Korea.

      7. The persons referred to in paragraph 1 shall not be liable
to pay income or corporation taxes to the Government of Korea or to
any other taxing agency in Korea on any income derived under a
contract with the Government of the United States in connection with
the construction, maintenance or operation of any of the facilities
or areas covered by this Agreement. Persons in Korea in connection
with the execution of such a contract with the United States shall
not be liable to pay any Korean taxes to the Government of Korea or
to any taxing agency in Korea on income derived from sources outside
of Korea nor shall periods during which such persons are in Korea be
considered periods of residence or domicile in Korea for the purposes
of Korean taxation. The provisions of this paragraph do not exempt
such persons from payment of income or corporation taxes on income
derived from Korean sources, other than those sources referred to in
the first sentence of this paragraph, nor do they exempt such persons
who claim Korean residence for United States income tax purposes
from payment of Korean taxes on income.

4

0254

8. The persons referred to in para 1 shall be subject to those provisions of Article (XXII) and the Agreed Minutes thereto which pertain to members of the civilian component, and to dependents.

AGREED MINUTES

1. The execution of contracts with the United States in addition to those specified in paragraph 1 of Article XVIII shall not exclude the persons provided for in Article XVIII from the application of that Article.

2. Contractor employees who are present in Korea on the effective date of this agreement and who would qualify for the privileges contained in Article XVIII but for the fact that they are not ordinarily resident in the United States shall be entitled to enjoy such privileges so long as their presence is for the purpose stated in paragraph 1 of Article XVIII.

5

0255

MILITARY PAYMENT CERTIFICATES

ARTICLE (XIX)

1. (a) United States military payment certificates denominated in dollars may be used by persons authorized by the United States for internal transactions. The Government of the United States will take appropriate action to insure that authorized personnel are prohibited from engaging in transactions involving military payment certificates except as authorized by United States regulations. The Government of Korea will take necessary action to prohibit unauthorized persons from engaging in transactions involving military payment certificates and with the aid of United States authorities will undertake to apprehend and punish any person or persons under its jurisdiction involved in the counterfeiting or uttering of counterfeit military payment certificates.

(b) It is agreed that the United States authorities will to the extent authorized by United States law, apprehend and punish members of the United States armed forces, the civilian component, or their dependents, who tender military payment certificates to unauthorized persons and that no obligation will be due to such unauthorized persons or to the Government of Korea or its agencies from the United States or any of its agencies as a result of any unauthorized use of military payment certificates within Korea.

2. In order to exercise control of military payment certificates the United States may designate certain American financial institutions to

0256

maintain and operate, under United States supervision, facilities for the use of persons authorized by the United States to use military payment certificates. Institutions authorized to maintain military banking facilities will establish and maintain such facilities physically separated from their Korean commercial banking business, with personnel whose sole duty is to maintain and operate such facilities. Such facilities shall be permitted to maintain United States currency bank accounts and to perform all financial transactions in connection therewith including receipt and remission of funds to the extent provided by Article.......paragraph 2, of this Agreement.

2

0257

ARTICLE

MILITARY POST OFFICES

1. The United States may establish and operate, within the facilities and areas in use by the U.S. armed forces, United States military post offices for the use of members of the United States armed forces, the civilian component, and their dependents, for the transmission of mail between United States military post offices in Korea and between such military post offices and other United States post offices.

AGREED MINUTE

1. United States military post offices may be used by other officers and personnel of the United States Government, and their dependents, ordinarily accorded such privileges abroad.

0258

ARTICLE

1.   The United States armed forces shall not be subject to taxes or similar charges on property held, used or transferred by such forces in Korea.

2.   Members of the United States armed forces, the civilian component, and their dependents shall not be liable to pay any Korean taxes to the Government of Korea or to any other taxing agency in Korea on income received as a result of their service with or employment by the United States armed forces, including the activities/organizations provided for in Article   .   Persons in Korea solely by reason of being members of the United States armed forces, the civilian component, or their dependents shall not be liable to pay any Korean taxes to the Government of Korea or to any taxing agency in Korea on income derived from sources outside of Korea, nor shall periods during which such persons are in Korea be considered as periods of residence or domicile in Korea for the purpose of Korean taxation. The provisions of this Article do not exempt such persons from payment of Korean taxes on income derived from Korean sources, other than those sources referred to in the first sentence of this paragraph, nor do they exempt United States citizens who claim Korean residence for United States income tax purposes from payment of Korean taxes on income.

3.   Members of the United States armed forces, the civilian component, and their dependents shall be exempt from taxation in Korea on the holding, use, transfer inter se, or transfer by death of movable property, tangible or intangible, the presence of which in Korea is due solely to the temporary presence of these persons in Korea, provided that such exemption shall not apply to property held for the purpose of investment or the conduct of business in Korea or to any intangible property registered in Korea.

0259

ARTICLE

Health and Sanitation

Consistent with the right of the United States to furnish medical support for its armed forces, civilian component and their dependents, matters of mutual concern pertaining to the control and prevention of diseases and the coordination of other public health, medical, sanitation, and veterinary services shall be resolved by the authorities of the two Governments in the Joint Committee established under Article _____.

0260

Local Procurement

1. The United States may contract for any materials, supplies, equipment and services (including construction work) to be furnished or undertaken in the Republic of Korea for purposes of, or authorized by, this Agreement, without restriction as to choice of contractor, supplier or person who provides such services. Such materials, supplies, equipment and services may, upon agreement between the appropriate authorities of the two Governments, also be procured through the Government of the Republic of Korea.

2. Materials, supplies, equipment and services which are required from local sources for the maintenance of the United States armed forces and the procurement of which may have an adverse effect on the economy of the Republic of Korea shall be procured in coordination with, and, when desirable, through or with the assistance of, the competent authorities of the Republic of Korea.

3. Materials, supplies, equipment and services procured for official purposes in the Republic of Korea by the United States armed forces, including their authorized procurement agencies, or procured for ultimate use by the United States armed forces shall be exempt from the following Korean taxes upon appropriate certification in advance by the United States armed forces :

    a. Commodity tax;

    b. Traffic tax;

    c. Petroleum tax;

    d. Electricity and gas tax;

    e. Business tax.

With respect to any present or future Korean taxes not specifically referred to in this Article which might be found to constitute a significant and readily identifiable part of the gross purchase price of materials, supplies, equipment and services procured by the United States armed forces, or for ultimate use by such forces, the two Governments will agree upon a procedure for granting such exemption or relief therefrom as is consistent with the purpose of this Article.

0261

4. Neither members of the United States armed forces, civilian component, nor their dependents, shall by reason of this Article enjoy any exemption from taxes or similar charges relating to personal purchases of goods and services in the Republic of Korea chargeable under Korean legislation.

5. Except as such disposal may be authorized by the United States and Korean authorities in accordance with mutually agreed conditions, goods purchased in the Republic of Korea exempt from taxes referred to in paragraph 3, shall not be disposed of in the Republic of Korea to persons not entitled to purchase such goods exempt from such tax.

AGREED MINUTES

1. The United States armed forces will furnish the Korean authorities with appropriate information as far in advance as practicable on anticipated major changes in their procurement program in the Republic of Korea.

2. The problem of a satisfactory settlement of difficulties with respect to procurement contracts arising out of differences between Korean and United States economic laws and business practices will be studied by the Joint Committee or other appropriate representatives.

3. The procedures for securing exemptions from taxation on purchases of goods for ultimate use by the United States armed forces will be as follows:

a. Upon appropriate certification by the United States armed forces that materials, supplies and equipment consigned to or destined for such forces, are to be used, or wholly or partially used up, under the supervision of such forces, exclusively in the execution of contracts for the construction, maintenance or operation of the facilities and areas referred to in Article _____ or for the support of the forces therein, or are ultimately to be incorporated into articles or facilities used by such forces, an authorized representative of such forces shall take delivery of such materials, supplies and equipment directly from manufacturers thereof. In such circumstances the collection of taxes referred to in Article _____, Paragraph 3, shall be held in abeyance.

0262

b. The receipt of such materials, supplies and equipment in the facilities and areas shall be confirmed by an authorized representative of the United States armed forces to the Korean authorities.

c. Collection of the taxes on such materials, supplies and equipment shall be held in abeyance until

(1) The United States armed forces confirm and certify the quantity or degree of consumption of the above referred to materials, supplies and equipment, or

(2) The United States armed forces confirm and certify the amount of the above referred to materials, supplies, and equipment which have been incorporated into articles or facilities used by the United States armed forces.

d. Materials, supplies, and equipment certified under c (1) or (2) shall be exempt from taxes referred to in Article _____, Paragraph 3, insofar as the price thereof is paid out of United States Government appropriations or out of funds contributed by the Government of the Republic of Korea for disbursement by the United States.

4. Regarding Paragraph 3, it is understood that "materials, supplies, equipment and services procured for official purposes" refers to direct procurement by the United States armed forces or their authorized procurement agencies from Korean suppliers. "Materials, supplies, equipment and services procured for ultimate use" refers to procurement by contractors of the United States armed forces from Korean suppliers of items to be incorporated into or necessary for the production of the end product of their contracts with the United States armed forces.

0263

ARTICLE

Either Government may at any time request the revision of any Article of this Agreement, in which case the two Governments shall enter into negotiations through appropriate channels.

0264

U. S. DRAFT OF CLAIMS ARTICLE

1. Each Party waives all its claims against the other Party for damage to any property owned by it and used by its armed forces, if such damage —

    (a) was caused by a member or an employee of the armed services of the other Party, in performance of his official duties; or

    (b) arose from the use of any vehicle, vessel or aircraft owned by the other Party and used by its armed services, provided either that the vehicle, vessel or aircraft causing the damage was being used for official purposes or that the damage was caused to property being so used.

Claims for maritime salvage by one Party against the other Party shall be waived, provided that the vessel or cargo salved was owned by the other Party and being used by its armed services for official purposes.

2. (a) In the case of damage caused or arising as stated in paragraph 1 to other property owned by either Party, the issue of liability of the other Party shall be determined and the amount of damage shall be assessed, unless the two Governments agree otherwise, by a sole arbitrator selected in accordance with subparagraph (b) of this paragraph. The arbitrator shall also decide any counter-claims arising out of the same incidents.

    (b) The arbitrator referred to in subparagraph (a) above shall be selected by agreement between the two Governments from amongst the nationals of the Republic of Korea who hold or have held high judicial office.

0265

(c) Any decision taken by the arbitrator shall be binding and conclusive upon the Parties.

(d) The amount of any compensation awarded by the arbitrator shall be distributed in accordance with the provisions of paragraph 5(e) (i), (ii) and (iii) of this Article.

(e) The compensation of the arbitrator shall be fixed by agreement between the two Governments and shall, together with the necessary expenses incidental to the performance of his duties, be defrayed in equal proportions by them.

(f) Each party waives its claim in any such case up to the amount of 1,400 United States dollars or its equivalent in Korean currency at the rate of exchange provided for in the Agreed Minute to Article_____ at the time the claim is filed.

3. For the purpose of paragraph 1 and 2 of this Article the expression "owned by a Party" in the case of a vessel includes a vessel on bare boat charter to that Party or requisitioned by it on bare boat terms or seized by it in prize (except to the extent that the risk of loss or liability is borne by some person other than such Party).

4. Each Party waives all its claims against the other Party for injury or death suffered by any member of its armed forces while such member was engaged in the performance of his official duties.

5. Claims (other than contractual claims and those to which paragraph 6 or 7 of this Article apply) arising out of acts or omissions of members or employees of the United States armed forces, including those employees who are nationals of or ordinarily resident in the Republic of Korea, done in the

2

0266

performance of official duty, or out of any other act, omission or occurrence for which the United States armed forces are legally responsible, and causing damage in the Republic of Korea to third Parties, other than the Government of the Republic of Korea, shall be dealt with by the Republic of Korea in accordance with the following provisions:

(a) Claims shall be filed, considered and settled or adjudicated in accordance with the laws and regulations of the Republic of Korea with respect to the claims arising from the activities of its own armed forces.

(b) The Republic of Korea may settle any such claims, and payment of the amount agreed upon or determined by adjudication shall be made by the Republic of Korea in won.

(c) Such payment, whether made pursuant to a settlement or to adjudication of the case by a competent tribunal of the Republic of Korea, or the final adjudication by such a tribunal denying payment, shall be binding and conclusive upon the Parties.

(d) Every claim paid by the Republic of Korea shall be communicated to the appropriate United States authorities together with full particulars and a proposed distribution in conformity with sub-paragraph (e) (i) and (ii) below.

In default of a reply within two months, the proposed distribution shall be regarded as accepted.

(e) The cost incurred in satisfying claims pursuant to the preceding subparagraph and paragraph 2 of this Article shall be distributed between the Parties as follows:

3

0267

(i) Where the United States alone is responsible, the amount awarded or adjudged shall be distributed in the proportion of 25 percent chargeable to the Republic of Korea and 75 percent chargeable to the United States.

(ii) Where the Republic of Korea and the United States are responsible for the damage, the amount awarded or adjudged shall be distributed equally between them. Where the damage was caused by the armed forces of the Republic of Korea and the United States and it is not possible to attribute it specifically to one or both of those armed forces, the amount awarded by adjudged shall be distributed equally between the Republic of Korea and the United States.

(iii) Every half year, a statement of the sums paid by the Republic of Korea in the course of the half-yearly period in respect of every case regarding which the liability, amount, and proposed distribution on a percentage basis has been approved by the United States shall be sent to the appropriate authorities of the United States, together with a request for reimbursement. Such reimbursement shall be made in won within the shortest possible time.

(f) Members or employees of the United States Armed Forces, including those employees who are nationals of or ordinarily resident in the Republic of Korea, shall not be subject to any proceedings for the enforcement of any judgment given against them in the Republic of Korea in a matter arising from the performance of their official duties.

(g) Except insofar as subparagraph e of this paragraph applies

4

0268

to claims covered by paragraph 2 of this Article, the provisions of this paragraph shall not apply to any claims arising out of or in connection with the navigation or operation of a ship or the loading, carriage, or discharge of a cargo, other than claims for death or personal injury to which paragraph 4 of this Article does not apply.

6. Claims against members or employees of the United States armed forces (except employees who are nationals of or ordinarily resident in the Republic of Korea) arising out of tortious acts or omissions in the Republic of Korea not done in the performance of official duty shall be dealt with in the following manner:

(a) The authorities of the Republic of Korea shall consider the claim and access compensation to the claimant in a fair and just manner, taking into account all the circumstances of the case, including the conduct of the injured person, and shall prepare a report on the matter.

(b) The report shall be delivered to the appropriate United States authorities, who shall then decide without delay whether they will offer an ex gratia payment, and if so, of what amount.

(c) If an offer of ex gratia payment is made, and accepted, by the claimant in full satisfaction of his claim, the United States authorities shall make the payment themselves and inform the authorities of the Republic of Korea of their decision and of the sum paid.

(d) Nothing in this paragraph shall affect the jurisdiction of the courts of the Republic of Korea to entertain an action against a

5

0269

member or employee of the United States armed forces unless and until there has been payment in full satisfaction of the claim.

7. Claims arising out of the unauthorized use of any vehicle of the United States forces shall be dealt with in accordance with paragraph 6 of this Article, except insofar as the United States forces are legally responsible.

8. If a dispute arises as to whether a tortious act or omission of a member or an employee of the United States armed forces was done in the performance of official duty or as to whether the use of any vehicle of the United States armed forces was unauthorized, the question shall be submitted to an arbitrator appointed in accordance with paragraph 2 b of this Article, whose decision on this point shall be final and conclusive.

9. (a) The United States shall not claim immunity from the jurisdiction of the courts of the Republic of Korea for members or employees of the United States armed forces in respect of the civil jurisdiction of the courts of the Republic of Korea except in respect of proceedings for the enforcement of any judgment given against them in the Republic of Korea in a matter arising from the performance of their official duties or except after payment in full satisfaction of a claim.

(b) In the case of any private movable property, excluding that in use by the United States armed forces, which is subject to compulsory execution under Korean law, and is within the facilities and areas in use by the United States armed forces, the United States authorities shall, upon the request of the Korean courts, render all assistance

6

0270

within their power to see that such property is turned over to the
Korean authorities.

      (c) The authorities of the United States and the Republic of
Korea shall cooperate in the procurement of evidence for a fair disposition of claims under this Article.

    10. Disputes arising out of contracts concerning the procurement
of materials, supplies, equipment, services by or for the United States
armed forces, which are not resolved by the Parties to the contract
concerned, may be submitted to the Joint Committee for conciliation,
provided that the provisions of this paragraph shall not prejudice
any right, which Parties to the contract may have, to file a civil suit.

    11. Paragraphs 2 and 5 of this Article shall apply only to claims
arising incident to non-combant activities.

    12. For the purposes of this Article, members of the Korean
Augmentation to the United States Army (KATUSA) shall be considered as
members of the United States armed forces.

    13. The provisions of this Article shall not apply to any claims
which arose before the entry into force of this Agreement. Such
claims shall be processed and settled by the authorities of the
United States.

AGREED MINUTE

A. Unless otherwise provided,

   1. The provisions of paragraphs five, six, seven and eight of this article will become effective six months from the date of entry into force of this agreement as to claims arising from incidents in the Seoul Special City area.

   2. The provisions of paragraphs five, six, seven and eight will be progressively extended to other areas of Korea as determined and defined by the Joint Committee.

B. Until such time as the provisions of paragraphs five, six, seven and eight become effective in any given area,

   1. The United States shall process and settle claims (other than contractual claims) arising out of the acts or omissions of members or employees of the United States armed forces done in the performance of official duty or out of any other act, omission or occurrence for which the United States armed forces are legally responsible, which cause damage in the Republic of Korea to parties other than the two Governments;

   2. The United States shall entertain other non-contractual claims against members or employees of the armed forces and may offer an ex gratia payment in such cases and in such amount as is determined by the appropriate United States authorities; and

   3. Each party shall have the right to determine whether a member or employee of its armed forces was engaged in the performance of

8

0272

official duties and whether property owned by it was being used by its armed forces for official purposes.

C. For the purposes of subparagraph 2(d) subparagraph 5(e) shall be effective throughout Korea from the date of entry into force of this agreement.

9

ARTICLE

ACCOUNTING PROCEDURES

It is agreed that arrangements will be effected between the Governments of the United States and the Republic of Korea for accounting applicable to financial transactions arising out of this Agreement.

0274

기록물종류	일반공문서철	등록번호	940	등록일자	2006-07-27
분류번호	741.12	국가코드	US	보존기간	영구
명 칭	한.미국 간의 상호방위조약 제4조에 의한 시설과 구역 및 한국에서의 미국군대의 지위에 관한 협정 (SOFA) 전59권. 1966.7.9 서울에서 서명 : 1967.2.9 발효 (조약 232호) *원본				
생 산 과	미주과/조약과	생산년도	1952~1967	담당그룹	국제법률
권 차 명	V.42 후속 조치, 1966-67				
내용목차	1. 관계부처 후속조치 (p.2~90) 2. 협정문 배포 (p.91~147) * 일지 : 1953.8.7 이승만 대통령-Dulles 미국 국무장관 공동성명 　- 상호방위조약 발효 후 군대지위협정 교섭 약속 1954.12.2 정부, 주한 UN군의 관세업무협정 체결 제의 1955.1월, 5월 미국, 제의 거절 1955.4.28 정부, 군대지위협정 제의 (한국측 초안 제시) 1957.9.10 Hurter 미국 국무차관 방한 시 각서 수교 (한국측 제의 수락 요구) 1957.11.13, 26 정부, 개별 협정의 단계적 체결 제의 1958.9.18 Dawling 주한미국대사, 형사재판관할권 협정 제외 조건으로 행정협정 체결 의사 전달 1960.3.10 정부, 토지, 시설협정의 우선적 체결 강력 요구 1961.4.10 장면 국무총리-McConaughy 주한미국대사 공동성명으로 교섭 개시 합의 1961.4.15, 4.25 제1, 2차 한.미국 교섭회의 (서울) 1962.3.12 정부, 교섭 재개 촉구 공한 송부 1962.5.14 Burger 주한미국대사, 최규하 장관 면담 시 형사재판관할권 문제 제기 않는 조건으로 교섭 재개 통고 1962.9.6 한.미국 간 공동성명 발표 (9월 중 교섭 재개 합의) 1962.9.20~ 제1-81차 실무 교섭회의 (서울) 　1965.6.7 1966.7.8 제82차 실무 교섭회의 (서울) 1966.7.9 서명 1967.2.9 발효 (조약 232호)				

마 이 크 로 필 름 사 항			
촬영일자	롤 번호	화일번호	후레임 번호
2006-11-24	I-06-0071	02	1-147

0001

1. 관계부처 후속조치

0002

교   통   부

교항정 1554 *10175*   1966. 8. 19

수 신   외무부장관
제 목   미군 및 미군 군계약 항공기 운항

         미군 및 미군 군계약 항공기의 대한 취항에 관하여 현자
당해 항공기 운항시 교통부 항공당국의 허가 절차를 밟지 않고 운항
을 임의로 하고 있는 군용기 및 군 계약 민간항공기에 대하여 방임
상태에 있는바 이는 종전의 마아아 협정 및 현자의 한.미간 주둔군
지위 협정에 의거한 관례가 되어온 것인데

         1. 당부로서 향후 이러한 항공기에 대하여 운항권은 인정
하나 국내법에 의한 허가 절차는 취하도록 조치 위계인바 전기한
협정상 가능한 것인지의 여부

         2. 미군 군계약 항공기 일지라도 민간항공기 임으로 착륙료
등을 포함한 공항시설 사용료를 징수하려고 하는바 이도 가능한지의
여부

이상을 회시하여 주시기 바라며 아울러 관계협정처도 수부 송부하여
주시기 바랍니다. 끝.

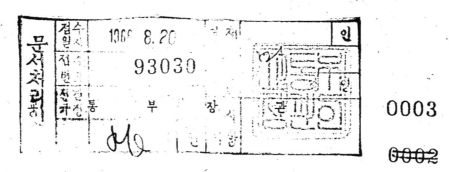

0003

~~0002~~

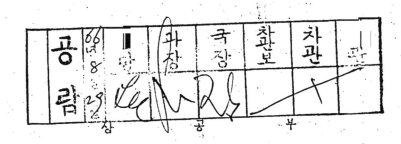

상역정 1313 1886   1966. 8. 25

수 신   수신처참조

제 목   회의소집

다음과 같이 회의를 소집하오니 참석하여 주시기 바랍니다.

· 다 음

가. 일시   66. 8. 30. 14.00

나. 장소   상공부상역국장실

다. 안건   한미간 합중국 군대지위협정에 관한 국회

집의에 대한 정부 답변에 관하여

라. 참석범위   외무부 미주과장

재무부 관세과장.

상공부 사정과장, 경공업과장, 중공업과장. 끝.

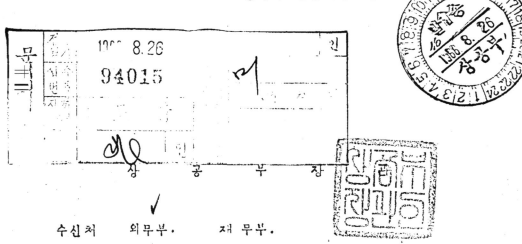

수신처   외무부.   재무부.

0004   ~~0003~~

기 안 지

기 안 자	미주과 이군필	전화 번호			공보	필요	불필요
	과 장	국 장	차 관 보	차 관	장 관		
	(서명)	(서명)	(서명)	(서명)			
협 성 자명	조약과 (서명)					보존 년한	
기 안 년월일	66. 8. 26.		시행 년월일		통 제 정 서 기 장		
분류기호 문서번호	외구미 722.2-						
경 유 수 신 참 조	교통부 장관			발 신 장 관			
제 목	미군 및 미군 군계약 항공기 운항						

　　귀부에서 1966. 8. 19 일자 교항정 제1554-10175 호 공함으로
문의하신 미군용기 및 미군과의 계약하에 운항되는 항공기에 대한
국내법에 의한 허가 절차 시행 및 착륙료 징수 가능성 여부에 관하여
다음과 같이 회시 합니다.

　　　　1. 지난 7월 9일 한.미간에 체결된 주한 미국 군대의 지위에
관한 협정의 제10조 제1항은 "합중국에 의하여, 합중국을 위하여 또는
합중국의 관리하에서 공용을 위하여 운항되는 합중국 및 외국의 선박과
항공기는 대한민국의 어떠한 항구 또는 비행장에도 입항료 또는

착륙료를 부담하지 아니하고 출입할수 있다……"라고 규정하여, 이러한
항공기가 공용으로 우리나라 비행장에 출입할수 있는 권리를 인정하고
있음으로 이러한 항공기의 우리나라 비행장에의 공용 출입에 대하여서는
우리나라가 허가 여부를 결정할수 있는 재량권을 가지는 것이 아니며
따라서 우리나라 관계 법령이 요구하는 허가 절차로 부터 면제되어야
한다고 사료됩니다.　　　　　　　　　　　　　　　　　　0005

　　　　2. 또한 이러한 항공기가 공용으로 우리나라 비행장에

출입할 때에는 협정 제10조 제1항에 규정된바에 따라 비행장 착륙료로 부터 면제됩니다.

    3. 상기 두가지 문의사항을 포함한 협정 제10조의 규정은 미·일협정 제5조의 규정과 동일하며 일본국의 동 조항 운영 현황도 또한 상기 회시 내용과 같읍니다.

    4. 한편, 항공 교통관제 및 운항 보조시설에 관한 제12조 제1항에 의하여 모든 민간 및 군용 항공 교통관제에 관한 협조 및 통합을 이룩하는데 필요한 절차는 양 정부의 관계당국간에 성립되는 약정에 의하여 선정하게되어 있음으로 교통관제를 위하여 귀부에서 필요로 하는 운영세칙은 미측과의 협의하에 결정하게 되어 있읍니다.

    5. 기타 협정 운영상 필요한 모든 상호 협의 사항은 앞으로 설치될 합동위원회에서 검토될 것임으로 귀부의 소관 사항인 항공기의 귀착에 대한 세부 운영사항은 수시 동 위원회의 협의 대상이 될수 있을것 입니다.

유 첨 : 7월 9일자 협정문 1부.

0005
0006

외 무 부

외구미 722.2-   1966. 8. 30.

수 신 : 교통부 장관

제 목 : 미근 및 미근 근계약 항공기 운항

　　　귀부에서 1966. 8. 19일자 교항정 제1554-10175호 공한으로
문의하신 미군용기 및 미근과의 계약하에 운항되는 항공기에 대한
국내법에 의한 허가 절차 시행 및 착륙료 징수 가능성 여부에 관하여
다음과 같이 회시 합니다.

　　　1. 지난 7월 9일 한·미간에 체결된 주한 미국 군대의 지위
에 관한 협정의 제10조 제1항은 "합중국에 의하여, 합중국을 위하여
또는 합중국의 관리하에서 공용을 위하여 운항되는 합중국 및
외국의 선박과 항공기는 대한민국의 어떠한 항구 또는 비행장에도
입항료 또는 착륙료를 부담하지 아니하고 출입할수 있다......"
라고 규정하여, 이러한 항공기가 공용으로 우리나라 비행장에
출입할수 있는 권리를 인정하고 있음으로 이러한 항공기의 우리나라
비행장에의 공용 출입에 대하여서는 우리나라가 허가 여부를 결정할수
있는 재량권을 가지는 것이 아니며 따라서 우리나라 관기법령이 요구
하는 허가 절차도 그대로 면제되어야 한다고 사료됩니다.

　　　2. 또한 이러한 항공기가 공용으로 우리나라 비행장에
출입할 때에는 협정 제10조 제1항에 규정된바에 따라 비행장

0007　　~~0006~~

착륙료로도 부터 면제됩니다.

3. 상기 두가지 문의사항을 포함한 협정 제10조의 규정은 미·일협정 제5조의 규정과 동일하며 일본국의 동 조항 운영 현황도 또한 상기 회시 내용과 같읍니다.

4. 한편, 항공 교통관제 및 운항 보조시설에 관한 제12조 제1항에 의하여 모든 민간 및 군용 항공 교통관제에 관한 협조 및 통합을 이룩하는데 필요한 절차는 양 정부의 관계 당국간에 성립되는 약정에 의하여 설정하게되어 있음으로 교통관제를 위하여 귀부에서 필요로 하는 운영계획은 미측과의 협의하에 결정하게 되어 있읍니다.

5. 기타 협정 운영상 필요한 모든 상호 협의 사항은 앞으로 설치될 합동위원회에서 검토될 것임으로 귀부의 소관 사항인 항공기의 귀착에 대한 세부 운영사항은 수시 동 위원회의 협의 대상이 될수 있을것 입니다.

유 첨 : 7월 9일자 협정문 1부. 끝.

외 무 부 장 관

0008

非歳出資金機関関係資料

（美八軍 提供）

1966. 9. 3

合衆國軍隊의 非歳出資金機関活動은 合衆國軍隊의 本質的
이며 緊要한 部分을 이룩하고있으며, 이러한 機関은 合
衆國軍隊의 士氣昂揚, 厚生, 및 誤業関係事業을 맞고 있
음

本協定 第13條에 規定된 非歳出資金機関은 合衆国軍当
局에 依하여 公的으로 認定되고 規制되고 一般歳出資金
機関과 同一하게 緊密한 監督下에 있음.

韓国内 非歳出資金機関現況은 다음과 같다.

1. P. X.

(1) 合衆国軍隊의 韓国内、大小、P. X는 總191 伯所이
며 그 規模는 큰것은 現代的施設로 부터 적은것은「트
레이러」車 또는 天幕의 一部로 되어있는것도 있으며

~1~

0003 ~~0008~~

化粧品類를 비롯하여 其他 日常必需品을 取扱하고 있음

(2) 큰 規模의 것은 다음 地域에 있음:

1. 서 울 龍山

2. 富 平

3. 烏 山

4. 大 邱

5. 釜 山

6. 第一軍司令部

7. 第二師團 本部

8. 第7師團 本部

2. 劇 場

(1) 3 5미리 필림을 上映할수 있는 劇場이 41個所 있으며 合衆国 陸軍 및 空軍의 motion picture Service 에 依하여 運営 되고 있음

數百名以上을 收容할수 있는 큰 規模의 것은 다음地区에 있음:

~2~

~~0009~~

0010

1. 서울 龍山地区에 2伯所

2. 富 平

3. 議 政 府

4. 烏 山

5. 大 邱

(2) 其外에도 16미리필림 上映劇場은 185伯所인바 이中 56伯所는 無料上映함

3. 食 堂

101伯所의 將校食堂과 198伯所의 士兵食堂이 있으며 이들은 33伯의 Open - mess System 에 依하여 運営되고 있음

0011

~3~

(1) NATO 協定諸國의 裁判权 拋棄統計

(美國防省 統計資料)

國家名	接受國의 裁判权에 屬하는 犯罪件数			拋棄件数			拋棄率(%)		
	62年度	63	64	62	63	64	62	63	64
Belgium	42	56	57	37	56	55	88.1	100	96.5
Canada	415	401	797	21	19	10	5.1	4.7	1.3
Denmark	2	5	1	1	3	0	50	60	0
France	4,454	4,625	4,244	3,841	3,928	3,544	86.2	84.9	83.5
Germany	-	6,188	17,658	-	5,512	14,131	-	89.1	80.0
Greece	36	45	86	35	36	66	97.2	80.0	76.7
Italy	305	271	274	100	163	158	32.8	60.1	57.7
Luxembourg	26	43	14	3	10	0	11.5	23.3	0
Netherlands	119	247	274	119	247	273	100	100	99.6
Norway	1	4	0	1	0	0	100	0	0
Portugal	0	0	-	0	0	-	0	0	-
Turkey	95	116	105	6	54	16	6.3	46.6	15.2
U.K	2,037	1,640	1,304	345	144	74	16.9	8.8	5.7
Total	7,532	13,641	24,214	4,509	10,172	18,327	59.7	74.6	73.9

(註) 独逸은 1963年 7月 1日에 NATO SOFA의 当事國이 되었다.

0012

~~0011~~

(2) 其他 協定諸國의 裁判權抛棄統計

〈美國防省 統計資料〉

國家名	接受國의 裁判権에 屬하之 犯罪件数			抛棄件数			抛棄率 (%)		
	62年度	63	64	62	63	64	62	63	64
Australia	0	1	—	0	—	—	0	0	—
Iceland	56	105	135	2	9	1	3.6	8.6	0.7
Japan	3,191	3,433	2,010	2,906	3,090	1.627	91.1	90.0	80.9
Morocco	33	42	8	18	20	8	54.5	47.6	100
New Zealand	23	29	20	22	28	20	95.6	96.6	100
Nicaragua	1	0	—	0	0	—	0	0	—
Philippines	85	67	132	77	52	104	90.6	77.6	78.8
Spain	16	122	158	10	99	148	62.5	81.1	93.7
West Indies	172	227	—	4	7	—	2.3	3.0	—
West Pakistan	—	1	—	—	1	—	—	100	—
Total	3,577	4,027	2,463	3,039	3,306	1,908	85	82.1	77.5

(註) 上記 抛棄統計는 処理를 위하여 美軍当局에 移送한 軍屬 및 家族関係事件 件数와 不起訴処分件数를 包含함.

0013 ~~0012~~

駐韓 美軍関係犯罪発生統計

（内務部 治安司）

年度 犯罪	殺人	強盗	強姦	窃盗	暴行	傷害	器物毀壊	其他	計
1962年度	13	3	0	0	107	64	0	31	218
1963 〃	6	2	0	0	105	48	6	48	215
1964 〃	9	6	3	2	118	59	7	20	224
1965 〃	5	3	2	2	153	50	13	10	238
1966. 7.10現在	1	3	3	8	102	13	20	22	172
計	34	17	8	12	585	234	46	131	1.067

0013

0014

駐韓美軍當局의 請求權處理統計

(1959年 6月1日 부터 1966年 6月30日 까지)

年 度 別	請求權接受件数	支 拂 額
1959年 6月1日以後	517	$ 282,688.28
1960年	2,125	727,696.22
1961年	1,163	361,801.26
1962年	979	187,633.75
1963年	839	148,185.86
1964年 9月1日까지	911	101,433.52
1965年	1,123	167,884.86
1966年 6月30日까지	626	78,148.77
計	8,283	$ 2,055,472.52

〔註〕 1. 美軍当局이 支拂한 賠償總額을 275対1로 換算하면 다음과 같으며 年間 約8千万원을 支拂한 것이 됨

$ 2,055,472.52 × ₩ 275 = ₩ 566,255,542.00

0015

<u>駐韓美軍非歲出資金機関(P.X)所在地</u>

(美8軍 提供)   (1966年7月22日現在)

1 主要 P.X   10.個所

(1) 서   울

(2) 仁   川

(3) 東 豆 川

(4) 汶 山 里

(5) 議 政 府

(6) 鳥   山

(7) 富   平

(8) 春   川

(9) 大   邱

(10) 釜   山

2. 小規模 P.X는 約50個가 全國에 散在한 部隊에 設置되어 있음.

0016

美軍 招請契約者 名單

(1966年 6月 30日 現在)

1. Adrian Wilson & Associates
2. Associated American Engineers Overseas, Inc.
3. Bendix Field Engineering Corporation
4. Collins Radio Company
5. D. F. Fischer & Sons, Ltd.
6. Dynalectron Corporation
7. Federal Electric Corporation
8. General Electric Company
9. Gilfillan Corporation
10. Hiller Aircraft Company
11. Hughes Aircraft Company
12. International Dairy Engineering Company
13. James S. Lee Company, Inc.
14. Motorola, Inc.
15. Northrop Corporation, Norair Division
16. Pacific Architect & Engineers, Inc.
17. Philco Corporation
18. R. M. Towill Corporation
19. Raytheon Company
20. Stolte, Inc.
21. Trans-Asia Engineering Associates, Inc.
22. University of Maryland

註; 1. 招請契約者数   22

2. 美國人雇傭員   314 名

3. 第3國人雇傭員   21 名   내역

0017

1. 제3국인 내역

2. 계약자의 영황

~~0018~~

한·미국 간의 상호방위조약 제4조에 의한 시설과 구역 및 한국에서의 미국군대의 지위에 관한 협정(SOFA)
전59권. 1966.7.9 서울에서 서명 : 1967.2.9 발효(조약 232호) (V.42 후속 조치, 1966-67)   297

유엔軍土地 및 建物徵發量 및 要補償額調書

(國防部 提供)　　　　　　　1966年 1月現在

区 分	件 数	坪 数		計
		國 公 有	私 有	
	件	坪	坪	坪
建 物	721	59,211	26,400	85,611
土 地	約30,000	25,400,000	75,000,000	100,400,000

1965年度補償額　　87,601,500 원 (國軍. 유엔軍包含)

1966年度予算　　94,000,000 원 (　　〃　　)

0018

유 엔 軍 (土地, 建物) 徵發量 및 要補償額 調書

REAL ESTATE ACQUIRED BY U/N FORCES (LAND, BUILDING) & BUDGET REQUIRED FOR REIMBURSEMENT

(土地 Land)

區分 Division	50	51	52	53	54	55	56	57	58	59	60	61	62	63	64	認計 Total
에이카 Acres	240.30	1,659	4,471	5,791	51,761	52,444	52,046	53,133	57,258	57,581	57,435	57,674	57,724	57,724	57,724	627,674
補償額 Budget for Reimbursement	2,266	25,243	101,114	153,948	500,449	872,966	1,185,804	1,486,580	1,506,808	1,598,908	1,815,222	2,157,223	2,246,747	2,278,186	2,468,181	18,401,131

(建物 Building)

區分 Division	50	51	52	53	54	55	56	57	58	59	60	61	62	63	64	認計 Total
에이카 Acres	6.21	14.02	22.84	23.27	23.32	23.35	23.35	23.35	28.47	28.47	28.54	28.54	28.56	28.56	28.56	360.03
補償額 Budget for Reimbursement	₩20.4	11,822	38,614	47,226	64,140	118,556	158,074	187,713	213,802	228,859	265,672	301,900	302,132	503,553	629,442	3,074,321

(註)
1. 本調書는 全部 民有이며 現在 使用中인 것 임
2. 補償額은 坪 50年 各2 32坪으로 算出함
3. 6.25 당時 土地台帳 燒失로 因한 未復旧로 所有者未詳의 財産이 約 50万坪 確認된 것으로 地積과 補償額이 增額될 것으로 推定됨
4. 徵發使用하다가 過去 解除된 것은 計上되지 않았으며 現在 把握中이나 現使用量의 約 3倍로 推定됨
5. 建物은 現在 測量中에 있으므로 測量完了와 同時 正確된 것이 判明될 것임

~2~

한·미국 간의 상호방위조약 제4조에 의한 시설과 구역 및 한국에서의 미국군대의 지위에 관한 협정(SOFA)
전59권. 1966.7.9 서울에서 서명 : 1967.2.9 발효(조약 232호) (V.42 후속 조치, 1966-67) 299

徵發地地目別明細

DETAILS OF TYPE OF LAND

區 分 Division	空 地 Flat Land	田 Dry Land	畓 Rice paddy	林 野 Mountain	其 他 Others	總地積 Total	備 考 Remarks
에이카 Acres	994.75	11.227	4.233.43	58.292.83	7.296.74	82.529.75	
坪 Pyong	1.193.099	13.941.857	5.181.698	71.356.547	9.543.219	101.016.420	

~3~

0020

所有区分別明細
DETAILS OF OWNERSHIP

区分 Division	所有区分 Ownership		民有의 地目別明細 Type of Land, Civilian Owned					總地積 Total	備考 Remarks
	國有 Gov't	民有 Civilian	空地 Flat Land	田 Dry Farm	畓 Rice paddy	林野 Fild & Mount.	其他 Other		
에이커 Acres	24,790 04	57,724 99	769 50	11,188 14	3,818 41	41,493 50	455 44	82,529 75	
坪 Pyong	30,343,021	70,655,391	941,880	13,694,293	4,673,745	50,788,046	557,435	101,016,420	

0026

0021

~4~

徵 發 建 物 年 度 別 明 細

DETAILS OF ACQUIRED BUILDING EACH YEAR

區分 Division	50	51	52	53	54	55	56	57	58	59	60	61	62	63	64	總計 Total	備考 Remarks
에이카 Acres	6.71	14.09	22.91	23.27	23.32	23.35	23.35	23.35	28.49	28.49	28.54	28.54	28.56	28.56	28.56	360.13	
坪 Pyong	8,221.7	17,249.3	28,048.4	28,487.6	28,552.5	28,587	28,587	28,587	34,853.1	34,853.1	34,942.2	34,942.2	34,969	34,969	34,969	440,818.1	

구 입 토 지 年 度 別 買 收 實 績

區分 Division	57	58	59	60	61	62	63	64	總計 Total	備考 Remarks
에이카 Acres	32	65	309	636	529	202	120	360	2,301	
土地代金 Cost of Land	10,258	82,264	218,019	194,199	154,090	37,183	41,903	204,337	942,253	

0022

기 안 용 지

분류기호 문서번호	외구미 720	(전화번호)	전결규정 **구미국종** 항 전결사항
처리기한		기안자	결 재 자
시행일자		미주과 민 67. 4. 12.	ㅋ
보존년한			

보 조 기 관	미주과장	ㅆ	

협 조				
경 수 참	유 신 조	내부처 참조	통 제 [검열 1967.4.13 용재신]	발 송	정 서

제 목	한.미 군대 지위협정 관계 조치 자료

    1. 한.미 군대 지위협정의 원활한 시행을 위하여 한.미 양측은

서로 각자가 취한 동 협정관계 각종 조치의 내용을 알려 줌으로서 상호간

타방의 협정 시행 상황를 파악할수 있게 하기로 합의한바 있읍니다.

(군대 지위협정 교섭 회의록 제82차 회의록 참조)

    2. 이 "각종조치"에는 입법조치, 예산상 조치 및 기타

행정조치가 모두 포함되는 것으로 양해되어 있으며, 특히 우리측이 제공할

것 에는 협정 제29조 2항의 "모든 입법상 및 예산상의 조치"를 위시하여 행정

각부의 규정 및 문서까지도 포함되는 것입니다.

    3. 따라서, 귀부에서 이미 제정하신 군대 지위협정관계

특례법 이나, 또는 기타 행정상의 조치에 관한 문서 내지 규정이 있으시면

공통서식 1-2-1 (갑)   0023   (18절지)

한·미국 간의 상호방위조약 제4조에 의한 시설과 구역 및 한국에서의 미국군대의 지위에 관한 협정(SOFA)
전59권. 1966.7.9 서울에서 서명 : 1967.2.9 발효(조약 232호) (V.42 후속 조치, 1966-67)   303

4월 20일까지 당부로 보내 주시되, 영문 번위문이 있으시면 첨부하여

주시기 바랍니다.　　　　끝

배부처 :　경제기획원장관, 내무부장관, 재무부장관, 법무부장관,

　　　　국방부장관, 상공부장관, 교통부장관, 체신부장관, 노동청장.

0028

0024

경 제 기 획 원

경기획 720 -126

1967.4.19

수 신 외무부장관

제 목 한미 군대 지위 협정 관계 조치 자료

　　　1. 외구미 720_7427 (67.4.13)에 대한 회신입니다.

　　　2. 본건에 대하여 당원이 취한 입법조치나 기타행정조치는 없으며 예산조치에 대하여는 현재 추진중에 있으니 양지하시기 바랍니다. 끝

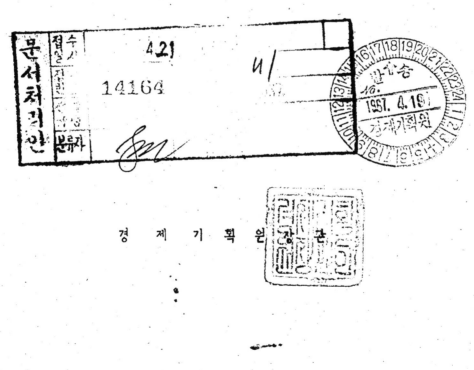

경 제 기 획 원 장 관

0025　　0029

재   무   부

재세국 1244.14-1728 (구 ㄴ 3911)   1967.   4.   20.

수 신 외무부장관

제 목 한·미군대지위협정 관계 조치 자료

    1. 외구미 720-7427 (67. 4. 13)에 관한것입니다.

    2. 동 협정의 시행을 위하여 당부에서 제정한 특례법
및 기타 행정상의 조치를 별첨하여 송부하오니 적절한 조치를
취하여 주시기 바랍니다.

첨 부 특례법 (법율제1898호) 한·영 각 1부.

    휴가장병 휴대품검사요청   1부.   끝

14464

0026

가리 경제

0030

法律 第1898號　　　　1967年 3月3日公布

大韓民國과　아메리카合衆國間의　相互防衛條
約第4條에　의한　施設과　區域　및　大韓民
國에서의　合衆國軍隊의　地位에　관한　協定
의　實施에　따른　<u>關稅法등의　臨時特例에</u>
<u>관한　法律</u>

第 1 條 (目 的)　이　法은　大韓民國과
아메리카合衆國間의　相互防衛條約第
4 條에　의한　施設과　區域　및　大
韓民國에서의　合衆國軍隊의　地位에
관한　協定 (이하　" 協定 " 이라　한
다) 을　實施하기　위하여　關稅法・
臨時特別關稅法・噸稅法・物品稅法・
酒稅法・石油類稅法　및　藏置期間經

~1~　0027 0031

~2~

過物品處理法의 特例를 規定함을
目的으로 한다.

第2條(定義) ① 이 法에서 "軍用
船"이라 함은 協定第10條의 規
定에 의한 公用을 위하여 運航되
는 船舶을 말한다.

② 이 法에서 "軍用機"라 함은
協定第10條의 規定에 의한 公用
을 위하여 運航되는 航空機를 말
한다.

③ 이 法에서 "免稅機關"이라 함
은 協定第9條의 規定에 의한 關
稅 및 기타의 課徵金이 賦課되지

0028 0032

아니하는 合衆國軍隊, 그 公認調達 機關과 非歲出資金機關을 말한다.

④ 이 法에서 "免稅對象者"라 함은 協定第 1 條의 規定에 의한 合衆國軍隊의 構成員·軍屬 및 그들의 家族 또는 協定第 1 5 條의 規定에 의한 招請契約者를 말한다.

⑤ 이 法에서 "非免稅對象者"라 함은 免稅機關 및 免稅對象者 이외의 者를 말한다.

⑥ 이 法에서 "軍納品"이라 함은 免稅機關이외의 者가 合衆國軍隊의

~3~   0029 ~~0033~~

專用에 供하거나 合衆國軍隊가 사
용할 物品 또는 施設에 最終的으
로 合体하기 위하여 輸入하는 物
品으로서 당해 物品을 이러한 目
的에 使用하기 위하여 合衆國軍隊
가 受領한다는 合衆國軍隊의 權限
있는 機関의 證明이 있는 것을
말한다.

第3條 (噸稅등의 徵收) ① 軍用船이
協定에 의하여 関稅가 免除되지
아니하는 物品을 積載하고 있을
때에는 당해物品의 重量이 全積載
物品의 重量에 대하여 차지하는

0034
0030

比率을 噸稅法에 의하여 算出한

당해 船舶의 噸稅相當額에 乘하여

算出된 額의 噸稅를 徵收한다

② 前項의 規定은 軍用船이 不開港

에 入港하는 경우와 軍用機가 通

關飛行場에 의하지 아니하고 外國

에 往來하는 경우에 關稅法의 規

定에 의하여 納付하여야 할 許可

手數料의 徵收에 관하여 이를 準

用한다

第 4 條 (噸稅免除節次) 噸稅의 免除

를 받고자 하는 軍用船의 船長은

당해 船舶이 軍用船이라는 것을

~5~

0031 ~~0035~~

~6~

稅關에 證明하여야 한다

第5條 (入出港節次) ① 軍用船 또는

軍用機에 대하여는 関稅法第139條

第140條, 第142條 내지 第

147條, 第164條 내지 第166

條와 第248條의 規定은 適用하

지 아니한다 다만, 同法 第142

條에 規定된 入港報告, 積荷目錄·

船用品目錄 및 旅客名簿, 同法 第

164條에 規定된 着陸報告· 積荷

目錄· 機用品目錄 및 旅客名簿, 同

法 第143條에 規定된 出港報告

와 同法 第165條에 規定된 離

0032 0036

陸報告에 관하여는 예외로 한다.
② 軍用船 또는 軍用機가 協定第9
條의 規定에 의하여 稅關撿査를
행하지 아니하는 物品을 積載하거
나 旅客을 搭乘시키고 있는 경우
에는 前項但書의 積荷目錄과 旅客
名簿에 그 趣旨와 해당物品의
總重量 및 旅客人員數만을 記載한다
第6條 (関稅등 諸稅의 追徵) 協定
第9條의 規定에 의하여 関稅·
臨時特別関稅 (이하 ·特関稅· 라
하다) 또는 内國消費稅 (物品稅·
酒稅 및 石油類稅를 말한다 이하

〈2〉 0033 ~~0037~~

같 다) 의 免除를 받은 軍納品이

稅關長이 指定한 期間內에 合衆國

軍隊에 引渡되거나 合衆國軍隊가

사용하는 施設 또는 物品에 合体

된 事實이 合衆國軍隊의 權限있는

機關에 의하여 證明되지 아니한

때에는 당해 物品을 輸入한 者로

부터 免除된 關稅·特關稅 또는

內國消費稅를 即時 徵收한다. 다만

당해 物品이 天災地變 기타 부득

이한 事由로 인하여 滅失되었음을

稅關長이 인정할 때에는 예외로

한다

0034

第7條 (關稅免除物品의 製造등) ⓪

協定 第9條의 規定에 의하여 關

稅·特關稅 또는 內國消費稅의 免

除를 받은 軍納品을 合衆國軍隊에

引渡하거나 合衆國軍隊가 사용할

施設 또는 物品에 合体하기 전에

당해 物品을 改裝·區分·分割·合

倂 기타 類似한 作業을 하거나

당해 物品에 加工하거나 다른 物

品과 混合하거나 당해 物品을 原

料로 하여 다른 物品을 製造하고

자 할 때에는 稅關長이 期間을

定하여 承認한 場所에서 행하여야

~9~   0035 ~~0039~~

한다.

② 稅關長은 前項의 規定에 의한 物品의 搬出入·作業·加工·混合 또는 製造를 確認하기 위하여 당해 物品의 輸入者로 하여금 필요한 書類를 제출하게 하거나 소속 공무원으로 하여금 당해 物品을 檢查하게 할 수 있다.

第 8 條 (關稅免除物品의 讓渡制限)

① 免稅對象者 또는 免稅對象者이었던 者가 協定의 規定에 의하여 關稅의 免除를 받은 物品을 大韓

0036 ~~0040~~

民國內에서 非免稅對象者에게 讓渡(讓渡를 위하여 그 委託을 받은 者 또는 斡旋을 하는 者에게 所持시키는 것을 包含한다. 이하 같다.)하고자 할 때에는 稅關長에게 申告하여 讓渡의 承認을 받아야 한다.

② 稅關長은 前項의 規定에 의한 承認을 하기 위하여 필요한 때에는 당해 물품을 保稅區域(關稅法 第55條 第1項의 規定에 의하여 稅關長이 許可한 場所를 包含한다.

~ll~   0037
                          0041

이하 같다) 에 搬入 시키거나

소속 公務員으로 하여금 당해

物品을 檢査 하게할 수 있다.

③財務部長官은 필요하다고 인정

할 때에는 第1項의 規定에 의한

讓渡의 承認을 할 수 있는 범위

를 告示한다.

④第1項의 規定에 의한 承認을

받지 아니하고 物品을 讓渡한

者는 關稅法 第114 條의 規

定에 의한 免許를 받지

0038 0042

아니하고 物品을 輸入한 者로 본다. 이 경우에는 關稅法 第198條의2 및 同法 第198條의3 第2項의 規定을 適用한다.

⑤ 關稅法 第213條 내지 第246條의 規定은 前項의 경우에 이를 準用한다.

第9條 (免稅物品의 讓受와 關稅등의 徵收) ① 非免稅對象者가 免稅機關 免稅對象者 또는 免稅對象者이었던 者로부터 協定의 規定에 의하여 關稅의 免除를 받은 物品 (당해 物品을 사용하여 製造된 物品 또

~13   0039

-14-

는 그 副産物을 포함한다) 을

大韓民國내에서 讓受 (讓渡 또는

讓受의 委託을 받거나 그 斡旋을

위하여 所持하는 것을 포함 한다

이하 같다) 하고자 할 때에는

그 讓受를 輸入으로 보고 關稅法

臨時特別關稅法·物品稅法· 酒稅法

및 石油類稅法을 適用한다.

③ 非免稅對象者가 前項의 規定에

의한 物品을 輸入의 免許를 받지

아니하고 讓受한 때에는 (당해

物品이 關稅法의 規定에 의하여

沒收되거나 物品納付의 通告處分이

0040　0044

履行된 경우를 제외한다)

당해 物品에 대한 關稅·特關稅

및 內國消費稅는 그 讓受人을 納

稅義務者로 하고, 讓受의 날에 適

用되는 法令과 그 당시의 物品의

性質 및 數量에 의하여 徵收한

다. 다만, 關稅·特關稅 및 內國

消費稅의 完納전에 당해 物品이

再讓渡된 때에는 그 關稅·特關稅

및 內國消費稅는 最初의 讓受人으

로 부터 徵收할 수 없는 경우에

限하여 그 物品의 所有者 또는

占有者로 부터 徵收한다

~15~   0041   0045

③ 稅關長은 前項의 規定에 의한 讓受人·再讓受人 또는 당해 物品을 所有 또는 占有하고 있는 者에 대하여 期限을 定하여 그 物品을 保稅區域에 搬入할것을 命할 수 있다. 이경우에 期限내에 그 物品이 保稅區域에 搬入되지 아니한 때에는 소속 公務員으로 하여금 그 物品을 保稅區域에 搬入하게 하고 그 運搬 및 保管에 所要된 費用을 搬入命令을 받은 者로부터 徵收할 수 있다.

④ 稅關長은 前項의 規定에 依하여 保稅區域

0042 0046

에 搬入된 物品이 前條第 3 項의
規定에 의하여 告示된 物品일 때
에는 지체없이 納稅의 告知를
하여야 하며 告示되지 아니한 物
品일 때에는 그 物品을 藏置場所
에 留置한다.

⑤ 保稅區域에 搬入된 物品 (前項
의 規定에 의하여 留置된 物
品을 포함한다)

이 關稅法에 規定된 藏置期
間을 경과한 것인 때에는
당해 物品을 藏置期間經過物品
處理法 第 3 條 6 號의 規定에

~17~ 0043

의한 物品으로 본다 이 경우
에 同法 第7條의 規定에 의
하여 賣却하는 物品에 대한
關稅, 特關稅 및 內國消費稅는
賣却한 날에 適用되는 法令과
그 당시의 物品의 性質 및
數量에 의하여 徵收한다.

⑥ 前5項의 規定의 適用을 받
는 物品은 關稅法의 規定에 의
한 外國物品으로 보며 第2項
및 前項의 規定에 의하여 關稅,
特關稅 및 內國消費稅를 徵收할 때
에는 당해 物品은 關稅法의 規定에

0044 0048

의한 輸入의 免許를 받은 것으로 본다.

⑦ 前條 第1項의 規定에 의한 讓渡의 申告 및 承認, 同條 第2項의 規定에 의한 檢査, 第1項의 規定에 依한 輸入申告, 檢査 및 免許는 당해 物品을 保稅區域에 搬入한 때에는 一括하여 할 수 있다.

第10條 (關稅의 課稅價格) ① 前條 第1項·第2項 또는 第5項의 경우에 讓受物品의 課稅價格은 關稅法의 規定에 불구하고 다음 各號의 時期에 去來되는 당해 物品과

~19~

0045 ~~0049~~

同種 또는 類似한 物品의 國內

通常價格에서 關稅 기타의 課徵

金 및 通常去來費用을 控除한 額

으로 한다.

1. 前條第1項의 경우에는 輸入申

告한 때

2. 前條第2項의 경우에는 讓受한때

3. 前條第5項의 경우에는 賣却한때

② 讓受物品이 合衆國軍隊가 所有하

는 物品으로서 大韓民國과 免稅機

關이 合意하여 處分한 것인 때에

0046

~~0050~~

는 前項의 規定에 불구하고 그
處分價格을 課稅價格으로 한다.
第11條 (特關稅의 課稅標準) 이 法
에 의하여 臨時特別關稅法을 適用하
는 경우에는 同法 第2條의 規定에
의한 用語의 定義는 다음 各號에
의한다.

1. 外國換對換라 함은 前條 第1項에
規定된 通常去來價格에서 關稅
와 內國消費稅와 正常費用을 控
除한 價格을 正常到着外貨價格으로
除한 數値를 말한다.

2. 正常到着外貨價格이라 함은 前條

0047
~321~
~0051~

~22~

에 規定된 關稅의 課稅價格을

이에 相應하는 同條第1項 各號

에 規定될때의 外國換對顧客賣渡率

로 除한 數値을 말한다.

3. 一定率이라함은 前條에 規定된

關稅의 課稅價格을 이에 相應하는

同條第1項各號에 規定될 때의

外國換對顧客賣渡率에 100分의30

을 加算한 率을 말한다.

4. 正常費用이라함은 前條에 規定

된 關稅의 課稅價格의 100分의

5를 말한다.

第12條 (內國消費稅의 課稅標準)

0048 ~~0052~~

第9條第2項 및 第5項의 規定에 의하여 徵收하는 物品稅와 石油類稅의 課稅標準은 第10條에 規定된 關稅의 課稅價格에 關稅相當額을 合算한 金額과 通常利潤(關稅의 課稅價格에 關稅相當額을 合算한 金額의 100分의 10)을 合算한 金額으로 한다

附 則

① (施行日) 이 法은 協定의 效力이 發生하는 날로 부터 施行한다

② (經過措置) 이 法 施行당시 合

~23~

0049 0053

合衆國軍隊, 그 公認調達機關, 非歲出
資金機關, 合衆國軍隊의 構成員, 軍屬
과 그들의 家族 또는 招請契約者가
大韓民國 내에 搬入한 物品 (당해
物品을 사용하여 製造된 物品 또는
그 副産物을 포함한다) 은 協定의
規定에 의하여 關稅, 特關稅 및 內
國消費稅의 免除를 받고 輸入한 物
品으로 본다 다만 당해 物品에 對
하여 이미 關稅 特關稅 및 內國消
費稅를 徵收하였거나 非免稅對象者에
게 讓渡된 후 關稅의 免除處分을
받은 것은 예외로 한다.

0054
0050

TEMPORARY SPECIAL LAW OF CUSTOMS AND OTHER LAWS FOR THE ENFORCEMENT OF THE AGREEMENT UNDER ARTICLE IV OF THE MUTUAL DEFENSE TREATY BETWEEN THE REPUBLIC OF KOREA AND THE UNITED STATES OF AMERICA, REGARDING FACILITIES AND AREAS AND THE STATUS OF UNITED STATES ARMED FORCES IN THE REPUBLIC OF KOREA

MINISTRY OF FINANCE

0051

TEMPORARY SPECIAL LAW OF CUSTOMS AND OTHER LAWS FOR THE ENFORCEMENT OF THE AGREEMENT UNDER ARTICLE IV OF THE MUTUAL DEFENSE TREATY BETWEEN THE REPUBLIC OF KOREA AND THE UNITED STATES OF AMERICA, REGARDING FACILITIES AND AREAS AND THE STATUS OF UNITED STATES ARMED FORCES IN THE REPUBLIC OF KOREA.

Law number : 1898, Promulgated March 3, 1967 ;

Article I. (Purpose) This is to prescribe exceptions of Customs Tariff, Temporary Special Customs Duty, Tonnage Tax, Liquor Tax, Petroleum Tax and Disposition of Unclaimed and Other Articles, in order to enforce the Agreement under Article IV of the Mutual Defense Treaty between the Republic of Korea and the United States of America, regarding facilities and areas and the status of United States Armed Forces in the Republic of Korea (hereafter referred as "the Agreement").

Article II. (Definition) ① "Military vessel" in this law means the vessel operated for official purposes as mentioned in Article X of the Agreement.

② "Military aircraft" in this law means the aircraft operated for official purposes as mentioned in Article X of the Agreement.

③ "Duty-free organization" in this law means the United States Armed Forces, their authorized procurement agencies and their non-appropriated fund organizations which are entitled to be free from customs duties and such other charges in accordance with the provisions of Article IX of the Agreement.

④ "Duty-free person" in this law means the members of the United States Armed Forces, the civilian component and their dependents as provided for in Article 1 of the Agreement, or the invited contractor as provided for in Article XV of the Agreement.

⑤ "Non-exempt person" in this law means the individual or the organization other than those described in above.

⑥ "Military procurement article" in this law means the article imported by any individual or any organization other than duty-free persons or duty-free organizations for the exclusive use by the United States Armed Forces, or is ultimately to be incorporated into articles and facilities used by such forces, and is certified by the proper authorities of the United States Armed Forces that delivery thereof is to be taken by such forces for the purposes above.

0052 ~~0056~~

Article III. (Collection of Tonnage Tax and Others) ① When any military vessel carries with the articles which are not entitled to be free from customs duties under the provisions of the Agreement, the ratio of the weight of such articles to that of its total cargo determines the dutiable sum on its tonnage under the provisions of Tonnage Tax Law and shall be collected as tonnage tax on such vessel.

② The preceding shall apply to the collection of entrance fee from any military vessel and aircraft entering from abroad by way of undesignated port of entry under the provisions of Customs Law.

Article IV. (Tonnage Tax Exemption Procedures) The master of any military vessel who desires his vessel to be exempted from tonnage tax, shall furnish the customs authorities with appropriate certification that his vessel falls under the categories of the military vessel under the provisions of this law.

Article V. (Clearance of Vessel and Aircraft) ① The provisions of Customs Law's articles 139 and 140, articles 142 through 147, articles 164 through 166 and article 248 shall not be applied to military vessels and military aircrafts. Provided, That the provisions regarding entry report, cargo manifest, list of vessel's supplies and stores, and passenger list provided by article 142 of the same law; landing report, cargo manifest, list of aircraft's supplies and stores, and passenger list provided by article 164 of the same law; departure report provided by article 143 of the same law, and take-off report provided by article 165 of the same law, shall be applied.

② When any military vessel or any military aircraft carries articles and passengers that are entitled to be free from customs examination under the provisions of Article IX of the Agreement, the captain of the vessel or the aircraft shall so declare, together with the weight of cargo in gross tons and number of passengers, in the manifest and the passenger list as mentioned in the preceding provision.

Article VI. (Post-Collection of Customs Duties and Other Such Charges) Unless military procurement articles which are free from customs duty, temporary special customs duty (hereafter referred to as special customs duty) and domestic excises (means commodity tax, liquor tax and petroleum tax, hereafter referred to with the same meaning) are delivered to the United States Armed Forces, or are incorporated into facilities and articles used by such forces, and are so certified by the proper authorities of the United States Armed Forces, within such period as the Collector of Customs shall designate, customs duty, special customs duty and domestic excises already exempted therefrom shall promptly be collected from the importer of such articles. In case the Collector of Customs confirms that such articles were destroyed by disaster or other unavoidable causes, the preceding shall not be applied.

— 2 —

0053 ~~0057~~

Article VII. (Manufacture of Duty-Free Articles and Others) ① When military procurement articles, which were exempted from customs duty, special customs duty and domestic excises pursuant to the provisions of Article IX of the Agreement, are desired to be repacked, sorted, segregated, combined, or otherwise manipulated, and processed, mixed with other articles, manufactured into other articles with the same, prior to the delivery to the United States Armed Forces and incorporated into facilities and articles used by such forces, such operations as specified above shall be done within the period and the place as the Collector of Customs shall designate.

② The Collector of Customs may request the importer of such articles mentioned in the preceding paragraph to produce necessary documents or dispatch customs officers to examine the articles in order to confirm that the articles are taken in and out of the designated place, manipulated, processed, mixed or manufactured pursuant to the preceding provisions.

Article VIII. (Limitation for Disposal of Duty-Free Articles) ① When any duty-free person or any person whose status has changed from a duty free basis, (or their designated agents), desires to dispose of in any manner, directly or indirectly, by sale, loan, or otherwise, any duty exempted articles, under the provisions of the Agreement, in the Republic of Korea, such person shall notify and obtain consent from the Collector of Customs.

② When the Collector of Customs considers it necessary in executing the provisions of the preceding, he may request such articles to be taken into customs bonded area (including any other place he may designate pursuant to paragraph 1, in article 55 of Customs Law, hereafter referred to with the same meaning), or designate customs officers to examine such articles.

③ In case the Minister of Finance, considers it necessary, shall publish a list of articles that may be disposed of under the preceding paragraph.

④ When any person disposes of such articles without obtaining the consent provided in paragraph 1, he shall be regarded as an importer of articles without import permit provided in article 114 of Customs Law. In this case he shall be subject to the penalties of article 198—2 and paragraph 2 of article 198—3 of the same law.

⑤ The provisions in articles 213 through 246 shall be applied.

Article IX. (Acquisition of Duty-Free Articles and Collection of Customs Duty and Others) ① When any non-exempt person desires to acquire, whether by sale, loan or otherwise, any articles (including articles manufactured with the same and their by-products), which were exempted from customs duties under the provisions of the Agreement, in the Republic of Korea, from any duty-free organization, any duty-free

— 3 —

0054 ~~0058~~

organization, any duty-free person or any person whose status has changed from a duty free basis, such acquisition shall be regarded as an importation; and such articles shall be subject to Customs Law, Temporary Special Customs Duty Law, Commodity Tax Law, Liquor Tax Law and Petroleum Tax Law.

② Any non-exempt person who acquires without obtaining import permit any article as mentioned in the preceding paragraph (except when articles are confiscated under any provision of Customs Law and taken under customs custody under the notice provision) shall be liable for the payment of customs duty, special customs duty and domestic excises which shall be levied against such articles according to laws and regulations in effect, in the quantity and condition of such articles at the time of acquisition. Provided, That when such articles are re-disposed of prior to the full payment of customs duty, special customs duty and domestic excises thereon, such taxes shall be collected from the owner or possessor of the articles only in case it is impossible to collect from otherwise liable person.

③ The Collector of Customs may order the acquirer or secondary acquirer, or the owner or the possessor of such articles as mentioned in the preceding paragraph, to take the same into customs bonded area within the period he shall designate. In case that the articles are not taken into the bonded area within the designated period, the Collector of Customs may have customs officers to take the same into the bonded area and collect the expenses for transportation and storage of such articles from the person liable.

④ In case that articles taken into the bonded area according to the preceding paragraph fall under the categories of the published list pursuant to the provisions prescribed in paragraph 3 of the preceding article, the Collector of Customs shall promptly issue and deliver the payment notice; when such articles do not fall under the categories specified above the articles shall be detained in the storage place.

⑤ When the storage period for such articles taken into the bonded area (including the articles detained under the preceding provisions) is terminated, such articles are subject to the provisions of paragraph 6 in article 3 for Disposition of Unclaimed and Other Articles. In this case customs duty, special customs duty and domestic excises on the articles offered for sale pursuant to the provisions in article 7 of the same law, shall be collected according to laws and regulations in effect, in the quantity and condition of the articles at the time of such disposal.

⑥ Articles subject to the preceding paragraph 5 shall be regarded as foreign merchandise under the provisions of Customs Law, and such articles on which customs duty, special customs duty and domestic excises have been collected pursuant to the provisions

— 4 —

0055 0059

of paragraph 2 and the preceding of this article shall be regarded as the merchandise duly imported under the provisions of Customs Law.

⑦ In case that articles taken into the bonded area and stored therein declartion and consent for disposal under the provisions in paragraph 1 of the preceding article, examination under paragraph 2 of the same article, import declaration, examination and permit under paragraph 1, shall be executed concurrently.

Article X. (Assessment Criteria of Customs Duty)　① Regardless of other provisions of Customs Law, the assessment criteria for acquired articles relating to paragraph 1, 2, and 5 of the preceding article, shall be the normal price of identical or similar articles on the domestic market-less customs duties, domestic excises and normal expenses at the time indicated in the following;

1. In case of goods under paragraph 1 of the preceding article, at the time when the import declaration is filed.

2. In case of goods under paragraph 2 of the preceding article, at the time when the same is acquired.

3. In case of goods under paragraph 5 of the preceding article, at the time of disposal.

② Regardless of the preceding, the assessment criteria for the acquired articles shall be the disposal price in case the same was owned by the United States Armed Forces and disposed according to agreement between the Republic of Korea and the duty-free organization.

Article XI. (Assessment Criteria for Special Customs Duty)　For the assessment of Temporary Special Customs Duty Law in conjunction with this law, article 2 of the same law shall be defined as follows;

1. The foreign exchange index means the result of the division of the normal price less customs duties, domestic excises and normal expenses with the normal arrival price expressed in foreign currency.

2. The normal arrival price expressed in foreign currency means the result of the division of the assessment criteria of customs duty prescribed in the preceding article with an appropriate foreign exchange selling rate of the Bank of Korea prevailing at the time indicated in respective sub-paragraph of paragraph 1 of the preceding article.

3. The fixed rate means the rate, foreign exchange selling rate of the Bank of Korea prevailing at the time indicated in respective sub-paragraph of paragraph 1 of the preceding article, plus 30%.

4. The normal expenses shall be 5% of the assessment criteria provided in the preceding article.

－ 5 －　　0056　　0060

Article XII. (Assessment Criteria of Domestic Excises) The assessment criteria for commodity tax and petroleum tax under the provisions of paragraph 2 and 5 of article IX shall be the same of customs duty's provided in article X, plus the amount of customs duty equivalent thereon with normal interest (10% of the assessment criteria of customs duty and customs duty equivalent).

Supplemental Provisions

① (The Effective Date) This law shall be effective from the date when the Agreement shall enter into force.

② (Transitional Disposition) In case the articles (including articles manufactured with the same and their byproducts) imported by the United States Armed Forces, their authorized procurement agencies, their nonappropriate fund organizations, members of the United States Armed Forces, the civilian component, their dependents, and the invited contractors prior to the time when this law enters into force; such articles shall be regarded as the articles duly imported and exempted from customs duty, special customs duty and domestic excises under the provisions of the Agreement. Provided, That customs duty, special customs duty and domestic excises already collected on such articles shall not be refunded; and customs duty, special customs duty and domestic excises shall not be assessed against such articles already exempted after transfer to a non-exempt person.

0057

0061

韓美軍隊地位協定에 따른 携帶品檢査事務 取扱要領

一. (目的)

　이 要領은 大韓民國과 아메리카合衆國間의 相互防衛條約 第4條에 依한 施設과 區域 及 大韓民國에서의 合衆國軍隊의 地位에 關한 協定 (以下 協定이라 한다) 第9條에 依하여 大韓民國에 出入하는 者의 携帶品通關節次를 規定함에 있다.

二. (檢査対象者)

　이 要領에 依하여 携帶品檢査를 받을 者는 다음과 같다.

1. 駐韓美軍人 及 軍屬으로서 休暇命令에 依하여 出入하는 者

2. 招請契約者 及 그의 雇傭員과 第三國雇傭員

~1~

0058

0062

3. 駐韓美軍人. 軍屬의 家族 및 上記 (2)項에 規定한

者의 家族.

三. (檢査要領)

1. 入國

가. 이 要領에서 定하는 檢査對象者의 携帶品檢査

는 美軍施設內 (*Passengers Terminal*) 또는

稅關檢査場에서 韓國稅關公務員이 行한다.

但. 美軍關係官이 立会할수 있다.

나. 稅關은 搭乘人員中 檢査對象者의 姓名. 階級.

所屬 및 最初入國年月日을 明記한 旅客名簿를 받

느다.

다. 檢査는 美軍側으로 하여금 檢査對象者 및 對象携

帶品을 指定된 檢査場所에 集合케 하고 開裝檢

査한다.

라. 開裝 및 再包裝은 稅關公務員의 指示에 依하여

~2~

0059 0063

旅行者가 開閉토록 한다.

　마. 檢査한后 通關이 許容된 物品은 稅關公務員의 檢査畢印을 捺印하여 通過시킨다.

　2. 出國

　　入國檢査要領에 準한다.

四. (通關要領)

　1. 入國

　가. 通關은 關稅法第35條第1項第9號의 規定에 依하며 協定 第9條第3項 但書의 規定에 依하여 免稅할 때에는 檢査對象者가 最初入國日로부터 6個月以內에 入國한다는 事實을 確認하여야 한다.

　나. 檢査對象者가 携帶入國하는 物品中 課稅對象物品은 現場通關하거나 또는 留置할수 있다.

　　留置할 때에는 留置調書를 作成하여 一通은

~3~

0060 ~~0064~~

旅行者에게 交付한다.

다. 檢査對象者가 携帶入國하는 物品中 關稅法 및 其他法令 違反으로 押收할때에는 그 要旨를 美軍 當局에 書面通告한다.

2. 出國

出國者의 身分에 相當한 物品에 對하여는 通關 을 許容하되 國外搬出에 關하여 特別히 規制된 物品의 搬出은 當該法에 依한 推薦 又는 許可받 은 分에 限한다.

五. (檢査畢印)

이 規定第3의 1項 (마)目에 指定한 携帶品檢査畢印 은 다음것으로 한다.

㉮ 丹型直徑 4 cm

内直徑 3 cm

㉯ AIRPORT 앞에는 비행장名

~4~

0061   0065

③ 船便入國時에는 AIR 를

SEA로 한다

5. (施行)

이 規定은 1967年 3月 16日 零時부터 施

行한다.

~5~

0062 ~~0066~~

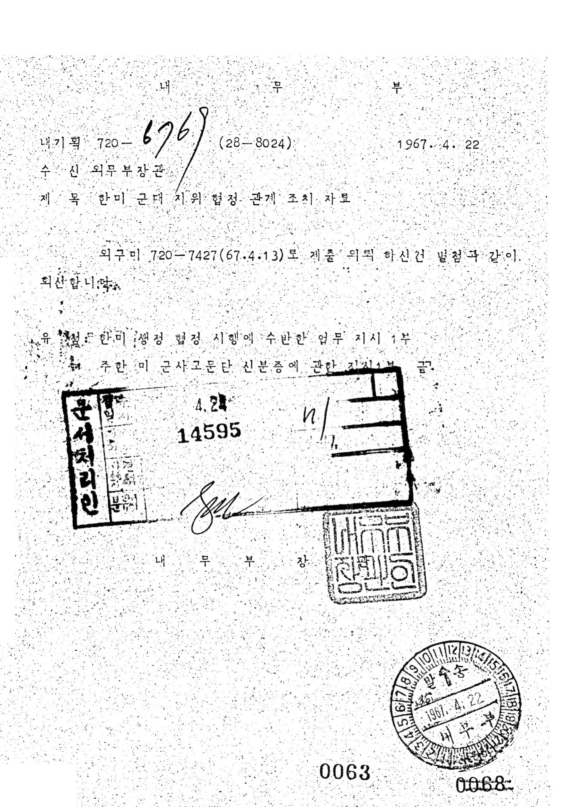

내　　무　　부

내기획 720-*6769*　(28-8024)　　　　　　　1967. 4. 22

수　신　외무부장관

제　목　한미 군대 지위협정 관계 조치 자료

　　　　외구미 720-7427(67.4.13)로 제출 의뢰 하신건 별첨과 같이
회신합니다.

　유 첨 : 한미 행정 협정 시행에 수반한 업무 지시 1부
　　　　　주한 미 군사고문단 신분증에 관한 지시 1부　　끝.

　　　　　　　　　　4.24
　　　　　　　　　　14595

내　무　부　장

0063

내　　무　　부

내치외 2068.4―　　　　　　　　　　　　　　　　　1967. 2.28.

수신　수신처 참조

제목　주한 미군사 고문단 신분증에 관한 지시

　　　　　대한민국과 아메리카 합중국간에 체결된 "주한 미군사 고문단
설치에 관한 협정 (1950.1.26)" 제4조에 의거 주한 미군사 고문단에
소속하는 단원(현역군인 군속)과 그 가족은 한국내에서 미국 대사관
의 일부로서 간주되며 이에 대등한 외교 특권이 부여되어 있음.
따라서 이들 주한 미군사 고문단원과 그 가족은 금반 발효된 한미
행정협정의 대상으로부터 제외되고 있음으로 (한미 행정협정 제1조
의거) 특히 다음각항에 유의하여 업무수행에 착오 없도록 할것

　　　1. 취급 요령

　　　　　가. 주한 미군사 고문단원과 그 가족 전원은 별첨 서식 (실제
크기― 가로 9.4센치, 세로 6.5센치, 황갈색)과 같은 특별 신분증
을 항시 휴대하고 있음으로 신분이 확인되면 외교관에 준하여 취급할것.

　　　　　나. 고문단원과 그 가족은 "주한 미국군사 고문단 신분증"
이외에 반드시 미군당국이 발행한 "군인 또는 군속 신분증" "미군 가족
신분증"이나 때로는 미국 정부가 발급한 여권을 소지하고 있음으로
해당자를 확인시 반드시 군대 가족 신분증 또는 여권의 번호와 사진을
대조 할것

　　　　　다. 주한 미군 고문단원 또는 그 가족으로 신분이 확인된자
에 대하여는 특별 신분증에 명시된바와 같이 다음사항에 유의하여야
한다.

　　　　　　　　　　2 ― 1　　　　　　　　0064

　　　　　　　　　　　　　　　　~~0069~~

  (1) 체포, 수색 또는 구금할수 없다.

  (2) 어떤 문서도 압수 할수 없다.

  (3) 신분확인에 필요한 이외의 검문을 할수 없다

  라. 주한 미군사 고문단원 또는 그 가족이 중대한 현행범을
법하였거나 사건과 관련되였을시는 인적사항 확인은 물론이며 보고
작성에 필요한 최소한의 집문을 할수 있다. 이런 경우에는 치안국
의사과로 사건개요를 직보하고 조치에 대한 지시를 받어야 한다

  2. 행정사항

  가. 본건 시행에 필요한 자체 교양을 철저히 실시하여 전
경찰관에게 취급요령을 주지케 하여 업무 수행의 정확을 기할것

  나. 서식은 제한된 수량을 미군사 고문단 당국으로부터 인수
한것임으로 미군사 고문단 주둔 지역 및 미군부대 주둔 지역 경찰관서
에 우선 배부하여 첨부케 할것.

첨부 서식 배정표 1부. 끝

        의명
          치 안 국 장

수신처
    나 1-11, 사 2, 바 6.8.9.11.12

            2 - 2

                              0065 ~~0070~~

주한 미군사 고문단 신분확인 배부표

구분 / 각시도	본국 과	학교	각서	지파출소	주둔지역 지파출소	계
치안국	(외사·수사) (경무·보·경비 수·정) 5 경전 5					10
서 울	2	2	13	60		67
부 산	2	2	6		4	14
경 기	2	2	20	70		94
강 원	2	2	16	50		70
충 북	2	2	10		1	15
충 남	2	2	16		14	34
전 북	2	2	13		4	21
전 남	2	2	23		2	29
경 북	2	2	27		6	37
경 남	2	2	20		9	33
제 주	1	2	2		1	6
계	31	22	166	180	41	440

0066 0071

嬌正交

내　　무　　부

내치외 2066.4 -

내친수 821 수신처 참조

참조　경찰국장

1967.　2.　6.

제목　한·미해정 협정 시행에 수반한 업무지시

　　　1967. 2.9 효력을 발생하게 되는 " 대한민국과 아메리카 합중국간
의 상호 방위 조약 제4조에 의한 시설과 구역 및 대한민국에서의 합중국
군대의 지휘에 관한 협정의 시행에 수반하여 경찰 업무중 외사 및 수사활동
에 관한 다음 각 유의 사항을 지시하니 시행에 만전을 기할것.

　　　본 협정 시행에 수반한 형사특별법을 국회에서 심의중에 있으며
개정되는 대로 법 및 시행령이 추후 시달될 예정임.　끝.

　　　내　　무　　부　　장　　관

수신처
　나 1 - 11　바 6 - 12　사 2.4

1 . 施設과 区域의 表識

警察官은 優先 管内에 所在하는 美合衆国軍隊의 施設과 区域에 対해서는 그 所在를 周知하고 있어야 될것이다

合衆国軍隊가 使用하는 施設과 区域의 境界線에는 누구나 認定될수있는 明白한 方法으로 合衆国軍隊가 管理하는 施設과 区域이라는 表識가 明示될것이며 이러한 施設과 区域은 次后 韓·美合同委員会의 議決을 거처 公表될것이며 関係 韓国政府機関에게도 通報될것임

2 . 身分証明書

가 . 合衆国軍隊要員은 行政協定第8条第3項(가)(나)에 依하여 身分証明書를 所持 携帯하여야하며 大韓民国의 関係 当局의 要求가 있으면 提示하게 되여있음 身分証明書의 様式은 아직 確定되지 않었으나 合衆国軍隊의 構成員들은 英文身分証明書以外에 韓·英国語로된 行政協定遵守事項카드를 携帯하고있음

나 . 行政協定第15条第3項에 規定되어있는 招請契約者에 対해서도 그 身分을 証明될수있는 文書가 交付될것임

다 . 合衆国軍人의 身分으로서 駐韓美軍事顧問団(KMAAG)에 所属하는 団員과 그家族은 行政協定第1条(가)에 依하여 行政協定適用対象으로부터 除外하기로 規定되여 있으며 1950.1.26 韓·美間에 締結된 〃駐韓美軍事顧問団設置에 関한 協定〃第4条에 依拠 韓国内에서 美国大使舘의 一部로서 看做되여 있으며 이에 対等한 外交特権

— / —　　　0068　~~0073~~

이 賦与되어 있으므로 警察은 一般的인 身分確認(特別身分証明書가 韓美両国語로 次后発給될것임) 以外에는 警察権을 行使 될수없음

顧問団員은 大部分現役軍人으로서 軍服을 着用하고 있으므로 一般美国軍人과 差誤를 이르키기 쉬우므로 特히 留意될것

　라. 行政協定合意議事録 才 8 条 才 1 項 에 依하여 合衆国軍隊의 法令執行機関員은 内務部例規 才 145号(62.1.31) 別紙 才 1号 書式과 같은 駐韓美軍憲兵身分証을 公務執行中 携帶하기로 되어있음 따라서 正服·私服着用与否에 拘碍없이 本身分証을 提示하는 者에 対하여는 法執行業務에 関하여 모두 可能한 協調를 提供될것

　3. 裁判権의 抛棄

　가. 合衆国側의 裁判権行使는 原則的으로 韓国側이 特定事件에 対해 裁判権을 行使함이 特히 重要하다고 決定을하여 法務部長官이 書面으로(韓国側이 犯罪発生을 通告받았거나 또는 認知한 時로부터) 15日以内나 또는 더短期間内에 合衆国側에 通告하지 않는限 合衆国側이 行使하게된다

　나. 韓国側이 裁判権을 行使함이 特히 重要하다고 認定되는 範囲는 原則的으로

　　① 大韓民国의 安全에 関한 犯罪

　　② 韓国人에 対한 殺人·致死·強盗·強姦

　　③ 前記各犯罪의 未遂또는 共犯等으로 되여있다

　다. 裁判権行使는 法務部長官의 書面要請이 必要하며 発

0069　0074

生또는 認知后 1 5日以内에 處理되어야 함으로 檢察로서는

該当 檢察과 上部機関에 迅速한 報告를 履行하며 指示를 받

아야 한다

4. 搜査要領

가. 合衆国軍隊要員(協定第1條 (가) 合衆国軍隊의 構成員

(나) 軍属 (다) 家族을 包含한다)의 逮捕(施設또는 区域外)

合衆国軍隊가 使用하는 施設또는 区域外에서의 韓国의 国内

法令을 違反하는 境遇 合衆国軍隊要員을 逮捕하는 權限은

韓国側과 合衆国側과의 双方에 認定되어있음

이런 境遇에는 逮捕現場에 臨한 韓美両側의 警察官의 相

互協調下에 犯人逮捕를 執行하여야 될 것임

나. 合衆国軍隊要員의 逮捕(施設또는 区域内)

① 合衆国軍隊가 使用하는 施設또는 区域内에있는

合衆国軍隊要員또는 韓国人被疑者를 韓国警察이 逮捕될 境遇

는 다음과 같은 節次에 依해서 執行한다

② 被疑者가 韓国人인 境遇에는 警察官은 営門警備

에 当하고 있는 美軍憲兵또는 警備兵에게 自己의 身分과

被疑者人的事項을 提示하고 逮捕를 要請하면 警察官은 美軍側

에 依해 憲兵隊와 警備隊에 案内되어 引継하게된다 営内에서

의 美軍側이 被疑者를 逮捕될時 韓国警察官은 美軍側과 同伴

하지 못하며 被疑者引継引受는 営門限界点에서 執行한다

③ 被疑者가 美国人또는 其他 外国人인 境遇는 韓

国警察은 逮捕要請書類와 같이 美軍側 法拘監에게 案内된后

-3-

0070 0075 0074

適切한 措置의 決定을 받어 執行한다.

다. 合衆國軍隊成員의 逮捕要請

合衆國側이 韓國警察에게 合衆國軍隊成員의 逮捕를 要請하는 事例는 比較的 드물것으로 思料되나 이런 境遇에는 隣近에 所在하고 있는 美軍憲兵隊長에 依해 警察署長에게 要請될것이며 原則的으로 公文을 使用될것이다. 이런 要請에는 積極 協調하며 被疑者逮捕에 努力하여 逮捕后 身병는 所定節次에 依해 引渡한다.

라. 身병引渡

① 身병引渡는 相互引渡原則에 入閣하여 施行하게 되어 있으므로 韓國側으르서는 合衆國側에 裁判權이 있는 者를 逮捕하였을 時는 遲滯없이 合衆國側에 通報하여 身병을 引渡하여야하나 事前에 반드시 檢察의 指導를 받어 實施될것.

② 이런 境遇 身병引渡는 被疑者의 所屬部隊에 拘傳됨이없이 隣近 美軍憲兵隊長또는 美軍憲兵司令官이 指定한 引受官에게 引渡하여야 한다.

③ 身병引渡時에는 (別表第1号) 樣式에 依한 身병引継書를 2通 作成하여 引継引受官의 署名捺印后 各各 1通 保管하며 寫本 2部를 作成하여 警察局長및 治安局長에게 各各 1通을 送付될것.

④ 이러한 身병引渡는 逮捕된 者가 合衆國軍隊의 成員을 確認한 后에 이루워져야한다. 따라서 逮捕된者가 身分証明書를 携帶치 않고 또提示도 하지않으며 그身分는 確認될

0071 0076

資料가 없을때는 一般行政協定에 規定된 身分을 明確치않은 一般外國人으로 看做하여 取扱한다

　　　마·合衆國軍隊의 財産에 対한 押收·搜索

　　　合衆國軍隊가 使用하는 施設또는 区域內에서의 押收·搜索에 対한 要請은 隣近의 憲兵隊長또는 対象과 関係있는 指揮官에 対해 本指示第4条나項에 準하여 実施한다

　　　바·警察官職務執行法의 適用

　　　①韓國警察官은 合衆國軍隊要員에 対하여 警察官職務執行法에 規定된 權限을 行使힐수있다

　　따라서 不審檢問(第2条) 保護措置(第3条) 犯罪의豫防과 制止(第5条) 武器의使用(第7条)等의 措置를 取힐수있다

　　　②合衆國軍隊要員을 逮捕時 手갑또는 捜察権等의 使用도 힐수 있으며 被疑者를 美軍에게 引渡힐 時까지의 処遇도 國內人과 同等히 取扱함이 마하나 愼重을 期함을 要함

　　5·其　他

　　　가·協定發効時(1967.2.9 0時)次后 發生한 合衆國軍隊要員의 犯罪發生報告는 此히 施行하고있는 節次에 準하되 特히 被疑者의 人的事項(英文으로 正確한 姓名·所属部隊名·階級·軍番·職位等)을 正確히 記錄하여 直報하여야 한다

0072　0077

─6─

나. 犯罪發生年月日時 및 發生通報接受日時는 裁判權抛棄·
要求期限의 起算点이 됨으로 正確히 期하여야하며 迅速 報告
되어야 한다

다. 本指示는 協定施行에 따른 特別法 其他 關係法規 等
이 制定될때까지 暫定實施되는것이며 協定과 關聯된 諸般業務
處理는 恒常 遲滯없이 管轄檢察当局의 指揮를 받어 執行될것

라. 本件施行은 外務·搜査·情報및 其他 各機能 相互間의
緊密한 協調가 切實히 要求됨으로 隨時 內部協調를하여 施行에
萬全을 期할것

0073

0078

逮捕被疑者引繼書

哥属.

(A) 被疑者	(1) 姓名		(2) 階級職業		(3) 軍番	
	(4) 所屬部隊 又는住所		(5) 年令	(6) 性別	(7) 國籍	

(B) 被疑事項	罪名 (8) 違反事項		犯行年月 日時 (9)		(10) 犯行場所	
	(11) 被疑事實要旨					
	(12) 逮捕事由					
	(13) 證拠物		(14) 證人姓名 住所			

(C) 逮捕事項	(15) 逮捕者		(16) 所屬部隊 官署名		(17) 留置場所	
	(18) 逮捕年月 日時		(19) 逮捕場所			
(D) 引繼	(20) 引繼年月 日時		(21) 引渡官 姓名捺印			印
	(22) 官職帶級		(23) 軍番		(24) 所屬部隊 官署	

(E) 引受	I hereby acknowledge receipt of the above mentioned person and certify that I am authorized to receive the said person into my custody. 本官은 上記 被疑者를 正히 引受하였음을 確認하며 同時에 被疑者引受官임을 證明함					
	(25) 官職階級		(26) 軍番		(27) 所屬部隊 官署名	
	(28) 引受年月 日時		(29) 引受官姓名		(30) 署名	
	(31) 保管物品		(32) 備考			

—7—

0074 0079

354 주한미군지위협정(SOFA) 서명 및 발효 15

8

作成時注意事項

本引継書는 原本 2 通를 作成하여 引継官과 引受官이 各各 1 通式

保管한다.

A 被疑者

  ① 英字姓名은 大文字로 韓國名은 漢字를 使用

  ② 美國軍隊構成員은 階級을 其他는 職位

  ③ 美國軍人 · 軍屬인 境遇만 記載

  ④ 美國人軍屬은 部隊名을 其他는 住所또는 宵署名

  ⑤ 年令   ⑥ 性別   ⑦ 國籍

B 被疑事実

  ⑧ 罪名 · 違反条項   ⑨ 年月日時는 正確히

  ⑩ 犯行場所   ⑪ 被疑事実의 概要   ⑫ 被疑者를 犯法者로 認定한 根拠

  ⑬ 押収証拠物의 名称 · 数量   ⑭ 証人의 姓名 · 住所

C 逮捕事項

  ⑮ A ― ① 게 準함   ⑯ A ― ④ 게 準함   ⑰ 留置場所

  ⑱ B ― 9 게 準함   ⑲ 逮捕場所

D 引 継

  ⑳ B ― 9 게 準함   ㉑ 捺印을 要함   ㉒ A ― 2 게 準함

  ㉓ A ― 3 게 準함   ㉔ A ― 4 게 準함

E 引 受

  ㉕ A ― 2 게 準함   ㉖ A ― 3 게 準함   ㉗ A ― 4 게 準함

  ㉘ B ― 9 게 〃   ㉙ A ― 1 게 〃   ㉚ 署名을 要함

  ㉛ 被疑者로부터 保管한 金品의 種類 · 数量

  ㉜ 其他參考事項

0075 ~~0080~~

INSTRUCTIONS

This form after completion in duplicate, shall be retained by the releasing and the receiving agencies.

A. Arrested Person; 1-For English name use the capitol letters and Chinese characters for Korean; 2-For US Armed Forces personnel enter rank for other persons enter occupation; 3-Applicable only to the US Armed Forces personnel; 4-For US Armed Forces personnel enter organization, and for others enter address or title of the office; 5-Age; 6-Sex; 7-Nationality.

B. Offense: 8-Name of offense; 9-Accurate year, month, date and time; 10-place of offense; 11-Summary of offense; 12-Reason for arrest; 13-Enter the name & quantity of the confiscated evidence if there is any; 14-Name and address of the witness.

C. Arrest Detail: 15-Same as A1; 16-Same as A4; 17-Place of detention; 18-same as B9; 19-Location of arrest made.

D. Delivery: 20-Same as B-9; 21-ROK side use seal; 22-Same as A3; 23-Same as A3; 24-Same as A4

E. Receiving; 25-Same as A2; 26-Same as A3; 27-Same as A4; 28-Same as B9; 29-Same as A1; 30-US side use signature; 31-List all personal property turned over to the receiving officer; 32-Enter other reference and pertinent information.

-9-

0076

0081

교   통   부

교기획720-4*93   1967.4.25

수신   외무부장관

제목   한,미군대지위협정 관계조치자료 제출

1. 외구미720 - 7427(1967,4,13)에대한 회신입니다.

2. 당부에 해당사항 없습니다. 끝

교   통   부   장   관

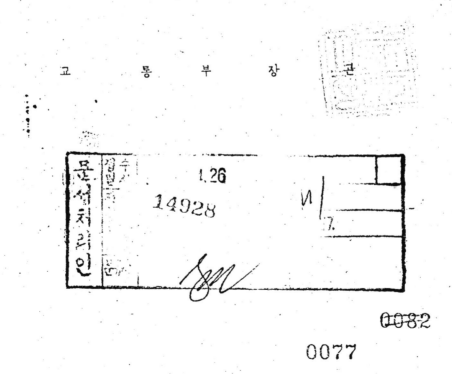

1.26
14928

0082
0077

국　　　방　　　부

국기정 911 - *196*　　　　　　　　　　　　　1967. 4 . 26

수신　외무부장관

제목　한, 미군대 지위협정 관계 조치자료

　　　1. 외구미　720 - 7427 (67.4.13)을　참조　바
랍니다.

　　　2. 한, 미군대 지위 협정 제 29 조　2 항에 따른
당부의 입법 조치 사항을 별첨과 여히 송부합니다.

유첨 : 법률 제 1905 호　1 부　　　끝

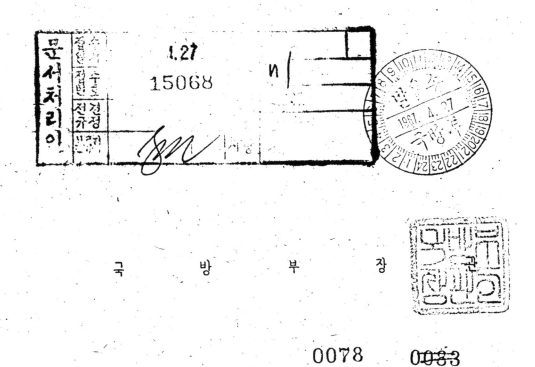

국　　방　　부　　장

0078　　0083

法律第1,905号　　　　　　　　　1967. 3. 3. 公布

大韓民國과 아메리카合衆國間의 相互防衛條約 第4條에 의한 施設과 區域및 大韓民國에 있어서의 合衆國軍隊의 地位에 관한 協定의 施行에 따른 **國家 및 地方自治団体의 財産의 管理와 処分에 관한 法律(案)**

第1條 (目的) 이 法은 大韓民國과 아메리카合衆國間의 相互防衛條約第4條에 의한 施設과 區域 및 大韓民國에 있어서의 合衆國軍隊의 地位에 관한 協定(이하 "協定"이라 한다)을 施行함에 있어서 아메리카合衆國(이하 "合衆國"이라 한다)의 軍隊에 供與하는 國家 및 地方自治団体의 財産의 管理와 処分에 관한 特例를 規定함을 目的으로 한다.

第2條 (供與決定의 通報 및 協議)
① 協定 第2條의 規定에 의하여 國家 또는 地方自治団体의 財産을 合衆國軍隊에 供與하기로 決定된 때에는 國防部長官은 財務部長官 및 당해 財産의 管理庁의 長 또는 地方自治団体의 長에게 이를 通報하고, 供與에 필요한 措置를 協議하여야 한다.

第3條 (供與財産의 管理) 協定 第2條의 規定에 의하여 合衆國 軍隊에 供與한 國家 또는 地方自治団体의 財産은 그 供與期間중에도 國防部長官이 이를 管理한다.

—3—　　　　0079 0081

才4条（管理換） ①国有財産의 管理庁은 才2条의 規定에 의한 国防部長官의 통보를 받은 때에는 지체없이 당해 財産을 国防部長官에게 移管（이하 ◦管理換◦이라 한다）하여야 한다.

②前項의 規定에 의한 管理換은 国有財産法 才14条의 規定에 불구하고 이를 無償으로 한다.

才5条（無償貸与） ①地方自治団體의 長은 才2条의 規定에 의한 国防部長官의 통보를 받은 때에는 지체없이 당해 財産을 国防部에 貸与하여야 한다.

②前項의 規定에 의한 地方自治団體의 財産의 貸与는 이를 無償으로 한다.

才6条（返還） ①才3条의 規定에 의하여 国防部長官이 管理하는 国家 또는 地方自治団體의 財産으로서 合衆国으로 부터 再使用한다는 留保条件없이 大韓民国에 返還된 때에는 国防部長官은 당해 財産의 原管理庁 또는 地方自治団體에 이를 管理換 또는 返還하여야 한다. 다만, 国防部長官은 軍事上의 目的을 爲하여 필요하다고 인정할 때에는 당해 財産의 原管理庁의 長과 財務部長官 또는 地方自治団體의 長과 協議하여 그 財産을 계속 管理할 수 있다.

②国防部長官은 前項의 規定에 의하여 国家 또는 地方自治団體의 財産을 管理換 또는 返還하는 때에는 原状回復의 責任을 지지 아니한다.

0080
~~0085~~

—4—

③ 第4條第2項의 規定은 第1項의 管理換에 이를 準用한다·

第7條 (施行令) 이 法 施行에 관하여 필요한 事項은 大統領令으로 정한다·

                    附   則

① (施行日) 이 法은 協定의 效力이 發生하는날로 부터 施行한다·

② (經過措置) 이 法 施行당시 合衆國軍隊가 使用하고 있는 國家 또는 地方自治團體의 財産은 이 法에 의하여 管理換 또는 讓與된 것으로 보고 이 法 施行日로 부터 90日이내에 第4條 및 第5條의 規定에 의한 節次를 밟아야 한다·

0081

—5—   0080   0086

체   신   부

체기획 720- 0006   1967.5.15

수신   외무부장관

참조. 구미국장

제목   한미간군대 지위협정 관계 조치자료 송부

    1. 외구미 720-7420(67.4.13)관련

    2. 위 관련문서로 요청한 자료를 별첨 송부합니다

첨부: 1. 미군사우체국과 간의 협정문(영문) 1부

    2. 한미간 미합중국 군대지위 협정에 따르는 우편물 취급요명(영문)1부. 끝.

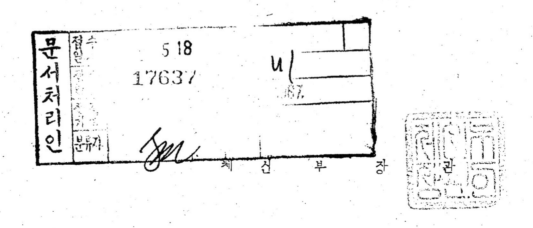

5 18
17637

체   신   부   장

0082

~~0087~~

1967. 5. 15

DEPARTMENT OF THE ARMY
HEADQUARTERS, EIGHTH UNITED STATES ARMY
APO SAN FRANCISCO 96301

EAAG-AM   3 August 1~~

SUBJECT: Implementation of the Military Post Office Article agreed
upon at the 40th Session of the SOFA Negotiations held on
January 24th, 1964.

TO: Mr. Seung Rok Shon
         Director of Posts
         Ministry of Communications
         Republic of Korea
         Seoul, Korea

Dear Mr. Shon,

       Reference is made to your letter, PB 1614-1, of July 6, 1965.

       I have reviewed your draft concerning the details of mail exchange
and in behalf of this headquarters find it most acceptable.

                                   Sincerely yours,

                                   RAYMOND G. MAYER
                                   Captain, AGC
Incl   Staff Postal Officer
Draft Implementation of
the Military Post Office
Article agreed on in the
40th session of SOFA

DATE Seoul, J... 6th 1965

...manding Officer
... the Eighth United
...ates Army in Korea,
.../o Postmaster APO 301,
...anf ...if, U.S.A.

...n: Postmaster, APO 301.

Subject: Implementation of the Military Post Office Article agree...
upon at the 40th session of the SOFA negotiation held on
January 24th, 1964.

.. Sir,

The attached, you will find a copy of draft concerning the .
...rinciple of detailed execution for the mail exchange under the
...greement referred in the subject.

Your immediate attention and any opinions or suggestions on
...is matter will be highly appreciated.

Sincerely yours,

Seung Rok Shon
Director General of Posts

0084

0083

PRINCIPLE OF MAIL EXCHANGE

In handling

(1) mails originated from the U.S.Military Post Office, the *senders* of which are priviledged to use the channel of the U.S.Military *Post* Office while the addressees residing or having their addresses in *Korea* are not entitled to use the Military addresses; or

(2) mails originated from post offices of Korea and intended for members of the U.S.Military Forces using the authorised U.S.Military Forces addresses while the senders are priviledged to use the channel of the U.S.Military Post Office (mails defined in the column 1 and 2 will be expressed hereunder simply as Military Mail),

under the Agreement between the Government of the Republic of Korea and the Government of the United States of America regarding the status of the United States Forces,

The execution of mail exchange will be regulated by:

 - The Universal Postal Convention
 - The parcel post agreement between the Republic of Korea *and the* United States of America
 - The Insured Parcel Post Agreement between the Republic of *Korea* and the United States of America

which are in force at the present between the Republic of Korea and the United States of America,

except the mails shown hereunder with the handling conditions *specified*

#=#=#=#=#=#=#=#=#=#=#=#

1. Category of mails

The term Military Mail applies to correspondence and parcel post and the former is again consisted of the following items.

(a) Letters
(b) Single and Reply-paid postcards
(c) Printed papers
(d) Small packets

0090
0085

2. Correspondence contained items subject to customs control of Korea.

Letter post contained items subject to customs duty will be excluded from the exchange.

3. Special handling

Special handling for Military Mail is limited to the following fields.

(a) Registration (limited only to letter post).

(b) Insurance (limited to parcel post).

(c) Advice of delivery (limited only to the advice of delivery to be forwarded by ordinary mail.... not by air or telegraphs. This service is limited to registered mail and insured parcel).

4. Special service

(a) Request of Enquiry (investigation or tracing for irregularity and lost items) on Military Mail will be accepted only when the addressee or the addressor asks the tracing to be transacted through ordinary mail, not by air nor by telegraphs. This service is limited only to registered items and insured parcels.

(b) Request of information, withdrawal from the post and alteration of address will not be accepted.

5. Postage fees

Postage fees applicable for Military Mail posting at any post offices of Korea will be as follows. The charges set out in this list are liable to change according to the inland postage rate revision of Korea.

CATEGORY	UNIT OF WEIGHT	CHARGE	LIMITS OF WEIGHT
		(won)	
(a) Letters			
first weight step	20 grams	4	6 kg
each succeeding step	20 grams	4	
(b) Postcards			
Single	/	2	/
Reply-paid	/	4	/
(c) Printed papers			
(1) A copy or a daily portion of news papers and periodicals			

0086

0091

which are published more than [illegible]
posted by the publisher.

first weight step	100 grams	4	[illegible]
each succeeding step	100 grams	40	

(2) News papers and periodicals more than a copy or a daily portion.

first weight step	100 grams	1	1.2 kg
each succeeding step	100 grams		

(3) The other printed papers

first weight step	100 grams	2	1.2 kg
each succeeding step	100 grams		

(d) Small packets

first weight step	100 grams	2	1.2 kg
each succeeding step	100 grams	2	

(e) Parcel Posts

first weight step	4 kg	30	6 kg
up to 6 kg	/	40	

6. Post office of Korea where they exchange Military Mail.

(a) Office of Exchange.

- Seoul International Post Office
- Inchon Post Office
- Pusan Post Office
- Taegu Post Office
- Kwangju Post Office
- Taejon Post Office
- Jaeju Post Office

The post offices mentioned above exchange mails directly with the nearby U.S. Military Post Offices in Korea.

(b) Posting of mails

Military Mail may be posted at any post offices in Korea.

7. Definition of the personnel authorized to use the channel of the U.S. Military Post Office.

   (a) Members of the United States Armed Forces, the civilian components and their dependents (the U.N. Forces included).

   (b) Staffs of the United States Government and their dependents accorded with the priviledges for use of the U.S. Military Post Address.

8. Customs control.

   (a) Small packets, parcel posts and printed papers, posted at post offices of Korea and addressed to the U.S. Military Post Offices in the territory of the Republic of Korea will not subject to customs inspection of Korea.

   (b) Small packets, parcel posts and printed papers contained items subject to customs control, originated from the U.S. Military Post Office and addressed to any exchange post offices of Korea are liable to customs duty or other restriction according to the Customs Law of Korea.

9. Terminal credits of parcel posts.

   Terminal credits concerned for the parcel posts addressed to the U.S. Military Post Office will not be shown on Parcel Bill while it is necessary for the parcels to be redirected or returned.

10. Exceptional handling.

    Standing operational procedure for the foreign mails of Korea may be applicable for the items which were not specified above.

0088
0083

MINISTRY OF COMM...

SEOUL KOR...

HOC/1614.1

5 May 1967

Commanding Officer
Hqs., the Eighth United States Army
in Korea,
c/o Postmaster APO 301,
San Francisco, California

Dear Sir,

In reference to our letter HOC/1614-116) dated July 6, 1965 concerning the mail exchange between our two countries in accordance with the Agreement regarding facilities and areas and status of the United States Armed Forces in the Republic of Korea, I have the honor to inform you the following alterations in mail handling procedure by our post office.

1. The exchange office for the U.S. military mails will be only Seoul International Post Office and Busan Post Office for the time being.

2. Parcel post service shall be limited only to the ordinary parcel except the insured parcel addressed to the post office of Korea accepted and sent from the U.S. military post office.

3. Parcel posts and insured parcels mentioned in the paragraph 2 above shall be subject to the customs inspection and customs clearance charge, 44 won, to be collected from the addressee for each parcel forwarded to the U.S. military post office from our post offices. The customs clearance charge and other duties imposed by the customs shall be collected from the addressee for the items forwarded to our post offices from the U.S. military post office.

4. Registered monetary and commodity items shall not be accepted.

0094

0089

5. Items addressed to the addressees who have changed their addresses are redirected to the place of new destination. In case the address of items despatched to the U.S. military post office from our post office is unknown, those should be returned to sender. The redirection charge and return charge shall be collected separately according to the inland postage rate. The redirection charge or return charge of registered mails is 13 won.

The redirection charge or return charge of parcel is as follows:

Limit of weight	Charge
4 kg	60 won
6 kg	80 won

6. Indemnity

a. When registered article is lost ------------------ 200 won
b. When insured parcel or ordinary parcel is lost--- 500 won
c. The actual loss below 200 won in case of registered mails and below 500 won in case of parcel post shall be compensated in its market price.
d. The indemnity between Korean post office and U.S. military post office is settled in Korean currency.

7. Small packet in ordinary mails except items forwarded to our post office from the U.S. military post office shall not be accepted. These items shall be subject to customs clearance duty and tax imposed; customs clearance charge 53 won to be collected form the addressee.

Sincerely yours,

Seung Rok Shon
Director General of Posts

0095

0090

2. 협정문 배도

0091

대 법 원

기획제 86 호   1966. 7. 18.

수신 외무부장관   귀하

제목 한미행정협정 관계자료 송부 의퇴

　'66. 7. 9. 자토 체결된 " 대한민국과 미합중국간의 주한합중국
군대의 지위에 관한 협정 " 과 동합의의사톡 및 그 부속문서 (양
해각서등) 일체는 동협정 발효후, 사법부 산하의 각급법원의 민형사
재판사건면에 직접 간접으토 관계가 있을 것이므토, 그에 대비코자
하오니, 동책자를 200 부만 조속히 보내 주시기 바랍니다. 끝.

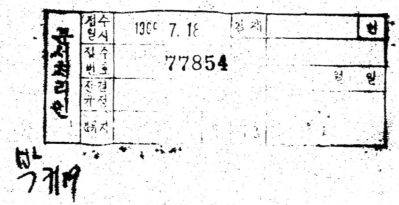

법 원 행 정 처 장   전

6106

0092

受領함

韓美行政協定 條約文
5巻

조히 受領함

1966. 7. 21.

財務部稅制局

李鍾奎

「領收証」

合衆 행정협정 조약집 2권

한 부를 正히 領收함

1966. 7. 21

통상진흥과 ㉓

0108

0094

노　　　동　　　청

노정노 1853 - 이○22 - 4295　　　　　　　1966. 7. 23.

수신　외무부장관

참조　구미국 미주과장

제목　한미행정 협정 유인물 배부 요청.

　　　당청의 업무수행상 필요하오니 귀부에서 간행하는 한미행정
협정서 유인물의 여분이 있으시면 다음과 같이 배부하여 주시기 바랍
니다.

　　　1.　배부요청수량 : 400부.

　　　2.　사용처　　가.　노동청 비치용
　　　　　　　　　　나.　전매외국기관 노동조합 및 동산하 지부분회
　　　　　　　　　　다.　미8군 예하 한국인 하청업체. 끝.

노　　동　　청　　　　　장

0109
0095

법 무 부

법무법 741 - 17157 (22- 4072)   1966 . 8 . 1 .

수신   외무부장관

참조   방교국장

제목   조약문 송부 의뢰

　　　　 당부 (관하 출입국사무소 및 동출장소 포함) 업무
수행에 필요한 " 대한민국과 아메리카합중국간의 상호방위
조약 제 4 조에 의한 시설과 구역 및 대한민국에서의 합중
국군대의 지위에 관한 협정 및 동부속문서 " 50부를 송부
의뢰 하오니 선처하여 주심을 바랍니다 · 끝

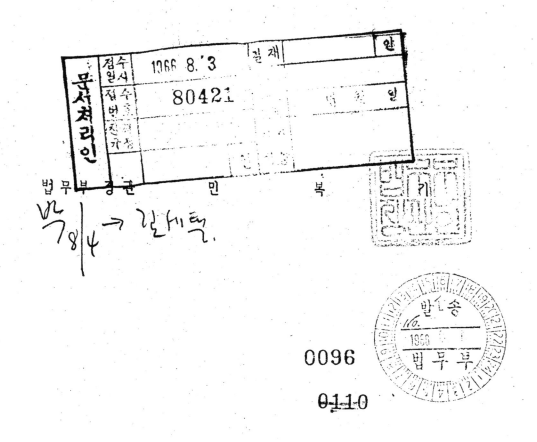

0096

~~0110~~

내   무   부

내치외 2068.4-13687   1966. 8. 3.

수 신 외무부 장관

제 목 자료수집 협조 의뢰

　　1. 67년도 한 미 행정협정 발효에 따라 당부 산하 외사관계
신무자들의 교양을 위하여 귀부에서 반행되는 <u>한미 행정 협정에 관한
해선서</u>를 요청하오니 다음 사항에 의거 송부하여 주시기 바랍니다.

　　2. 필요사항 (내역)

　　　가. 각국 , 서 , 배부용 11개국   185개서 (218) 부

　　　나. 교재용, 경찰전문학교, 서울분교 (50)부

　　　　　각도경찰학교 (11 개학교)   220부   계270부

　　　다. 신무자용 (치안국 각과) 20부   총계 508부.

　　　　　　　　　　　　　　　　　　　　　　　　　　　　끝

문서처리인

1966. 8. 4
80623

내   무   부

0111
0097

한·미국 간의 상호방위조약 제4조에 의한 시설과 구역 및 한국에서의 미국군대의 지위에 관한 협정(SOFA)
전59권. 1966.7.9 서울에서 서명 : 1967.2.9 발효(조약 232호) (V.42 후속 조치, 1966-67)   377

기 안 지

기 안 자	조약과 김세택	전화번호	74-2474	공보	필요	불필요

과장	국장	차관보		차관		장관
	전결					

협조자 서명				보존년한	
기안년월일	1966.8.5.	시행년월일		통제관	정서 기장
분류기호 문서번호	외방조 741-				
경유 수신 참조	법무부 장관		발신	장 관	
제 목	협정문 송부				

법무법 741-17157(66.8.1.)호로 요청하신 "대한민국과

아메리카 합중국간의 상호 방위조약 제4조에 의한 시설과 구역 및

대한민국에서의 합중국 군대의 지위에 관한 협정 및 동 부속문서"를

별첨 송부합니다.

유첨: 협정문 50 부 끝.

0112

0098

공통서식 1-2(갑)   (18절지)

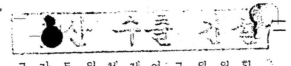

국가동원체제연구위원회

안보총 764-3l　　　（75-0409）　　1966. 8. 10

수　신　외무부 장관

제　목　연구자료 제출 의뢰

　　　　당국가동원체제연구위원회에서 업무상 필요한 연구자료를
본 위원회 규정 제11조에 의거 하여 다음과 같이 요청하오니
1966. 8. 18 까지 당위원회에 제출하여 주시기 바랍니다.

　　　　　　　　　　　다　　음

요구자료	내　용	부수
한미행정 협정서 （개정편）	국가동원계획을 수립함에 있어 한미간의 협정내용을 참고코저 함.　끝.	2 부

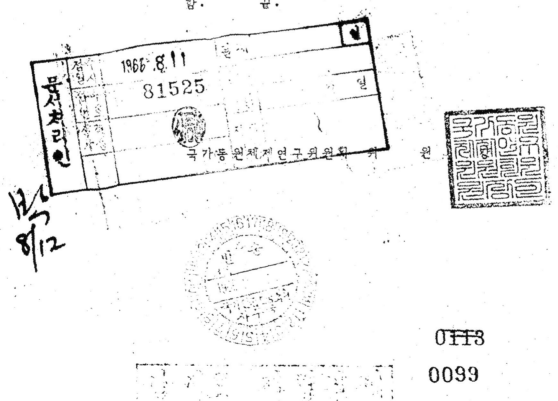

숭 심 대 학

숭대제 549 호   1966. 8. 24

수 신.   의무부장관 귀하

제 목.   한미행정 협정문 송부의뢰의 읽

　　　본 대학 학생들의 참고자료로 도서관에 비치코저 하오니 2부만
보내주시옵기를 앙원합니다.

　　　숭 심 대 학 장   고 병

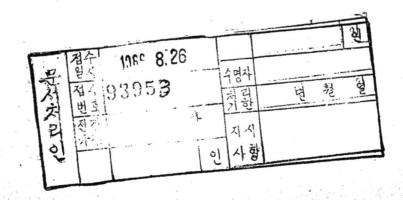

0114
0100

공　보　부

공문해 1752 *P43* (72 —6121)　　　　　　1966. 9. 1

수　신　외무부 장관

제　목　한·미 행정협정문 (영문) 송부 요청

　　　주미 공보관으로 부터 현지 각기관의 요청이 있어

한·미행정협정문 (영문)이 필요하다 하오니 가능한 한 다량

송부하여 주시기 바랍니다　　끝.

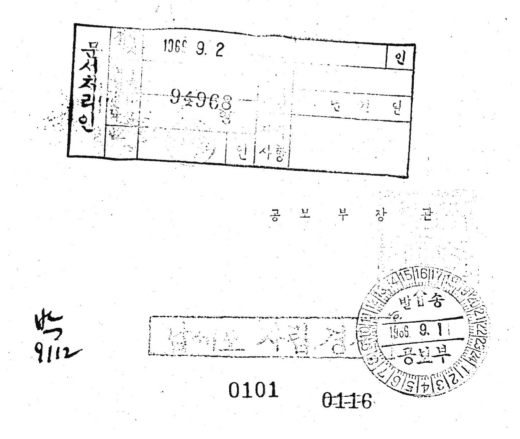

공　보　부　장　관

0101　　　0116

기 안 지

기 안 자	조약과 박원철	전 화 번 호			공 보	필 요	불필요
과 장	국 장 전결		차관보	차 관			장 관

협조 성 자명				보 존 년 한	
기 안 년 월 일	1966.9.16.	시 행 년월일	1966.9.	통 제 관	정 서	기 장
분 류 문 서 기 호 번 호	외방조.741-					
경 수 참 유신 조	" 내 부 결 재 "	발 신				
제 목	한·미 간 군대지위협정 협정문 배부					

지난 7월 9일에 서명한 표기 협정문은 우선 제 1차로 별지
배부 미스트에 따라 재외공관, 관계부처 및 각 대학교 도서실 등에
배부하고저 합니다.

유 첨 : 1, 공판 안, 2부,

2. 배부 미스트, 끝.

16684
1966 9. 20

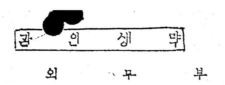

외 무 부

외방조741-   1966. 9.   .

수신 : 수신처 참조

제목 : 한·미 간 군대지위협정 협정문 배부

　　　지난 7월 9일에 서명한 표기 협정문을 송부하오니,

참고하시기 바라며, 동봉한 수령증을 송부하시기 바랍니다.

유 첨 : 1. 협정문,   부,

　　　　2. 수령증,   끝.

수신처 : (별지 배부 미스트에 의함.)

　　　　　　외 무 부 장 관   이   동   원

0118
0103

수 령 증

1. 수령 품명 : "대한민국과 아메리카 합중국 간의 상호 방위조약
            제4조에 의한 시설과 구역 및 대한민국에서의
            합중국 군대의 지위에 관한 협정 및 동 부속 문서"
            책자

2. 수령 부수 :   부

   상기 물품을 정히 수령하였음을 이에 선명 남인하여 증명함

                  1966 년   월   일

                  기관 명

                  위 수령인   (인)

외무부 장관 귀하

01:20
0104

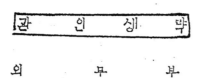

외　무　부

외방조741-   1966. 9.   .

수신 : 수신처 참조

제목 : 한·미 간 군대지위협정 협정문 배부

　　　지난 7월 9일에 서명한 표기 협정문을 송부하오니,
사무 처리에 참고하시기 바랍니다.

유 첨 : 협정문, 부,   끝.

수신처 : (재외공관에 배부함)

　　　　외　무　부　장　관　　　이　　동　　원

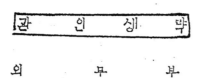

0121
0105

배부 계획표

외무부
재외공관
본부
장관실 1부 외교연구원 2부
차관실 1부 도서실 3부
차관보실 1부 기자실 3부 각과 각1부 (22부)

관계부처 (부서 각 2부)

청와대비서실 1부   상공부 특허국 1부
감사원 (원장실, 도서실) 2부 무역진흥공사 1
국무총리실 (법제담당) 1부 문교부 1
안전보장이사회 1   농림부 1
기획조정실 1   무임소장관실 1
경제과학심의회 1   수산청 1
원자력원 1   법제처장 50 (요청에 의함)
중앙정보부 1   공보부 1
보사부 1   체신부 1
경제기획원 1   정부간행물위탁
노동청 5   판매센터 1
재무부 1   법무부 20
국방부 1   교통부 1
국세청 1   철도청 1
육군본부 1   내무부 1
해군본부 1   총무처 1
공군본부 1   중앙공무원교육원 2
조달청 1   건설부 1
전매청 1   서울특별시 1

113부

(計)

0106   0123

<u>구 도서관 명세서</u>

국립중앙도서관 3 부   전북대학교 도서관 1 부
남대문도서관 1 "   부산대학교 도서관 1 "
종로도서관 1 "   충남대학교 도서관 1 "
한국연구도서관 1 "   조선대학교 도서관 1 "
인천시립도서관 1 "   한양대학교 도서관 1 "
전북도립도서관 1 "   동아대학교 도서관 1 "
광주시립도서관 1 "   건국대학교 도서관 1 "
대구시립도서관 1 "   √ 대구대학교도서관 1 "
청주시립도서관 1 "   √ 한국외대 도서관 1 "
서울대학교 중앙도서관 2 "   육군대학교 도서관 1 "
√ 서울상대대학교 도서관 1 "   육군사관학교 도서관 1 "
√ 서울법과대학교 도서관 1 "   해군사관대학도서관 1 "
√ 서울행정대학원 도서관 1 "   공군사관학교 도서관 1 "
연세대학교 도서관 1 "   공군대학교 도서관 1 "
고려대학교 도서관 1 "   국방대학원 도서관 1 "
중앙대학교 도서관 1 "   이화여자대학교 도서관 1 "
숙명여자대학교 도서관 1 "   성균관대학교 도서관 1 "
경희대학교 도서관 1 "   동국대학교 도서관 1 "
전남대학교 도서관 1 "   √ 진주농과대학교 도서관 1 "
단국대학교 도서관 1 "   마산대학교 도서관 1 "
√ 서울문리실과대학 도서관 1 "   √ 경기대학교 도서관 1 "
경북대학교 도서관 1 "   √ 부산시립도서관 1 "
국학대학도서관 1 "   √ 국제대학 도서관 1 "
한국학생도서관 1"(서울특별시 중구 묵정동 18)숭실대학   1 부

(계. 50 부)

언 론 기 관

동아일보　　1부
서울신문　　1 〃
경향신문　　1 〃
조선일보　　1 〃
대한일보　　1 〃
대한공론　　1 〃
한국일보　　1 〃
중앙일보　　1 〃
신아일보　　1 〃
한국경제신문　　1 〃
서울중앙방송국　　1 〃
서울중앙방송국 테레비방송국　　1 〃
서울 국제방송국　　1 〃
동아방송국　　1 〃
기독교방송국　　1 〃
동양방송국　　1 〃
동양텔레비 방송국　　1 〃
문화방송국　　1 〃

국가동원체제 연구위원회 1부.　(계 18부)

0108　~~0125~~

내　　　무　　　부

내치수(3) 822.2 - 17333   1966. 10. 11

수신 외무부장관

참조 방교국장

제목 한미 행정 협정에 대한 해설 책자 배부 요청

　　　경찰관의 교양자료로 각시도에 배부코저 하오니 동 협정에 대한 책자
200부를 제공 하여 주시기 바랍니다. 끝.

내　　　무　　　부　　　장　　　관

0109   1966.10.11   0126
0126

서 울 민 사 지 방 법 원

총무 제 205호   1967. 1. 14.

수신 외무부 장관

제목 한미협정문 (책자) 송부의뢰

　　　당원에서 재판사무 수행상 필요하오니" 대한민국과 아메리카 합중국
간에 상호방위 조약 제4조에 의한 시설과 구역 및 대한민국에서의 합중국
군대의 지위에 관한 협정"(해설 및 협정문) 의 책자 150부를 송부하여 주시
기 바랍니다. 끝.

지 방 법 원 장   주   재

0110   0128

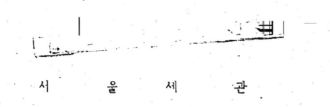

서 울 세 관

서관시 1274-403   (23.3382-4)   1967. 1. 26.

수 신   외무부 장관

참 조   조약 과장

제 목   한미 행정 협정 유인물 송부

    본년 2월 9일자로 발효되는 한미 행정 협정에 대하여 당관에서 업
무 수행상 본 협정 유인물이 필요 하오니 15부 송부하여 주시기 바랍니다.

첨 부   수령증 1매. 끝

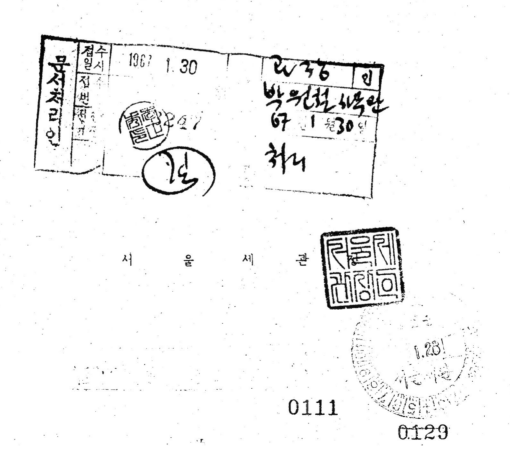

서 울 세 관

0111

0129

수　　령　　증

1967. 1. 26

수 신　외무부 장관

품 명　한미 행정 협정 유인물
수 량　15부

상기와 같이 정히 수령합니다.

서울 세관장　　김　유

0112　0130

부 전 지

1967. 2. 11.

수신 조약과장

발신

제목 공문 이송

(내용)

　열원 "도서 혜증 의뢰" 공함을 송부
합니다.　당과 소관 사항은 이미
처리되었기 알지 바랍니다.

미주과장 印

이미 통과하였을 [?] 通報요함
[?] 2社

MR. PARK

행통서식 1-13 　　　　　　(36전지)

0113　0113

대 법 원

법 행 조 제   83   호   1967. 2. 3.

수 신   외무부장관   귀 하
참 조   미주과장, 조약과장
제 목   도서혜증   의뢰

　　　　금 번   귀부 미주과及 조약과에서발 행 하 신   아 래
의   도 서 를   혜 증 하 여 주 시 면   존 의 에   부 응
토 록   최 선 의   관 리 하 에   영 구 히   보 존 하 여
법 원 직 원 의   연 구 에   공 하 고 자   하 오 니   이 에
혜 증 하 여   주 시 기 를   앙 청 합 니 다

　　　　　서 명

" 대한민국과 아메리카합중국 간의 상호방위조약 제4조에 의한 시설과 구역 및

　대한민국에서의 합중국 군대의 지위에 관한 협정 및 동 부속문서 "   10 부.

（미주과 발행 5부.   조약과 발행 5부）

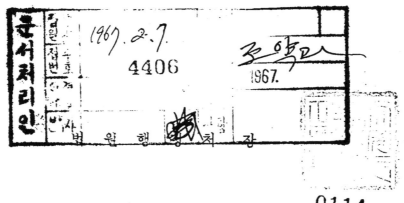

　　　　　　　　　　　　　　　　　0114   ~~0132~~

건   설   부

건기획 72\3─1/♂♂   1967. 2. 8.

수신   외무부 장관

제목   자료(책자) 송부 의뢰

         당부 업무 수행상 필요하여 참고 하고자 하니 아래 책자를 각각
10부 식 송부하여 주시기 바랍니다.

      1. 대한민국과 아메리카 합중국간의 상호 방위조약 제4조에 의
한 시설과 구역및 대한민국에서의 합중국 군대의 지위에 관한 협정(해설
및 협정문) 10부

      2. 대한민국과 아메리카 합중국간의 상호 방위조약 제4조에 의
한 시설과 구역및 대한민국에서의 합중국 군대의 지위에 관한 협정 및 동
부속문서 10부. 끝

                        건   설   부   장

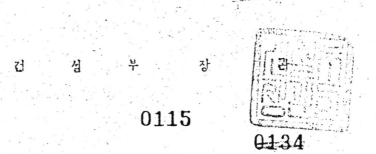

0115
0134

기 안 용 지

분류기호 문서번호	외방조 7**~	(전화번호 74-2474)	전결규정 9 조 6 항 전결사항

처리기한		기 안 자	결 재 자
시행일자		조약과 박염첨	
보존년한	3년		

보조기관	과 장	(서명)		

협 조						
경유		통제		발송		정서
수신	배부처참조		(직인)			
참조						

제 목 **한.미간 군대지위협정문 배부**

　　지난 7월 9일에 서명한 표기 협정문을 우선 제2차로 별지
배부 리스트에 따라 재외공관, 관계부처 및 대학교 도서실에 배부
하고저 합니다.

　　첨 부 : 1. 공문안, 2부.

　　　　　 2. 배부리스트. 끝.

(직인: 발송 No. 1967. 2. 9 외무부)

공통서식 1-2-1 (갑)　　　　　　0116　0135　　　　(18절지)

외   무   부

외방조741-   1967. 2. 8.

수신 : 수신처 참조

제목 : 한.미 간 군대지위협정문 배부

　　　　1966 년 7월 9일 서명되고 1967 년 2월 9일에 발효되는
표기 협정문을 송부하오니, 산하 관계 기관에 이를 배부하시어
집무 상 참고하도록 적의 조치하여 주시기 바랍니다.

　　유 첨 : 협정문,   부

　　　　　　　　　　외 무 부 장 관

첨부 : 협정문,   부

수신처 : 대법원 행정처, 대검찰청, 내무부 치안국, 재무부 세관국,
　　　　노동청, 교통부 해운국, (................... 장)

　　　　　　　　　　　　　　　　　　　　　　　　0117   0136

배부 리스트

1. 법원 (대법원 행정처)   675 부

2. 검찰 (대검찰청)   338 부

3. 경찰 (내무부 치안국)   ~~2,000부~~   1600부

4. 세관 (재무부 세관국)   100부

5. 노동청 (노동청 노정국)   290 부

6. 지방해운국 (교통부 해운국)   12부

0118   ~~0137~~

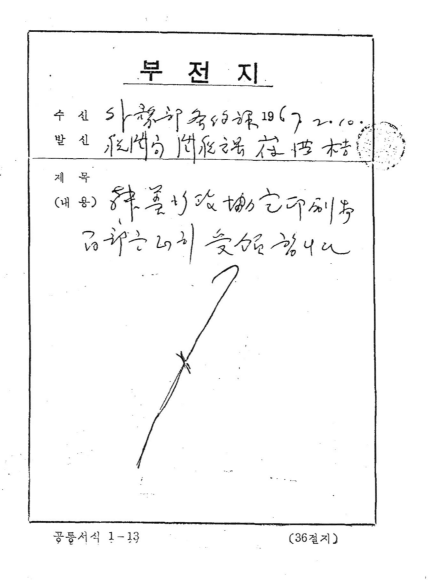

부 전 지

수 신 外務部 을 第○○號 1967. 2. 10.

발 신 税 廳○ 間 稅 謀 在 世 楠

제 목

(내 용) 韓 美 刑 政 協 定 에 刑 務

○ 務 를 以 下 受 領 하 나 니

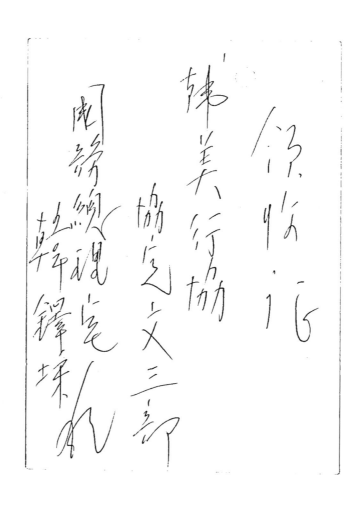

領收証

韓美行政協
定完文三部

閔續頒視完
韓錤珠

0120

수　명　증

1. 수명 품명 : "대한민국과 아메리카 합중국 간의 상호 방위
　　　　　　　조약 제4조에 의한 시설과 구역 및
　　　　　　　대한민국에서의 합중국 군대의 지위에 관한
　　　　　　　협정 및 동 부속 문서" 책자

2. 수명 부수 ㄴ338부

　　　　　상기 품품은 정히 수명하였음을 이에 서명 날인하여
증명함.

　　　　　　　　　　　　　1967년 2월 7일

　　　　　　　　　기관명　大檢察廳總務課

　　　　　　　　　위 수명인：朴朱澤

외무부 장관 귀하　　　　　　　　0121　　　0140

수　　령　　증

1. 수령 품명 : "대한민국과 아메리카 합중국 간의 상호 방위
   조약 제 4조에 의한 시설과 구역 및
   대한민국에서의 합중국 군대의 지위에 관한
   협정 및 동 부속 문서" 책자

2. 수령 부수 : 290 부

　　　　상기 품목을 정히 수령하였음을 이에 서명 날인하여
증명함.

　　　　　　　　　　　　　　1967 년 2 월 9 일

　　　　　　　　　　　　　　기관명　노동청

　　　　　　　　　　　　　　위 수령인 : 김용순 (인)

외무부 장관 귀하

　　　　　　　　　　　　　　　　　　　　0122　0141

수   령   증

1. 수령 품명 : "대한민국과 아메리카 합중국 간의 상호 방위
   조약 제 4조에 의한 시설과 구역 및
   대한민국에서의 합중국 군대의 지위에 관한
   협정 및 동 부속 문서" 책자

2. 수령 부수 : 100 부

　　　상기 물품을 정히 수령하였음을 이에 서명 날인하여
증명함.

　　　　　　　　　　　1967 년 2 월 10 일

　　　　　　　　기관명　배교부 최민규

　　　　　　　위 수령인 : 서 흥호

외무부 장관 귀하

0123　　　　　　0142

증 명 증

1. 수명 중명 : "대한민국과 아메리카 합중국 간의 상호 방위
　　　　　　　조약 제4조에 의한 시설과 구역 및
　　　　　　　대한민국에서의 합중국 군대의 지위에 관한
　　　　　　　협정 및 등 부속 문서" 역자

2. 수명 자수 : 675字

　　　상기 문증은 길이 수명하였음은 이에 지방 논인과이
증명함.

19??년 2월 10일

기관명 법원행정처
　　　　　조사과

위소명인 김 동 수

0124　　　0143

수   명   증

1. 수명 품명 : "대한민국과 아메리카 합중국 간의 상호 방위
             조약 제4조에 의한 시설과 구역 및
             대한민국에서의 합중국 군대의 지위에 관한
             협정 및 동 부속 문서" 책자

2. 수명 부수 : 1,400 부

       상기 품목은 정히 수명하였음을 이에 서명 날인하여
증명함.

                    1967년 2월 10일

            기급별 내무부 치안국 외사과

            위 수명인 : 홍효 미경 경무역

수 령 증

1. 수령품명: "대한민국과 아메리카 합중국간의 상호 방위
조약 제 4 조에 의한 시설과구역 및 대한민국
에서의 합중국 군대의 지위에 관한 협정 및
동 부속문서 " 책자

2. 수령부수: 200부

상기 물품을 정히 수령하였음을 이에 서명 날인하여
증명함.

1967년 2월 15일

기관명: 내무부치안국 외사과

위 수령인: 경감 고명중 ㉞

외무부 장관 귀하

0145
0126

전기복 740

수신: 외무부장관

제목: 한·미 행정협정 조약문 배부의뢰

　　당청에서 업무에 참고코자 하오니 위 조약문 10부를
배부하여 주시기바랍니다. 끝

전 매 청 장

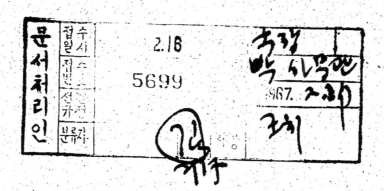

'67 2 16 13 51

0127

1.	외아교.741-16807(66.9.21)	450부.	조회批准에대한 동의案
2.	〃	50부.	조출外에 所要員數 尹榮卓
3-1.	〃	50부.	大法院刑事課 李興秀
3-2.	〃	150부.	서울民事地法 姜榮覺
4.	외아교741-2599(67.2.8)	3,015부.	
		675.	大法院行政處
		338.	大檢
		1,600	外事課
		600	税關
		290.	勞動廳
		12	交通部海運局
5.	〃	20부	陸軍憲兵監察家 憲兵搞少領
6.	〃	50 〃	
7.	〃	7 〃	法務部出入國管理課 安泰根
8.	〃	205 〃	搜査指導課 禹鉉鍵
9.	〃	50 〃	外事課 이용구
10.	〃	10 〃	〃 최상호
11.	〃	5 〃	市警外事課 宋爲壽
12.	〃	10 〃	財務部關稅課 孫炳英
13.	〃	5 〃	〃 税制 李鍾奎
14.	〃	2 〃	〃 税關句 宋昌學
15.	〃	15 〃	서울税關監視課 金鎭喚
16.	〃	15 〃	서울税關長
17.	〃	50 〃	公報部海外課 김口口
18.	〃	40 〃	法務課長 吳一俊
19.	〃	10 〃	〃
20.	〃	2 〃	법무부법조실 朴承窒
21.	〃	1 〃	서울地檢 李魏元
22.	〃	10 〃	建設部法務課 呂昌雲

0128

2부.
1 "
3 "
5 "
5 "
2 "
5 "
1 "
1 "
3 "
1 "
1 "
20 "
7 "
15 "
20 "
5 "
4 "
5 ";

統一商은劃 //晚.
法令管室.

壽寬祈.
意合往許長官室.
總務於忌은 每同期諸室.
總理秘処.
서울市元.
商工部건화知品室
保政安頃室
產房取引調查元个
勞初所 勞政場
美大使舘
和紀逸 "
日本 "
中本 "
美8軍惠支司.
駐韓美軍新清本部政.
"

嗣 南 無
趙 良 照
喜 戒 龍
이 合 길
意 思 興
羊 報 得
升 外 植
無 名 稀
이 재 記
김 명 수
정 선 기
외 성

우 물 심
堀
숭 元福
氣 呂 植

朴 東 莫
"

한·미국 간의 상호방위조약 제4조에 의한 시설과 구역 및 한국에서의 미국군대의 지위에 관한 협정(SOFA)
전59권. 1966.7.9 서울에서 서명 : 1967.2.9 발효(조약 232호) (V.42 후속 조치, 1966-67) 409

한미간군대지위 협정문 배부상황

(1967. 2.25 현재)

[一] 一차 일괄배부

배부처	총부수	배부근거
관계부처 외무부본부 재외공관 도서관 언론기관	√248부	외방조741-16684(66.9.19)공문

[二] 二차 개별배부

배부처	총부수	내 역	배부근거
○ 국회	√5○○부	(1) 비준동의안. 45○부 (2) 외무위원회심의용.5○부.	외무조741-16807(66.9.21)공문 변첨1
○ 법원	895부	(1) 1교 50부 (2) 2차 √150부 (3) 3차 695부√	수령증 별첨 2 수령증 별첨 3-1 수령증 별첨 3-2 외무조741-2599(67.2.8)공문 변첨4
○ 검찰	338부√		외무조741-2599(67.2.8)공문 변첨4
○ 헌병감실	7○부√		수령증 별첨 5-6
○ 출입국관리소	7부√		〃 〃 7
○ 경찰	1,870부	(1) 1차 27○부√ (2) 2차 1,6○○부√	〃 〃 8-11 외무조741-2599(67.2.8)공문 변첨4
○ 재무부	17부	0130	수령증 별첨 12-14 〃 〃 15-16
○ 세관	730부	(1) 1차 3○○부 (2) 2차 1○○부	외무조741-2599(67.2.8)공문 별첨4

외협조741-2599(67.2.8)공문
별첨4
외협조741-2599(67.28)공문
별첨.4

- 지방해운국.   12부 ✓
- 노동 청   290부. ✓

- 공보부.   50부.✓
- 법무부.   53부.✓

- 건설부   10부 ✓
- 경제기획원   6부 ✓
- 전매청   5부 ✓

- 기타 부처.
  - 무임소장관실   5부
  - 총리기획조정실   2부
  - 총 무 처   5부
  - 서울시청   1 부
  - 상공부 법무관실 1부
  - 정전위원회   3부
  - 한국산업은행   1
- 외국기관.
  - 미국대사관   20부
  - 독일대사관   7부
  - 일본 "   15부
  - 중국 "   20부
  - 비8조 잠정시행시   5부)
        위정위원회   9부
- 외무부내.   59부
- 외무부 출입기자 및 기타. 37부

수령증 별첨 17.
  同 "   " 18-21
  "   " 22
  "   " 23-25
  "   " 26
  "   " 27
  "   " 28
  "   " 29
  "   " 30
  "   " 31
  "   " 32
  "   " 33
  "   " 34
  "   " 35
  "   " 36
  "   " 37
  "   " 38
  "   " 39
  "   " 40-41
  "   " 42
  "   " 43.

총계. 4610부
      4692부
      4642부

조약` 388

0131

0150

1126

한·미 대사관 하 협정문 발정 및 매매 상황 (1967. 2. 25. 현재)

1. 이와 위한 협정문

매 체 명	총 부 수	배 부 처 기 관
관계부처	248	외방조 741-16684 (1966.9.19) 공문
해외공관		
재외공관		
도서관		
언론기관		

2. 2차 매매 상황

매 체 명	총 부 수	내 역	배 부 처 기 관
단행본	500 부	(1) 비준 동의안 450부	외방조 741-16807(66.9.21) 공문 별첨)
		(2) 하우하원회 신이화 응 50부	수방중 별첨 2
책자	875 부	(1) 1차 50부	수방중 별첨 3 - 1.
		(2) 2차 150부	수방중 별첨 3-2
합계		(3) 3차 675부	외방조 741-2599(67.2.8)공문 별첨 4

0132

0151-010

구분	부수	비고
관 청	338 부	외방조 741-2599(67.2.8) 공문 별첨4.
국방각서	70 부	수령증 별첨 5-6.
출입국관리소	7 부	〃 〃 7.
공 항	1,870부 (1) 1차 270부 (2) 2차 1,600부	〃 〃 8 - 11.
세 관	17 부	외방조 741-2599 (67.2.8)공문 별첨 4.
검 역	130 부 (1) 1차 30 (2) 2차 100부	수령증 별첨 12 -14.
지방해운국	12 부	외방조 741-2599(67.2.8)공문 별첨 4.
노 동 청	290 부	외방조 741-2599(67.28.)공문 별첨 4.
보 건 부	50 부	외방조 741-2599(67.2.8) 공문 별첨 4.
건 설 부	53 부	수령증 별첨 17.
경제기획원	10 부	〃 18-21
전 매 청	6 부	〃 22
전 매 청	5 부	〃 23 -25
		〃 26

0133

0152

기타부처		수신처 별첨	27.
무임소장관실	5부	〃	28.
총리기획조정실	2부	〃	29.
총 무 처	5부	〃	30.
서울시청	1부	〃	31.
상공부 발명관실	1부	〃	32
경제과학심의회	1부	〃	33
한국산업은행	1부	〃	34
노동청	1부	〃	
외국기관			
미국대사관	20부	〃	35
주일대사관	7부	〃	36
일본 〃	15부	〃	37
중국 〃	20부	〃	38
미8군 헌병사령부	5부	〃	39
〃 소청위원회	9부	〃	40 - 41
외무부 구주내	79부	〃	42 -
외무부 총의가가 및 기타.	37부	〃	43.

주 일 대 사 관

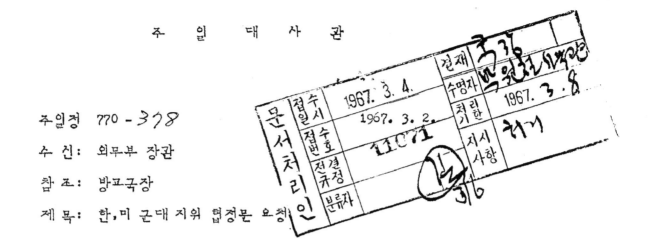

주일정 770 - *378*

수 신: 외무부 장관

참 조: 방교국장

제 목: 한,미 군대 지위 협정문 요청

　　　　당관 집무 수행에 참고하고자 하오니 표제 협정문 (1966. 7. 9. 서명)
을 10부 정도 송부하여 주시기 바랍니다. (외방교 741 - 16684로 1부 수령
한적 있읍니다) 끝.

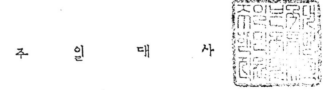

　　　　　　　　　주 　 일 　 대 　 사

0154
0135

대한민국 외무부

착신전보

종 별

수 신 인: 장 관

발 신 인: 주 월 대 사

주재국 정부의 요청이 있아오니 한미행정 협정 6부를 다음
파우치편으로 송부바람.

(방조)

mr. Park

'67 3 15 9

비서	아주	통상	상공	청와대	보사부	중정1		
총무	구미	경기	농림	총리실	문교부	중정2		
의전	정보	문화	조달	노동청	수산청			
여권	방교	재무부	외연	공보부	해외개			
육군	해군	공군	해병	합 참	무역진			

수신시간:

검인

배포일시 196 .

09

※ 주무장관 허가없이 전문내용을 타부에 누설함을 엄금함

0136 ~~0155~~

韓·美間 軍隊地位協定冊子
配付表.

一次包括配付 (外協조 741-16684 (66.9.19)).

　　　　總　248 部　｛
関係各處 113
外務部本部 . . . . 22. ✓
在外 公館 . . . . . 45. ✓
圖書館 . . . . . . 50. ✓
言論機関 . . . . . 18 ✓

個別配付
ㄱ. 関係部處.　　　　總 1133 部
1. 國會　　✓ 500 部. ｛ 450　序去議審議用.
　　　　　　　　　　　　　50　外협參贊用 ".

2. 서울民事法院.　✓ 150 部.　(총무제 205호 (67.1.14) 에 따라서 手交)

3. 法務部.　　[103 部.] ｛
50. (법무장 741-17157 (66.8.1) 에 따라서)
　　法務課長 (出入國管理처 18部 包含)
40.　법조쏘.　—　9.22.
2.　金 一 個課長 — 7.19.
　서울地檢　李鍾元 — 67.1.12.

4. 內務部.　　[271 部] ｛
50.　治安局外事課　이응구. — 9.20
205.　搜査指導課 ✓　李 謹健 — 11.3
10.　外事課 ✓　최 18옥 — 8.4
5. ✓ 市警外事課 ✓　朱 勇로 —67.1.21
1.　서울市府 庶務課、尹 君杉— 67.1.21

5. 公報部.　　50 部　　　海外課.　김 대수 — 9.22.

6. 財務部.　　17 部 ｛
5.　稅制句　　廖 鍾堂. 2.21
10.　稅関句　　朱 品岩. "
2.　　"　　이 재선 7.19.

0138　0157

配付年月日	配 付 処	配付数	受 領 者 印
1966. 9. 9	駐韓 瑞逸大使館	7卷	유분식
" 9. 9	勞動予勞政課	1卷	한 서철
1966. 9. 10	美刊道法洋料設土觀室	1卷	김 종득
966. 9. 10.	銀出任書（國管理 訟放 一会 登録목록（외무弁護經協시）	1港	
1966. 9. 12	駐韓 中國大使舘	20卷	馬 元福
" 9. 13	駐韓 日本大使館	15港	木橋 과강성
1266. 9. 14	국제 민항라	4천	
1966. 9. 19	미주라	4천	이근탈 代理

李漢基 教授
司法大學院 敎校
條約 課 用

0158
0139

②

配付年月日	配付部数	配付処	受領者	備考
1966. 7. 20	25 部	歐美局 美洲課	李根八	美大使館 Kinney
1966. 7. 21	2 部	通商局 通商振興課	최세진	
"	5 部	財務部 税制局	李鍾奎	
"	10 部	財務部 税關局 關税課	孫炳美	別途
1966. 7. 19	2 "	財務部 税關局	宋昌學	
"	1 "	商工部 法務官室	이재화	
"	10 "	法務部 法務課長	李一俊	張 收
1966. 8 4	1 "	國大 강사	이종연	
1966. 8. 4	10 "	내무부 (外事課室)	최상욱	慶
1966. 8. 8	3 "	외무부 통상진흥과		
1966. 9. 10	1 "	管理能書課回覧室	屋金管録	
1966. 9. 16	3 部	정신기 김교육 대령		
1967. 1. 12	1 部	서울地檢	李鍾元	BOG
1967. 1. 13.	3부	육군과 경리과서	唐京煥	
"	1	중제 기관서	이사영	李
67. 1. 18	(20	陸軍本部 憲兵監室	少領 崔尙錫	
67. 1. 20		東亞出版社 編輯部	元容睾	Won.
67. 1. 21.		市警 外事課	宋義圭	宋, 이
67. 1.	1	市庁 北会壇	金君材	방윤희
67. 1. 23	5	서울 税黃	金州帆	
67. 1. 24	2	經済協力課	남호구	
67. 1. 24	1		김상옥	
67. 1. 24	5	通商振興課	박근로	
67. 1. 24	3	總務処人事制度課	朴氏拉	

52

115 部

0140   0159

③

配付 年月日	配付部數	配付處	受領者	備考
67. 1. 25	10部	서울龍壽醫製凍 全벙기		
67. 1. 28	2部	亞洲局 柔業亞緯	최용근	
67. 2. 1	1부	경향신문	유지은	
67. 2. 2	2부	경향신문	장 승	
67. 2. 7	1부	그만 비서실	이게활	
67. 2. 8	1부	이 기계	안종국 (金룡필)	안
67. 2. 8	10부	建設部 法務官室		
67. 2. 8	5部	US Armed Forces Claims Service, Korea	박동영	Reg.
67. 2.	1부	검오과	오영	
67. 2. 10	10부	미주과	김기조	
67. 2. 13	1부	北續보인과	이이병	
67. 2. 13	1部	經濟 수레 법 法務官室	한류우	
67. 2. 13		情報課	전인행	
67. 2. 13		紐約事 總領事	金俊坤	
67. 2. 15	1部	유럽局		
67. 2. 15	"	기록관리실		김대랑
67. 2. 22	"	同和通信社 서울 新聞社	초221	
		總務 4692部 醫務院51部		
67. 3. 2	1部	光州地檢 김기층감사	천영련	천
67. 3. 8	1部	調査課 梯材課	이용구	
67. 3. 9	1部	TBC 진옥조기자		
67. 3. 17	1部	공보관실 조기성	조기성	

0141 ~~0160~~

配布年月日	配布部数	配布先	査読者	受領印
1967. 3. 18.	10부	駐日 大使館	외무부741—	
"	6부	駐越大使館.	외무부741—	

0142

기 안 용 지

분류기호 문서번호	외방조741-	(전화번호 74-2474)	전결규정 국장 조 항 전결사항		
처리기한	1967.3.	기 안 자	결	權	자
시행일자	1967.3.18.	조약과 박원철			
보존년한	1 년	1967.3.18.			
보 조 기 관	과 장				
협 조					
경유수신참조	주일대사	통 제	발 송	정 서	
제 목	한.미간 군대지위협정 (약칭) 문 송부				

(대: 주일정 770-378(67.3.2.))

표기 협정문을 송부하오니, 집무수행에 참고하시기 바랍니다.

유첨: 표기 협정문 10부 끝.

발송
5621

0162
0143

공통서식 1-2-1 (갑)   (18절지)

외 무 부

외방조741-   1967.3.20.

수 신 : 주일대사

제 목 : 한.미간 군대지위협정 (약칭)문 송부

(대: 주일정770-378 (67.3.2)

표기 협정문을 송부하오니, 접무수행에 참고하시기

바랍니다.

유 첨 : 표기 협정문 10부   끝.

외 무 부 장 관

0144   0163

기 안 용 지

분류기호 문서번호	외방조741-	(전화번호 74-2474)	전결규정 **국장**조	항 전결사항
처리기한	1967.3.	기 안 자	결	재 자
시행일자	1967.3.18.	조약과 박영철		
보존년한	1 년	1967.3.18.		

보 조 기 관	과 장	

협 조				
경 수 참	유신조	주월대사	통 제	발 송	정 서

제 목   한·미간 군대지위협정 (약칭)문 송부

(대: VNW - 0367(67.3.14))

표기 협정문을 송부하오니, 집무수행에 참고하시기 바랍니다.

유첨: 표기 협정문 6부   끝.

발 5622
1967. 3. 20

0164

외 무 부

외방조741-   1967.3.20.

수 신 : 주월 대사

제 목 : 한·미간 군대지위협정 (약형)문 송부

(대 : VNW- 0367 (67.3.14)

    표기 협정문은 송부하오니, 집무수행에 참고하시기

바랍니다.

유 첨 : 표기 협정문 6부   끝.

                         외 무 부 장 관

0146

수 령 증

1. 수령 품명: "대한민국과 아메리카 합중국 간의 상호 방위조약 제 4 조에 의한 시설과 구역 및 대한민국에서의 합중국군대의 지위에 관한 협정 및 동 부속문서" 책자

2. 수령 부수: ㄹ 부

상기 물품을 정히 수령하였음을 이에 서명 날인하여 증명함.

1967년 4 월 20일

기관명: 홍口 요이화 郵

위 수령인: 黃 은 자

외무부 장관 귀하

외교문서 비밀해제: 주한미군지위협정(SOFA) 15

주한미군지위협정(SOFA) 서명 및 발효 15

초판인쇄 2024년 03월 15일
초판발행 2024년 03월 15일

지은이 한국학술정보(주)
펴낸이 채종준
펴낸곳 한국학술정보(주)
주 소 경기도 파주시 회동길 230(문발동)
전 화 031-908-3181(대표)
팩 스 031-908-3189
홈페이지 http://ebook.kstudy.com
E-mail 출판사업부 publish@kstudy.com
등 록 제일산-115호(2000. 6. 19)

ISBN 979-11-7217-026-4 94340
     979-11-7217-011-0 94340 (set)